S0-BOE-918

ISBN 978-1-64416-986-5 (hardcover)
ISBN 978-1-64416-987-2 (digital)

Christian Faith Publishing, Inc.
832 Park Avenue
Meadville, PA 16335
www.christianfaithpublishing.com

Printed in the United States of Americ

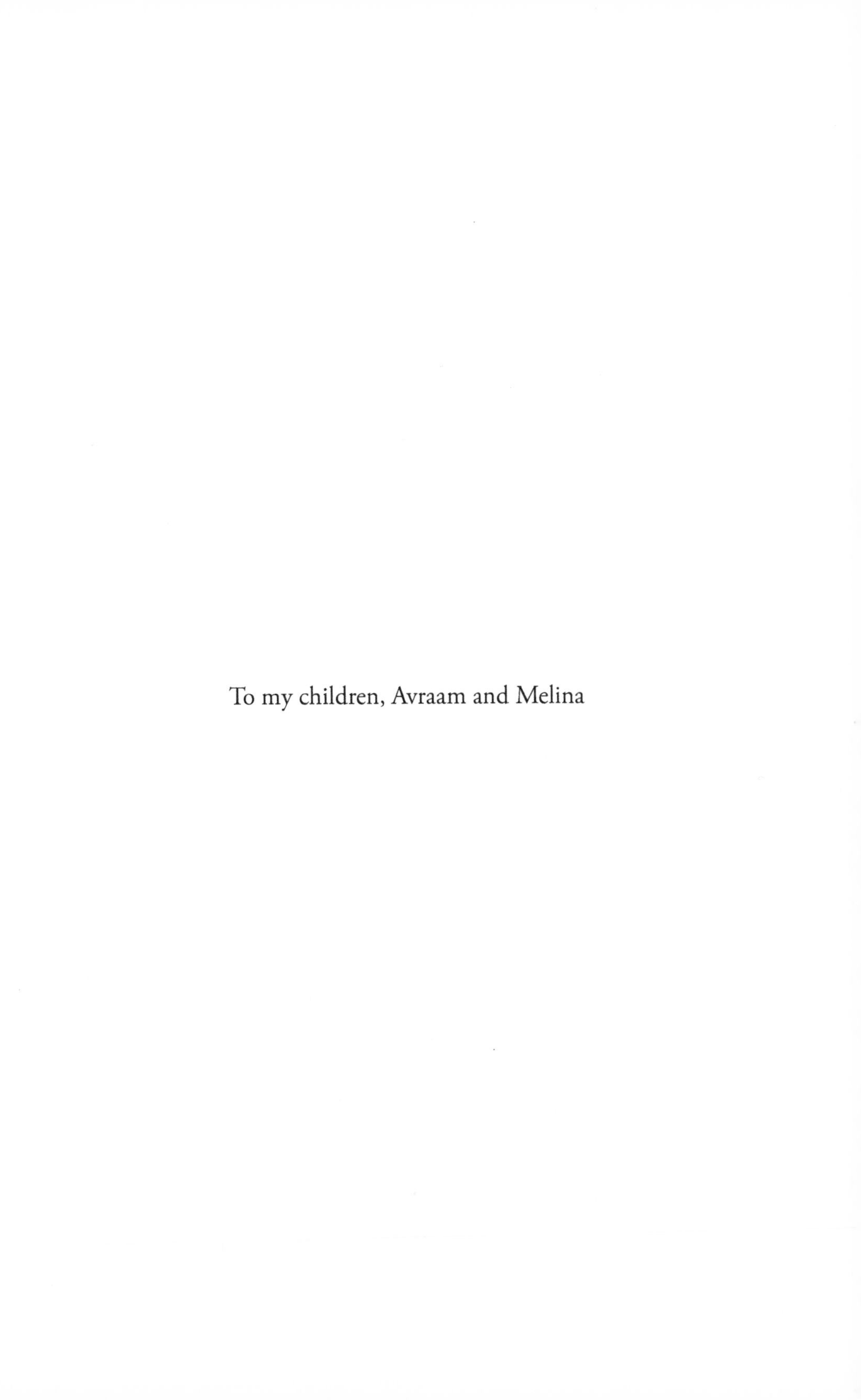

To my children, Avraam and Melina

Evriviades, Kimberly K. Holtz, Clarissa Ingram, James Ingram III, Professor Hasan Kayali, William S. King, M.D., Ambassador Frixos Kolotas, Ambassador Andreas Kyprianides, Ambassador Efstathios Lagakos, Professor Arend Lijphart, Vassos Lyssarides, Professor Marianne McDonald, Professor Victor V. Magagna, Professor David Mares, Christos Moustra, Nitsa Neophytou, Professor Paul Papayoanou, Polyvios Polyviou, Machael Sarris, Professor Gershon Shafir, Patroklos Stavrou, Ambassador Byron Theodoropoulos, Attorney General Michalakis Triantafyllides, Theodore Tsakiris, and Professor Eric Van Young.

Finally, yet as importantly, I am indebted to my family—my mother Maria Karamanou and my brothers Argiris, Sotiris, Konstantinos, and Ioannis—who have broken through the confines of our family's traditions by allowing me the opportunity to pursue my educational goals in the United States and experience life in a new and different environment. Their encouragement and support has been an inspiration to me. I conclude by acknowledging someone who is not last in my thoughts or appreciation—Elliot Grossman—whose patience and understanding kept me going through the difficulties I faced in undertaking this project.

Katerina Karamanou
UC San Diego

CONTENTS

PREFACE

> The fact is that when great prosperity comes suddenly and unexpectedly to a state, it usually breeds arrogance; in most cases it is safer for people to enjoy an average amount of success rather than something which is out of all proportion.
>
> —Thucydides

Cypriot liberation from British colonial rule occurred "suddenly and unexpectedly."[1] Independence was born not as a result of the efforts of a united Cypriot people, but rather by a harsh compromise wrested from a violent struggle between the Greeks and Turks, each force striving to achieve its own objective of union while preventing the other from fulfilling partition. Ironically, the tumultuous environment from which Cyprus emerged as an independent entity ultimately sired her demise.

Cyprus, a small but strategically positioned island, is situated in the eastern Mediterranean Sea, 240 miles from Egypt, 60 miles west of Syria, 40 miles south of Turkey, and about 150 miles east of the Greek Dodecanese Islands. The third largest island in the Mediterranean Sea after Sicily and Sardinia, Cyprus is approximately 3,584 square miles in area and 59 miles in length on a north-south axis. Cyprus has a population that is approximately 80 percent Greek-speaking (Greek-Orthodox Christians), 18 percent Turkish-speaking (Sunni Muslims), and the remainder consists of a heterogeneous mixture of other minorities.

---

[1] This statement made by Cleon is cited in Thucydides, trans., *History of the Peloponnesian War*, by Rex Warner (London: Penguin Books, 1972) 215.

Cyprus has been subjected to more than a dozen foreign conquests over the past 3,500 years of recorded history. Notably, the Greeks inhabited Cyprus for over 3,000 years and successfully Hellenized the territory, transforming it into one of five great centers of Greek learning and tradition. Although Cyprus has been predominantly influenced by Greek culture, Turkey gained political control of the island in 1571 and retained its ruling status until 1878 when Great Britain began its occupation. In 1914, Britain formally annexed Cyprus. The island became a crown colony in 1925 after Turkey acknowledged British sovereignty in the Treaty of Lausanne. British control of Cyprus persisted until 1955.

During the 1950s, serious dissension arose between Greece and Turkey over Cyprus. In 1955 British control over Cyprus was challenged when Greek Cypriots rebelled in an attempt to sever ties with Britain and gain their independence. The large Greek population on Cyprus organized a revolutionary movement with the goal of enosis, or the union of Cyprus with Greece. Neither Britain, which regarded the island as a vital defense base, nor Turkey, which feared that a change in the status quo of Cyprus would pose a security threat, would grant the Cypriots the right of enosis. In 1959, Greek and Turkish representatives met in London to participate in negotiations with Britain concerning Cypriot independence. This independence was granted to the island in 1960. Despite its newly acquired independent status, Cyprus was beset with a constitutional crisis in 1963. The crisis continued and came to a head in 1974 when the Cypriot war broke out.

Since 1974, Cyprus has been a divided island, and Greece and Turkey have remained influential players in determining the fate of Cyprus. The events leading to bloodshed in Cyprus present us with a host of important questions. Why has the 1974 Cypriot Crisis endured? Do the politics of small states such as Greece and Turkey have a greater effect on the fate of small republics like Cyprus than do their own domestic politics? Is Cyprus's domestic structure the exclusive determinant of its internal stability? Or do international relations and even interaction between the island and its neighbors need to be considered? Does nationalism play a role in states like

Cyprus that are plagued by competing nationalities? Is Cyprus yet another example of the economically based relationships we have seen in Latin America?

To answer these questions, I turn to the literature of international relations and comparative politics. The former addresses the foreign policy components of the Cypriot Crisis of 1974, whereas the latter elucidates its domestic political dimensions. By combining these approaches and surpassing their narrow limits to make them engage each other, I have discovered a phenomenon I call transnational nationalism.

Transnational nationalism describes the situation when international leaders are involved in games that implicate the culture of their own countries as well as of those concerned. Cross-national cultural institutions obligate leaders to behave in certain ways, and are not merely reducible to pretexts for strategic choice. At the same time, strategic issues are real and do concern these decision makers.

Transnational nationalism treats the problem of cultures that cross national boundaries, as well as providing insight into cultures that do not coincide with national boundaries because they are subnational in character. In the new world order, it is subnational and transnational nationalism that will present real challenges to the leaders of the nation-state. Because of this, I will apply my insights to cases like Northern Ireland, Palestine, Lebanon, and Bosnia-Herzegovina after I have addressed Cyprus.

To test international relations and comparative theories, as well as my alternative transnational nationalist model which synthesizes both and brings culture back in, I rely on primary and secondary sources. In terms of primary sources, I conducted and collected a set of interviews of prominent officials who were key players in the 1974 Crisis. Some of the interviews were conducted by Michael Cacogiannis and are recorded on film; most of them I conducted myself.[2]

---

[2] My interviews do not have statistical significance because there are only a few of them, but they possess shaping significance because they are so strategic. The interviewees were key decision-makers who were active in the negotiations.

This work adheres to the following format: Chapter 1 offers a historiography of the Balkan region which serves to elucidate the conditions under which the Cypriot Crisis occurred. Chapter 2 addresses the limitations of international relations theory as applied to the Cypriot case. Chapter 3 demonstrates that merely examining the domestic structure of a state, as is done by the comparative theories, does not provide an adequate explanation of the Cypriot Crisis. Because a more comprehensive understanding of the crisis requires that other variables be examined, Chapter 4 discusses my alternative theory of transnational nationalism. This model applies the insights of game theory and the cultural approach. Chapter 5 reveals that cultural politics disrupt the harmony within other countries besides Cyprus when foreign and domestic forces strive to achieve transnational nationalism. Chapter 6 commences with an overview of the determinants of war and concludes with a discussion of various issues that have the potential to structure of the new world order.

The various positions of those interviewed ranged from president of Cyprus to ambassadors and public officials.

CHAPTER 1

THE BALKAN PENINSULA: USING HISTORY TO DEVELOP A THEORY OF TRANSNATIONAL NATIONALISM FOR UNDERSTANDING THE CYPRIOT CRISIS OF 1974

The olive trees with the wrinkles of our fathers
The rocks with the wisdom of our fathers
And our brother's blood alive on the earth
Were a vital joy, a rich pattern
For the souls who knew how to pray.[1]
—John Brademas

I. INTRODUCTION: PERSISTENT CONFLICTS IN THE BALKANS

Cyprus is not alone with its problems of ethnic strife and geographical significance. To fully understand its predicament in 1974, we must look at the history of the Balkan region itself. Greek and Turkish identities which split the island's inhabitants were formed by the same events which faced the Balkans as a whole. Turkish identity is partly a product of the Ottoman Empire, as Greek identity was produced by the Ottoman and Habsburg empires. The Cypriot situation from 1960 to 1974 represents in microcosm the dilemmas of the entire Balkan region from the eighteenth century to the present.

---

1 See George Seferes, trans., Amerikaniki Paideia Kai O Evriteros Cosmos, *A World No Longer Narrow: International Education of American Universities*, by John Brademas (Athens: Athens Academy, 1985) 495 and 511.

For this reason, we must understand Balkan history to comprehend the origins and significance of nationalism in Cyprus.

Conflicts among Balkan nation-states have existed ever since their emergence as political entities. Bitter memories of the bloodshed of loved ones cannot be erased. How did the Balkan nationalities break free from both Ottoman and Habsburg imperial control, establish independent nation-states, and venture into the even harsher realm of economic and social modernization? And how were Balkan cultures preserved amid the influx of foreign political, ideological, and economic forces? What was the mechanism that drove these people to the fulfillment of their dreams of autonomy? In order to address these questions, it is necessary to examine the history of the Balkan region at large.

Despite the similarities between the Balkan countries, disunity has perpetually plagued the region. The effects of such disunity are visible both internally, by the regional, ethnic, and territorial disputes, and externally, by the assorted alliances and foreign occupations of the past. One of the greatest sources of Balkan contention is the diverse pattern of historical development which is the legacy of centuries of Ottoman, Austro-Hungarian, and Russian domination.

In addition to the animosity created by history, strategic importance is another critical factor in the development of Balkan problems. Even though strategic values have changed, the routes affecting the Balkan region have retained their basic value over centuries. The strategic significance of the Balkans has driven the intervention by foreign powers in the region. No less significant is the role of Balkan ethnic complexity which exacerbates the problem of boundary demarcation and can be cited in support of "irredentist" claims. The interaction of these geopolitical factors has historically been and continues today to be a constant source of disunity among Balkan nations.[2]

---

[2] Huey Louis Kostanick, "The Geopolitics of the Balkans," in Charles and Barbara Jelavich eds., *The Balkans in Transition: Essays on the Development of the Balkan Life and Politics Since the Eighteenth Century* (Berkeley: University of California Press, 1963) 1–10.

Balkan national formation was shaped by the socio-ethnic structure and the religious identity engendered by the millet system. The term *millet* was used, according to Muslim religious court archives, to set Muslim elements of the population apart from the non-Muslim communities. The Christian element, including the Jewish population, was regarded as "non-millet." Conspicuous distinctions, such as segregated dwelling quarters and distinguishing attire, were enforced for purposes of tax imposition (more pronounced for non-Muslims) and allegiance to respective heads (also more pronounced for non-Muslims).[3]

The newly established states affixed themselves to geographical bonds of secular citizenship and memories of their past while their group identity, internal ties, and sociopolitical values as a nation were derived from their lengthy subjection to the millet system. The religious-communal experience within the millet gave birth to the ethnic-national identity of the states, while territory determined the secular concept of citizenship. Since their emergence, the Balkan nation-states have been plagued by political, social, and cultural crises, attributed principally to the incompatibility of the religious concept of nation and the secular notion of state rooted in the millet philosophy. Therefore, the dual process of state and nation formation, because of its antagonistic nature, created nation-states in which citizenship and nationality remained incongruous and at times hostile.[4]

Even though one autonomous and four independent Balkan states were established during the revolutionary age of nationalism from 1800 to 1875, the Balkan population was more profoundly affected by the four ensuing decades constituting the age of imperialism and capitalism. The great European powers pervaded the Balkans

---

3 Barbara Jelavich, *History of the Balkans: Eighteenth and Nineteenth Centuries* vol. 1 (Cambridge: Cambridge University Press, 1993) 48–53.

4 Kemal Karpat, "Millets and Nationality: The Roots of the Incongruity of Nation and State in the Post Ottoman Era," in Benjamin Braude and Bernard Lewis eds., *Christians and Jews in the Ottoman Empire* (New York: Holmes & Meier Publishers, Inc., 1982) 141–67.

diplomatically and especially economically as they increased the pace of colonial expansionism.

As Western European civilization expanded, the Balkan Peninsula's self-sufficient natural economy gave way to a money-based capitalist system. The new capitalism signified a break with the past as it produced fundamental changes in the political institutions, traditional social organizations, and everyday lives of the Balkan people. The ensuing disruption inevitably generated a host of new problems, namely rural overpopulation, fragmentation of peasant properties, peasant indebtedness, and hostilities between the city and the village; these problems persist even to the present day.[5]

The forthcoming survey offers an account of the dramatic and fateful history of the Balkan Peninsula. Over the course of Balkan history, predominant political and cultural frontiers intersected, as did the interconnected borders between the Eastern Byzantine and Western Roman empires, Christianity and Islam, Orthodoxy and Catholicism, and in more recent history, the military blocs of the North Atlantic Treaty and the Warsaw Pact. Each of these alignments represents conflicting social, political and economic systems. These rival external influences and significant internal pressures are complicated further by the Balkan passion for liberation, which could not be extinguished. Cypriot nationalism is enlightened by an examination of Balkan history. Its struggle for independence has likewise been hindered by domestic turmoil, but even more importantly by the clashing interference of Greece and Turkey. Let us now examine Balkan events to determine whether a combination of culture, domestic politics, and international relations explains the ageless unrest that characterizes the Balkan region.

---

[5] See L. S. Stavrianos, *The Balkans 1815–1914* (New York: Holt, Rinehart and Winston, 1966) 72–104. Additionally, see Stavrianos, 'The Influence of the West on the Balkans," *The Balkans in Transition* 184–221.

II. AN OVERVIEW OF BALKAN HISTORY: THE ROAD TO POLITICAL TRANSFORMATION

Centuries of nationalistic conflict have not only hindered the delineation of boundaries, but have prevented the Balkan nation-states from uniting for the purpose of warding off the advances of intruders. Moreover, these states have sacrificed some degree of economic and social progress in order to maintain competitive military forces. Consequently, the political, economic, and social development of the Balkan region is vulnerable to dominant external powers and world economic conditions.

Although this historical survey formally commences with the final decade of the seventeenth century, a recapitulation of the previous period is crucial because of the noteworthy role of the development of the Balkan nation-states. This geographic region, consisting of the five modern states of Albania, Bulgaria, Greece, Romania, and Yugoslavia, is inhabited by seven major nationalities. All of these nationalities speak different languages, and each is driven to effectuate a cultural revival of its respective pre-Ottoman histories.

A. The Ottoman and Habsburg Empires

The road to political transformation was a lengthy one. For hundreds of years the fortunes of the Balkan people were determined not simply by the economic, political, and social structures of the Ottoman and Habsburg empires, but also by the domestic and foreign issues that were current. Without doubt, the key political issue for Ottoman and Habsburg leaders in the eighteenth century was the relative balance of power between central and provincial authorities. But the Ottoman and Habsburg leaders responded to the problem differently. The Habsburg monarchy attempted to obtain control over feudal estates that it did not possess, while the Ottoman sultans strove to reassert the control they had previously exercised. Austrian centralism and absolutism encountered resistance from the nobility, whose lineage was on par with the Habsburg dynasty. The Ottoman Porte was challenged by Ayans, Beys, Christian and Muslim military leaders and bandits, all forces which had no historical claim to political power.

The perceived threat or reality of military defeat propelled both empires to initiate reform. Aimed at improving the military, which the Ottoman Empire implemented reforms in order to avert the fall of the central government to foreign aggression or internal subversion. The Ottoman situation was comparatively the more serious one because they faced threats from France, Austria, Russia, Persia, and Prussia that might have dismembered the empire. Habsburg efforts at domestic reform were directed toward enabling the central government to raise taxes and recruit soldiers with greater ease.[6]

With regard to the different systems of government in the region, a few assertions can be made about the relative positions of the Balkan people by comparing the circumstances of the two regimes. Christians living in Ottoman territory were considered second-class citizens. Ottoman Christians were not only subject to the millet system, but also to the local leaders of the village communities. The millet system emerged gradually as a solution to the difficulties of accounting for the structure and culture of the numerous religious ethnic groups that fell subject to the authority of the Ottoman administration. The system granted a degree of religious, cultural, and ethnic continuity within these communities, while simultaneously incorporating them into the Ottoman system. The system, a sociocultural and communal framework, was structured on religion which provided each millet with a universal belief system, and ethnic and linguistic differences which created the divisions and subdivisions within each of the millets. The elements comprising the sociocultural aspect of the millet were religion, language, community, ethnicity, and family, which stressed the universality of the faith by unaccentuating ethnic and linguistic differences without eliminating them.

In many communities, justice, the collection of taxes, and the police were under the control of local authorities. Christian nota-

---

6 Austrian reforms were based on the political ideology of the Enlightenment, which defined the role of leaders as one requiring responsibility to all of their people, in contrast to the Ottoman goal of a return to old traditions.

bles were held accountable to the Muslim provincial authorities or the representatives of the central government. Since the Ottoman Empire was unsuccessful at holding firm control over its territories, the prevailing lawlessness guaranteed a certain degree of freedom. The family unit, which was the principal social unit at this time, reflected the religious values and the ethnic and linguistic idiosyncrasies of its community. When the millets and communities began disintegrating, the family was the only structure that remained relatively intact. As a consequence, individuals began developing an identity and a sense of membership in the new sociopolitical units (urban communities and perceived nations) through the ethnic values, culture, traditions, and language preserved in the family. Thus, even though Christians were considered second-class citizens, they enjoyed a large degree of autonomy.[7]

In contrast, the manorial system in effect throughout Habsburg lands was characterized by a local government dominated by the nobility. Under the domination of the nobility, the peasant population was held in a state of servitude. Within the manorial system, status was dependent on social class rather than religion or nationality. The lord of the manor administered justice and tax collecting, and the peasants had no political rights nor any institution of self-government. Only in the Military Frontier, a system of village government, were immigrant Serbs allowed an organization of government within the monarchy that resembled the millet system.

Despite the similar problems shared by the two empires, their differences from a world perspective were profound. To the educated, the Ottoman Empire was a barbarous state notorious for its shocking executions, public displays of dismembered bodies, and a primitive sanitation system which fostered repeated epidemics of dangerous diseases and plagues. In addition, government corruption was bla-

---

[7] See generally Karpat, *Millets and Nationality: The Roots of the Incongruity of Nation and State in the Post-Ottoman Era* 141–67. For specifics on the role of religious and social institutions see generally Arnakis, "The Role of Religion in the Development of Balkan Nationalism," *The Balkans in Transition* 115–44; and Traian Stoianovich, "The Social Foundations of Balkan Politics, 1750–1941." *The Balkans in Transition* 297–345.

tant and law and security problems were rampant. In great contrast, the Habsburg empire was noted as one of the prominent centers of Baroque culture. It was characterized by the stability of law and order, a comfortable middle class, high standards of sanitation, and relatively honest and efficient public service officials.[8]

Of greater importance than political matters, however, was the issue of landholding, which concerned 90 percent of the Balkan people who were peasants. The major economic problems for most Balkans stemmed from the land and from agricultural production. At the beginning of the eighteenth century, the peasants in the Habsburg empire and the Danubian Principalities were enserfed, regarded as subordinates, and granted only traditional rights to work the land. In addition, they were required to make payments for their land use that were to carry the major burden of state and church taxes. Although reforms were introduced to alter peasant legal status, primarily for reasons of state interest, nothing was done to secure tenure or ownership of the plots of land that the peasants cultivated. Consequently, massive discontent among the peasant population was an ever-present problem until it exploded in 1848.

Despite their generally worse land and political conditions, some Ottoman Christian peasants actually fared better than Habsburg peasants in practical terms because they had advantages in the form of landholding. A large number of peasant households successfully gained free control of a plot of land to be farmed as they pleased within the Ottoman domains. Furthermore, because more unoccupied land was available in Ottoman domains than in the Habsburg region, Ottoman peasants benefitted from a heightened opportunity for movement.

---

[8] Karpat, *Millets and Nationality: The Roots of the Incongruity of Nation and State in the Post-Ottoman Era* 141–67.

B. Foreshadowing: National Conflict, Governmental Reorganization, and the Great Powers

Although fundamental changes in Balkan life did not take place until the nineteenth century, there were hints of what was to come. In the eighteenth century, leaders in both empires attempted to remedy the problems their empires faced. The Ottomans attempted to strengthen the military to enable the state to control local rebellions and to withstand foreign invasion. The Austrian monarchs initiated a fundamental reorganization of the government. Neither of these reforms was successful, however. By the close of the Napoleonic Wars, the conservatives reasserted their power positions, and the major issues of dispute were left unresolved. Specifically, the dangers of external aggression and internal dissolution persisted for the Ottoman sultan. Similarly, the Habsburg monarchy was unable to deal with the problems that resulted from attempts to unite the widely different provinces of the empire. Moreover, difficulties arising from the economic stagnation of the era compounded the existing instability of the region.[9]

The history of the Balkan Peninsula from 1804 to 1887 is characterized by the theme of national conflict and the establishment of new governments. The first national liberation movements were successful, although they did not accomplish what their founders had desired. Under Prince Milos, Serbia acquired many rights, but not a sovereign status. Even greater advances were achieved with the implementation of the terms of the Treaty of Adrianople. Despite the fact that both the Greek-led revolt and the peasant rebellion in Wallachia and Moldavia failed, the Phanariot regime terminated and a native government was installed. Ottoman sovereignty was further confined as a result of the Russo-Turkish War, and the resultant of enhanced Russian influence persisted throughout the country.

The benefits of the Greek revolution were not as obvious because the nation forfeited a great deal. Princes for the Danubian Principalities were no longer provided by Greece. Those that were

---

[9] See generally Jelavich, *History of the Balkans* 39–168.

still under Ottoman control were regarded as traitors, and most were forced to abandon their positions in business and commerce. Armenians, for the most part, replaced the Greeks in banking, while Bulgarians assumed the important responsibility of meeting state and military needs. Moreover, the territory that comprised the state since 1830 was devastated after ten years of civil war and foreign occupation. A Bavarian administration was employed and a mercenary army of foreigners was called upon to assume power.

The developments in Greece, Serbia, and the Principalities during this period closely resembled one another. The Serbian revolution was initiated as a defense mechanism against unbridled janissaries; the crisis in the Peloponnesus occurred because the peasants feared that the Ottoman bureaucracy might become vengeful; and Vladimirescu's revolt was never staged directly against Ottoman domination. Moreover, the leaders in each area imitated the Philiki Etairia (Friendly Society). Philiki Etairia was a revolutionary secret society that helped lay the organizational framework of the Greek revolt, with the ultimate goal of the establishment of a free Greece with broad boundaries.

By the close of the revolutionary period, the leadership of each region had clearly defined its desires to establish a nation-state with either an autonomous or independent status. To advance this goal, each area established a government capable of negotiating with the powers, and even more importantly, a government that appeared to the Porte to have united forces. In Serbia and Greece, central administrations replaced the scattered communal bureaucrats, and native princes governed the Principalities in lieu of the Greek agents of the Porte.[10]

The movements also paralleled one another in their implementation of terrorist methods for the advancement of their causes. For example, Christian insurgents were noted for massacring Muslims

[10] See generally, Richard Clogg, *A Short History of Modern Greece* (Cambridge: Cambridge University Press, 1979) 43–104; and C. M. Woodhouse, *A Short History of Modern Greece* (New York: Frederick A. Praeger, 1968) 125–86 for further developments in the Greek independent nation-states.

who were typically defenseless civilians rather than individuals guilty of committing cruel or unjust acts. Even though Ottoman authorities found it difficult to suppress Christian rebellion because they lacked the support of a regular army, the Porte exercised even harsher means of reprisal whenever possible.

Not only did Christian revolutionaries undertake cruel measures against their Muslim opponents, but they did so against uncooperative members of their own faith and nationality as well. In order to satisfy the need for military recruitment, Serbians would set fire to the homes of their more apathetic neighbors or hang a Turk on a neighbor's threshold, forcing them to flee to the hills where they would join the insurgents to avoid the consequences when the authorities found the body. Vladimirescu's peasants burned and looted the property of their own countrymen to propel participation in the revolts. The disintegration of law and order and insufficient police control gave criminals and violent revolutionists free rein to pillage and plunder.

Balkan history is saturated with accounts of cruelty to adversaries and atrocities against the defenseless, the defeated enemy, and prisoners. These stories reflect the extreme animosity that existed not only between the Christians and the Muslim authority, but among the nationalities themselves. Many of the customs, such as displaying severed heads or impaled bodies in public places, were repulsive to Western observers yet held great symbolic significance in these primitive areas.

Unquestionably, Serbia, Greece, Wallachia, and Moldavia gained a significant degree of freedom from Ottoman control during this period. Unfortunately, however, the power once held by the Porte was transferred into other hands which, if fully exercised, were even more difficult to endure. By 1830, Serbia and the Principalities found themselves under a recognized Russian protectorate, and Greece was subject to the three-power guarantee of Britain, France, and Russia. For an extended period of time, the political development of the Balkan states was greatly affected by the control exercised by the great powers.

The protectorate status of the great powers granted them the right to interfere in or control the domestic and foreign policies of another country. The effects of this status during the remainder of the century can be recapitulated as follows: the Principalities were initially under Russian protection until 1856 and were subsequently under great-power supervision until 1878. Likewise, Serbia fell under Russian and then great-power protection, but it then became a member of the Habsburg empire until 1903. Bulgaria was overseen by Russia from 1878 to 1886; and Greece had the misfortune of having these triple-protectorates until 1923.

Although the degree of influence exerted by Britain, France, and Russia varied based on the events and circumstances of the time, it can be generally said that the first governments of the Balkan states were assembled by the great powers to a greater degree, and by the national leaders to a lesser degree. Serbia was an exception in that the first administration was principally the work of Prince Milos. From the time of their respective inceptions, the powers repeatedly interfered with the internal affairs of each state. For many years, Balkan leaders had to concern themselves not only with the Porte, but also with the European powers, who were tremendously strong in military, political, and economic terms. The European great powers, either in unison or individually, organized the Greek kingdom in the 1830s, formulated of the Danubian Principalities in 1856, formed the government of autonomous Bulgaria in 1878, and established the Albanian administration in 1913.[11]

C. The Newly Established Balkan National Governments

By the 1860s, four Balkan areas established national governments. Greece was the only true independent state. Serbia and the Danubian Principalities were still theoretically under Ottoman control, but practically speaking, they were independent except for the payment of a tribute and other minor obligations regarding internal affairs. Montenegro maintained a unique position in that even

[11] See Jelavich, *History of the Balkans* 171–234.

though the state was officially recognized as part of the Ottoman Empire, the Porte could not exact a tribute nor could he control Montenegrin internal affairs. The Balkan governments performed in an equally independent fashion regarding foreign policy. Once again, in theory the Ottoman foreign ministry was responsible for handling the international relations of the entire empire, but in practice, the Balkan states conducted their own affairs through consistent and direct contact with other governments.

The newly established national regimes adhered to similar patterns in their internal development and therefore tended to face similar difficulties. Each state adopted a centralized bureaucratic monarchy as their governmental form and, as a result, political control shifted from the village communities and regional divisions to the capital. Naturally, this shift elicited a struggle to control the central authority and administrative network. The chief conflict flourished between the executive and legislative branches of government, or in other words, between the prince and his supporters and those who were excluded from power. The first demand of the excluded groups was for a council or assembly of notables who would be responsible for monitoring the power of the executive. Later, the idea of a representative assembly and constitutional government was considered. The average peasant, who had no direct political role in the state except as a revolutionary fighter, questioned whether a strong ruler or an oligarchy should hold the power to make decisions for the country.

Domestic controversies were enhanced when prominent individuals joined competing factions or parties in order to enhance their chances of gaining positions that would provide them with political power. Some organizations developed around a leader, while others developed out of issues such as alignment with or opposition to a prince, or issues dealing with domestic reform. Victory in an election extended far beyond the triumph of an individual or an idea. Victory both guaranteed the winning party would control the bureaucracy and assured appointments to major posts that meant access to the roots of real profit.

1. Governmental Corruption and European Influence

Guaranteed access to the bureaucracy and its major posts was important in order to put a check on corruption. Even though a government void of corruption is nonexistent, the entire Balkan society became severely restricted and weakened because of the corruption in political life. Corruption in government was not limited to the Ottoman political system, but was rampant in Christian states as well.

It must be remembered that corruption in office may be defined differently from one culture to the next. What may have been unacceptable to Western Europeans of that day may have been considered proper to the Balkan population. For example, nepotism was a common practice. It was considered standard behavior for an elected official to appoint members of his family to prestigious offices. Attachment and loyalty, or political patronage, was typically rewarded through assignment to public posts. Once securely in office, officials adhered to acceptable Ottoman practices while reaping the benefits of their positions. Payments for rendered services were expected. The term "bakshish" referred not only to the Western European custom of giving a tip, but to outright bribes. Officials in the lower echelons of the bureaucracy were frequently paid miserably and were therefore expected to supplement their incomes. In response to corruption and domestic controversies, and in an attempt to halt the disintegration of its empire, the Ottoman government began a policy of reform. By the 1870s, the Balkan government was forced to acknowledge that their aim to reconcile with the Balkan people still under the confines of Ottoman rule had failed. Balkan allegiance toward their national identities was too strong. Furthermore, in order to reinforce their influential positions, authorities in Greece and other autonomous principalities ensured that Ottoman horrors were not forgotten. Official propaganda and national mythology emphasized the concept of a "Turkish yoke" to incite the population under

Ottoman administration and to camouflage the defects of the Balkan governments.

Corruption and misgovernment were not the only problems plaguing the Balkan states; they were aggrieved by a high degree of interference by the European powers. Such interference was all legal and based on international treaties. As previously mentioned, Russia had the right to intervene in the Principalities and Serbia until 1856, and the three-power protectorate held rights over Greece until 1923. In addition, Austria and France could speak for the Catholics, as could Russia for the Orthodox, but what this arrangement entailed was never fully determined. Again the list of Balkan guarantors expanded, this time to include all of the signatories of the 1856 Treaty of Paris. The major powers of Russia, Austria, France, and Britain became key players in determining the fate of the Balkan states. In addition to exerting control over foreign relations, the major players penetrated local politics. Intervention was not evenly distributed among the Balkan states, nor was there a balance of power between consulates. Consequently, the ability of the Ottomans to run the empire was seriously hampered. In addition, the relations of the rulers in each nation with opposing politicians and the Porte became dreadfully strained.[12]

2. The Establishment of Austria-Hungary

Like Ottoman rule, the Habsburg empire began crumbling in 1867 when its history took a decisive turn. The Ausgleich Compromise, which segregated the empire into two distinct political units, represented an extensive reorganization of the empire which would prevail until the death of the monarchy in 1918. Additionally, the Ausgleich Compromise rewarded Hungary, which had been the most active and aggressive nationality in the empire, with the benefits of an administrative system

[12] Jelavich, *History of the Balkans* 235–99.

assistance was decisive in delineating the final political status, the revolutionary bands seized national lands and established governments. The Danubian Principalities and Bulgaria, on the other hand, gained freedom from Ottoman control as a result of shrewd negotiations in Romania's case, and of Russian War advancements in Bulgaria's.

The situation facing the nationalities inside the Habsburg Monarch prior to 1867 was naturally a different one. They were not able to ask for foreign assistance; however, they could capitalize on the internal conflict between the imperial government in Vienna and the most powerful and nationally conscious group in the empire, the Hungarians. The competition for power between Budapest and the national groups, and between the Habsburg imperial government and the capital, terminated with the collapse of the monarchy in 1918.

1. The Role of the Great Powers in Regional Development

The great powers, as previously noted, played a substantial role in the development of the region. During the nineteenth century, they strove not only to preserve the balance of power in the Near East, but to extend their influence into a single state, or better yet, over the entire region. France had interests in Egypt and the Principalities and was joined by Britain and Russia in the contest for preeminence in the councils of the sultan. Over the course of the century, each and every Balkan nationality requested British, French, Habsburg, or Russian assistance. Even though the temptations of exploitation were great, for the most part a resistant stand was taken.

Another development was the creation of treaties agreed upon by the Porte that guaranteed governments individual or collective rights to intervene in the internal affairs of the Ottoman Empire or to confine the activities of Ottoman officials to their own area. These governmental rights became the basis for European intervention. The agreements were not confined to the local affairs of the nationalities, but frequently extended to the sanctioning of privileges in foreign trade. The first agreements were the treaties of Karlowitz and Kuchuk Kainarji, which stipulated the conditions under which external powers could speak on behalf of Ottoman Balkan subjects. The nineteenth-century agreements, such as the Convention of Akkerman in 1826, the 1829 Treaty of Adrianople, the Treaty of London of 1830, and the 1856 Treaty of Paris, tended to be far more threatening to the Porte in that they guaranteed the great powers' political protectorate status over Balkan lands.

Despite the obvious benefits enjoyed by those who were designated as protectorates, the protectorate status came with its share of disadvantages. Frequently, the Balkan people requested assistance and assumed it would be provided gratuitously and without any political implications. Negotiations regarding restitution inevitably aroused indignant reactions from the Balkan governments. Russia suffered the greatest losses. Although its repeated wars with the Ottoman Empire served as the decisive factor in the Balkan acquisition of autonomy, the benefits that accrued to Russia were negligible in comparison to the enormous price paid in the loss of money and human lives.

The Balkan Peninsula was not merely affected by direct diplomatic intervention; the newly adopted political institutions reflected a strong European influence as well. In every case, the new governments were structured on constitutions modeled after the West. The extent of this influence, however, is debatable. Although European liberalism was reflected in language formation and use, representative institutions were not a novelty to Balkan societies and therefore cannot be attributed to contemporary Western ideology.

Reflecting European influence, councils to defend the interests of the nobility and notables date back as far as the Medieval Ages; the divans in the principalities served in the same capacity. Peasant-class administrative involvement during the Ottoman period was of even greater importance. At the community level, leaders of peasant families directed local affairs. The institution of the skupstina in Serbia, where men of a community gathered to converse about problems, greatly influenced the evolution of the Serbian political system. The primitive areas of Montenegro practiced customs similar to those of other regions. These traditional institutions, that were based on direct representation, proved to be problematic for all the national regimes because they scrutinized and often opposed the reforms these outsiders sought to implement.

Even though representative councils were commonplace in Balkan history, centralized and secular Christian administrative systems were not. In almost all cases, the Balkan people of former years had been subject to indirect government control via agents of the central power, or by the local nobility who rivaled the titular regional master. As subjects of Ottoman rule, Christians were under the direct authority of their millet and communal leaders, rather than the Porte's representatives. Similarly, in Habsburg territory and the Danubian Principalities, Christians fell under the control of local nobles, not officials of the monarch.

With the nineteenth century came the adoption of centralized bureaucratic regimes which enlarged the powers of the central offices of state so as to control all citizenry and eliminate intermediary provincial or local institutions. Officials of the central government were directly responsible for serving the individual. This system took hold throughout the Balkan region because it was considered contemporary, innovative and sophisticated. The reforms of the Ottoman Tanzimat, the Bach system in the Habsburg empire, and the 1848–1849 and post-1867 Hungarian administrations were all structured with these principles in mind. The outgrowths of this novel approach were a greater restriction in the political power of the peasantry and a growth of the influence of the educated middle class. Strong, centralized bureaucracies in control of law enforcement agencies and the electoral process purged the region of all representative institutions in order to insure the command of the political process.[14]

[14] See generally, Jelavich, *History of the Balkans* 329–72; and Stavrianos, *The Balkans 1815–1914* 10–71.

The internal political systems of the Balkan states may have been in a guarded position, but the peninsula wavered precariously as its entanglement in the affairs of the great powers determined its fate. The predominant diplomatic alignment during the years prior to 1878 was the Three Emperors' Alliance. Extreme Russian dissatisfaction with the meager outcome of the Russo-Turkish War resulted in conflicts not with the outright British opposition, but rather with the Russian allies under the Three Emperors' Alliance, namely Germany. Russian authority maintained that the German government had failed to return in kind the assistance Russia provided during the period of German unification. When relations between the two countries became severely strained in 1879, the governments began searching for alternate diplomatic arrangements. This time, the partners were bound by written agreements specifying the obligations of the partners, rather than by an informal arrangement which had been the nature of the 1870s Three Emperors' Alliance. The Balkan states were drawn into the great-power alliances either directly through supplementary agreements, or indirectly through a relationship with a member nation.[15]

The first agreement, the 1879 Dual Alliance, obligated its German and Austrian-Hungarian members to wage war should either country be attacked by Russia. The treaty was particularly significant because it drew Germany into Balkan affairs and into a partnership with Vienna. Shortly thereafter in June 1881, Germany, Russia, and the Habsburg empire settled their differences as they revived the Three Emperors' Alliance, this time in the form of a written agreement. The general neutrality pact included clauses pertaining to the Balkans, including an agreement that all three powers were to consult each other regarding any changes in the peninsula. A third agreement, the Triple Alliance, linked Germany, Italy, and Austria-Hungary. Even though this agreement was initially directed against

[15] Stavrianos, "The First Balkan Alliance System, 1860-1876," *Journal of Central European Affairs*, II (October 1942) 267-90.

France, Italian statesmen soon expressed their intent to share an influencing in the Balkans. Italy's chief interest was the fate of the Albanian regions. Italy hoped it could influence the region as did Russia in the eastern part of the peninsula and Austria-Hungary in the West. Because the pattern of alliances was defensive in nature, alliance obligations did not conflict even though the players copartnered in a manner which on the surface appeared contentious. These alliances functioned to tie the Balkan states to Vienna and Berlin.

However, problems over a division of Bulgaria surfaced between the Russian government which supported the partition and the Habsburgs which opposed it. As a result, when the time came to renew the Three Emperors' Alliance in 1887, the renewal did not transpire. Instead, Russia and Germany re-allied under the Reinsurance Treaty. Germany assured the Russian government it would provide support to help secure a favorable regime in Bulgaria. Simultaneously, however, Germany approved the organization of a counteralignment consisting of Britain, Italy, Austria-Hungary, and Spain against French expansion in Northern Africa. The counteralignment reinforced the status quo in the Mediterranean and Black Sea regions, which directly conflicted with Russia's plans for Bulgaria.[16]

This complex alliance system was upset in 1890 when the German Emperor William II discarded the Reinsurance Treaty, leaving France and Russia isolated. In 1891, a military agreement was signed by these two powers and an alliance was established in 1894. The continent was truly divided into two diplomatic camps. Russia and France stood together on one side, while Germany and the Habsburg empire were joined by Italy through the Triple Alliance. Romania and Serbia were connected by way of supplementary agreements to what later came to be called the Central Powers. Meanwhile, Britain maintained a policy of "splendid isolation."

---

[16] Stavrianos, "The First Balkan Alliance System, 1860-1876." *Journal of Central European Affairs,* II (October 1942) 267-90.

Despite the existence of the two European alliance systems, interests in the Balkans were one and the same during the last decade of the century. Throughout this period, both alliance systems cooperated with each other in order to maintain the status quo in the region and to prevent the reopening of the Eastern Question. Two disturbances ensued, however: in 1897, Greece and the Ottoman Empire went to war following one of many Cretan uprisings; in addition, Macedonia was plagued with constant problems. To make matters worse, all of the great powers were occupied with the task of empire building in Asia and Africa and therefore did not wish to be distracted by Balkan events.[17]

Accompanying the turn of the century was an intensification of imperial world rivalries that affected the Balkans because of their increasing diplomatic significance. To worsen the situation, the different nationalities, largely disregarded during the Ottoman period, reared their heads in conflict. Boundaries of the Balkan states were difficult to define because the populations had intermixed during the period of Habsburg and Ottoman rule. Consequently, the new states were multinational, some to a greater degree than others. In addition, not one national leadership was content with their boundaries; each maintained they had legitimate claims on its neighboring territory. Each government became obsessed with foreign policy, military preparedness, and foreign alliances that would promote their goals.

At the same time, the great powers strove to advance their positions by seeking out client states that would further their

[17] For the effects of Russia and the West on the Balkan modernization process, see generally Cyril E. Black, "Russia and the Modernization of the Balkans," *The Balkans in Transition* 145–72. For an account of the Eastern Question and the revolt in Crete, see generally E. J. Dillon, 'The Fate of Greece," *Contemporary Review*. LXXII (July–December 1897) 1–34; Harold Temperley, "The Situation in Crete," *Contemporary Review*. (September 1896) 317; Harold Temperley, 'The Greco-Turkish War," *Harper's Weekly*. XLI (January–June 1897) 309–10; and Theodore George Tatsios, *The Megali Idea and the Greek-Turkish War of 1897: The Impact of the Cretan Problem on Greek Irredentism 1866–1897* (New York: East European Monographs, 1984) 29–137.

interests. Revolutionary conflict employed by oppressed minorities and militant nationalists was the most common means by which to oppose the alien authority to which they were assigned. World War I, with its near annihilation of Balkan lives and property, marked the culmination of this volatile period. But while the two great multinational empires had become a part of history, the question still remained as to whether the Balkan states could negotiate among themselves how to resolve their internal problems, which had become even more pronounced after years of warfare and deprivation.

E. The Aftermath of the World Wars: Balkan Developments and Attempts to Modernize

1. Nationalism and the Effects of World War I

With the conclusion of World War I, the fate of the Balkan Peninsula was again placed in the hands of the victorious great powers. The peace treaties, the work of the representatives of Britain, France, Italy, and the United States, defined the geographic boundaries that have subsequently remained relatively stable. However, significant issues such as internal organization and economic development remained unresolved. Even though the peninsula in its entirety was characterized by an agrarian economy, a few privileged individuals whose viewpoints were frequently quite different from those of the peasant majority held the political power of the capitals. The political decision makers were individuals who had obtained university educations and had acquired positions in the government, the army, the professions, business or other middle-class occupations.

The various interests of this educated group of individuals were reflected in the political parties that rivaled one another under the parliamentary system. As they strove to fulfill their own ambitions, the voice of the rural populations was left unheeded. For the most part, Balkan governments regarded the peasant majority as a source of taxes and conscripts for the army; rarely were attempts made to provide them with compensatory benefits. While the Balkan political systems have been frequently criticized for their failure to guarantee civil liberties, it is possibly the corrupt, centralized administrations that deserve the most condemnation.[18]

Even though the Balkan leadership neglected to consider some of their constituents' wishes, they did recognize the restrictive nature of their societies. Balkan leaders envisioned a progressive transformation and wished to emulate the industrialization and modernization taking place in the advanced Western European states, but were confronted with obstacles too large to overcome. The Balkan Peninsula lacked sufficient capital and the necessary raw materials and trained personnel, but even more difficult a problem was to undertake the radical social and political changes associated with an extreme economic transformation. Specifically, the Balkans, where a decentralized community and millet system had previously been in effect, could not adjust to the necessity of referring all decisions, large or small, to the central administrators rather than deferring to local administrators who were representatives appointed by the central government. Unfortunately, very few advances were made before the peninsula faced another devastating period of warfare. Meanwhile, as the regional population grew and greater restrictions on external emigration were implemented, agrarian problems intensified. As if the situation was not fragile enough, the collapse of world grain prices due to the Great Depression nearly shook the foundation out from under the Balkan nations.

The developments in the Balkan Peninsula since the eighteenth century clearly reveal that the greatest force influencing the political life of the Balkan people was the national idea. Nationalism became even further accentuated during the brief

[18] For a better understanding of the domestic developments in the Balkan nation-states, see generally Barbara Jelavich, *History of the Balkans: Twentieth Century* vol. 2 (Cambridge: Cambridge University Press, 1993) 121–37.

period between the two world wars. However, by 1941, nationalism developed features that were more negative than positive.

The national states of Albania, Bulgaria, Greece, and Romania originated as a result of the implementation of the nationalistic principle. Yugoslavia, on the other hand, was torn apart during wartime as the Croats, Serbs, and Slovenes refused to allow a Yugoslav nationality to come into existence. Serbian policies of centralization created bitterness and hostility among the region's inhabitants and led to a series of incredible wartime atrocities. Balkan passions regarding the control of lands claimed on the basis of history or nationalism were intense. All of the states engaged in territorial disputes with their neighbors. Generally regarded as the most serious disputes were the Macedonian issue among Bulgaria, Greece, and Yugoslavia, and that of Transylvania between Hungary and Romania. In addition, there were conflicts over Thrace, Epirus, Dobrudja, Bessarabia, Bukovina, Dalmatia, Istria, the Vojrodina, the Kosovo area, the Dodecanese Islands, Cyprus, and other small areas.

The rivalry between these lands created divisiveness between the Balkan peoples and served as a pretext for great-power intrusion. France, Britain, Italy, Germany and the Soviet Union all played on these mutual grievances to advance their own interests. Additionally, the French postwar system of alliances sustained the bitterness of the peace settlement and the resentment of the nationalities. These and other perceived injustices interfered with any attempts to unite the Balkan states or to concur on a plan to block great-power intervention.[19]

The Balkan political situation worsened as the Great Depression crippled the world economy. Plagued by multiplying social and economic problems, the Balkan states were unable to maintain their former parliamentary systems. An authoritarian regime was established in each state whereupon the monarchy and army took center stage. Each government

[19] Jelavich, *History of the Balkans* 192–243.

attempted to maintain internal order and preserve the existing social structure. The royal dictatorships strove to preserve the domestic status quo and to guard national interests during a time when the international arena was plagued with instability. When Europe once again thrust itself into war, the governments made a desperate attempt to stave off fighting from their borders, but to no avail.

With the entire region participating in the war, the summer of 1941 marked a turning point in the history of the Balkans. Romania and Bulgaria were involved in the hostilities as Axis allies, while Greece, Albania, and Yugoslavia were subject to German, Bulgarian, and Italian occupation. Romania's General Ion Antonescu was in full charge of the government and decided to participate in the German campaign against Russia to recover its Transylvanian territory, as well as its share in the spoils of victory.

In the year 1943, after the Stalingrad catastrophe, it became clear that Axis defeat was inevitable and the war would end in disaster for Romania. Romanian officials made efforts to arrange a separate peace with the Western Allied powers, but without success. By the beginning of August 1944, with Soviet troops fast approaching, Romania realized that it needed assistance from the Western Allies. With Allied assistance, Romania declared war on Germany on August 24, but the Soviet army had already entered Romanian territory. An armistice was signed in Moscow on September 12 that obligated the Romanian government to pay reparations and yield to Soviet occupation.

Unlike the Romanian military, Bulgarian troops did not participate in the Soviet Union campaign. Bulgarian contributions to the war effort consisted of providing garrison activity to territories conquered by German and Italian troops. As an Axis ally, Bulgaria occupied and then annexed Macedonia and Thrace at the onset of the war, and southern Dobrudja at a later time. In an attempt to raise the general cultural level of their new territories and to revive the population's Bulgarian nationality, the Bulgarian government instituted a massive pro-

Partisans dominated all other elements in the Serbian, Croatian, and Slovenian regions and actually took full control in the areas of Macedonia and Kosovo.

Albanian circumstances differed considerably from those in Yugoslavia because after the conquest of the Albanian lands in 1939, the Italian government established a constitutional monarchy. After the fall of both Yugoslavia and Greece in May 1941, Albania took control of the Kosovo region. As in Yugoslavia, the organization of resistance groups followed. Most importantly were those groups formed by the Communist Party and the rival National Front, or Balli Kombetar.

The Western government encouraged the partisan bands to unite in their campaign against the Axis, but with the Italian surrender in September 1943, German occupation was effectively established. Because the German government was primarily interested in securing a stable administration, they agreed to recognize Albanian independence, and a regency was selected. The state was declared neutral, and a state police and army were established. The political future of Albania was to be decided by external events, as was the case after World War I. The interests of its neighbors in Albanian territory were bound to resurface. When the German forces withdrew in November 1944, the National Liberation Movement (LNC) under Yugoslav direction established itself in power.

After the conquest of Greece in April 1941, the victorious powers divided the conquered regions. Bulgarian troops occupied most of Thrace and part of Greek Macedonia. The European military controlled Athens and other important centers, and Italian and Albanian troops held other regions. Even though the Axis organized a cooperative administration in the capital, Axis authorities did not try to govern the entire region; about two-thirds of the territory and half of the population were not under the authority of the central bureaucracy. Again, as in the other Balkan states, an anarchical environment prevailed, thus creating favorable conditions for the rise of resistance movements. Here, as in the neighboring states, the strongest forces were those under Communist leadership.

In the fall of 1941, guerilla bands developed throughout the mountain regions of Greece, most importantly the National Liberation Front (EAM) under Communist direction. Closely associated with the EAM was the military arm of government, the National Popular Liberation Army (ELAS). The most important rival to EAM/ELAS was the National Republican Greek League, or EDES, and there was a third, much smaller band, known as the National and Social Liberation (EKKA).[20]

British military and political decisions made to prevent Greece from falling prey to Communist-directed guerilla groups significantly influenced Greek circumstances. At the same time, in their efforts against the Axis enemy, British leaders deemed it necessary to take advantage of the resistance forces, whether directed by republicans or Communists.

In a sense, British military and political objectives were in conflict. Despite this conflict of interests, an attempt was made to implement a double line of policy. British officers began working with some of the resistance groups in order to establish a kind of federation of guerilla bands under British control. The guerilla bands eventually united under the National Bands Agreement to assist the British in some of their military operations. After several cooperative undertakings against the Axis, the partisan bands, particularly EAM/ELAS, gained significant strength through the acquisition of Axis equipment. Less dependent on Ally supplies, the band leaders adopted a more independent attitude. Predicting that the war would soon end and the British would attempt to restore the old regime, the EAM leadership decided to launch an attack on rival partisan groups. The purpose of the attacks was to gain full control of the country before the arrival of a British expeditionary force.

---

[20] Stavrianos, "The Greek National Liberation Front (EAM): A Study in Resistance Organization and Administration." *Journal of Modern History*. XXIV (March 1952) 42–55.

The October 1943 attacks marked the beginning of the first stage in the long Greek civil war that was to last until 1949.[21]

In September 1944, the German troops began leaving Greece and evacuated Athens by October 12. British occupation forces entered the city despite the possibility of a confrontation with the resistance groups. With the arrival of British reinforcements, EAM agreed to demobilize and accept an armistice to take effect on January 15. This document provided for the demobilization of all partisan bands in return for a guarantee of full political rights and an amnesty for all previous political activities. At the close of World War II, Greece had a coalition government that was based on the prewar parties and was supported by Britain.[22]

2. Major Changes in the Balkan Peninsula Following World War II

World War II ushered in major changes in the peninsula: most important was the diplomatic upheaval accompanying peace. No longer could Germany nor Italy, both defeated in war, nor France and Britain, both seriously weakened by the war, lay claims to the title of first rank. As such, the Soviet Union and the United States emerged as the title holders. Although neither the Soviet Union nor the United States had been very involved in interwar Balkan affairs, both found themselves in a position granting them power to determine the individual states' forms of government and even the ability to approve or disapprove of

[21] For an analysis of the British defeat of EAM generally, refer to Lars Baerentzen and David Close, 'The British Defeat of EAM, 1944–45," in David H. Close ed., *The Greek Civil War. 1943–1950: Studies of Polarization* (London: Routledge, 1993) 32–55. Additionally, for information regarding the Greek Communist Party of 1945–49, see Ole L. Smith, "The Greek Communist Party, 1945-49," *The Greek Civil War.* 1943–1950 129–50.

[22] For further details about World War II effects in the Balkan Peninsula, see generally Jelavich, *History of the Balkans* 247–84; and Clogg, *A Short History of Modern Greece* 133–65.

their leaders. Immediately following the peace settlement, the United States held the preeminent position in Greek politics while the Soviet Union functioned as the decision maker in the other countries. After 1948, however, the Soviet Union held direct control only in Bulgaria and Romania, and in Albania until 1960.[23]

Following the Greek civil war and the stabilization of Yugoslav–Soviet Union relations, world attention and the struggle for control shifted from the Balkan states to Asia and Africa. The political division of the Balkan Peninsula mirrored that of the rest of Europe, which was experiencing a division into two military and ideological alignments. The predominant issues in Europe at this time were economic unification within both the Western and Soviet blocs, the German dilemma, and Soviet military intervention in the Communist states of Hungary and Czechoslovakia.

Despite the active role the Balkan states took in world affairs, in actuality, they had lost their freedom of action. Former inter-Balkan grievances continued, but any governmental decision to wage war was not an option without the approval of its great-power patron. Even Yugoslavia, who claimed to be non-aligned (at least theoretically), had to closely monitor both great powers. With the twentieth century came a new set of rules by which the Balkan states were obligated to abide. They were no longer able to draw their great-power allies into war over local issues, nor could they match the pace of the new military technology due to their lack of finances and skills. The period of the Balkan guerilla fighters who were dependent upon local villages for rifles, grenades, and supplies had passed.

More important than the shift in the strategic significance of the Balkan nations was the revolutionary transformation in domestic policy during the postwar years. These alterations typically had a greater effect on the Balkan way of life than any

---

23 For information regarding the status of the great powers after World War II see generally, Jelavich, *History of the Balkans* 284–300.

change in the previous three centuries of Balkan development. In spite of the property damage and sacrifice of life that occurred as a result of the revolts and great wars, and in spite the population movement within the peninsula and emigration overseas, the basic social structure remained mostly undisturbed. The ideal for the majority of the agrarian peasant population was ownership of highly productive farms. Therefore, family and village relationships were of primary importance.

After the civil revolutions, the central bureaucracy attempted to exact greater political control over the countryside, but aside from a few superficial changes, its attempts were unsuccessful. Additionally, the new constitutional systems were as liberal as they were nationalistic in that they were directed toward individual liberation rather than social improvement. They did not provide rigid structure for the future, nor did they stipulate the role of the citizen. In contrast, the socialist systems focused on social advancement and economic modernization, and serious constraints were placed on the individual's designated role in the general scheme. The goal of the socialist system was neither liberty nor individuality but rather equality. Both the aim of socialism and its methods of attainment conflicted with the traditions and ideals of agrarian village life. Therefore, the discord in the Balkans was in essence not the Communist usurpation of political power, but the steady deterioration of traditional patterns of life. A similar change occurred in Greece when the countryside underwent extreme alterations in the interest of economic advancements.[24]

The crucial need for radical economic changes and development was recognized prior to 1945 by the monarchical governments, but governmental efforts were fruitless. The monarchical governments encountered obstacles in the very nature of their regimes and in the environment of the times. Even more significant obstacles surfaced because the political authorities lacked the ability to implement radical yet necessary alterations

[24] Jelavich, *History of the Balkans* 301–35.

in old patterns. The armies could restrain opposition, but they could not enact measures conducive to industrialization. Even though prewar Balkan authorities wielded their power to a great degree, they were incapable of maneuvering large segments of the population or delegating hundreds of undesirable tasks to their citizens. In contrast, the new socialist leadership was compelled to adhere to a plan devised by the Soviet Union and therefore experienced no such constraints. The socialist leadership was reinforced by the armed power of the state and maintained control over the means of coercion and propaganda. As a result, the leadership could implement measures without any regard for public opinion. They could execute extreme programs that previous regimes would not have dared to implement, such as severe reductions in living standards in order to finance factories or thwart all expression of political resistance.

The national governments that Communist systems replaced justified their right to rule based upon their role in the establishment of their independent status and their constitutional regimes. In turn, the independent status and constitutional regimes were legitimized by the theoretical concept of individual freedom and political, if not social or economic, equality. Naturally, Communists endeavored to replace the Christian principle of human destiny with Marxist doctrine, which asserts that each individual's life is automatically linked to a preordained pattern of historical development.

Communist systems have been criticized, particularly in the United States and Western Europe, for their harsher aspects, yet their positive attributes have been virtually ignored. To give credit where credit is due, Communist regimes have unquestionably brought many material advantages to their citizens, particularly in Yugoslavia, which adheres less to Communist doctrine than do other socialist governments. Specifically, significant advances have been made in the field of social services, such as the development of national health programs, educational systems available to all, subsidized housing, paid leisure time, and pensions for the sick and elderly. The citizens of

Albania, Bulgaria, and Romania have also enjoyed the assurance of full employment. In addition, modern housing has been constructed for a large percentage of the population and many more enjoy some of the most valued consumer goods, namely radios, television sets, and automobiles. Those nations that benefit from the proper administration of such social measures have been able to soften the harshness of the radical changes that have occurred and have been able to offer material advantages to a segment of the population who otherwise would not have received them.

Even though there have been many obvious benefits, the Communist system is ailing. All nations, including the Balkan states, suffered from the inflationary cost of world oil in the 1970s and continue to be restrained by the deficit of other basic raw materials such as coal and iron. Some of the Communist system's troubles are shared with the rest of the world, while others are indigenous to Balkan or socialist conditions. The vast array of problems that plague all industrialized societies are even more difficult to solve within the Balkans' relatively poor economic framework. In the political realm, problems associated with one-party rule and the suffocating consequences of a well-established bureaucracy are still being dealt with. Political stability has been attained, but the cost has been the imposition of extreme individual and social control. Additionally, like all those who preceded them in Balkan history, including the Greeks, Communist systems depend on the loyalty of their military, a loyalty which is always precarious.[25]

Of all the Balkan states, Greece has undergone the most varied political experience after 1945. Even though there was economic and social stability, the political changes were dramatic. The first government established after the civil war under General Alexandras Papagos and Konstantinos Karamanlis was a moderately conservative one. It was followed by the centrist liberal regime of George Papandreou, who was overthrown by a

[25] Jelavich, *History of the Balkans* 336–405.

military coup directed initially by Colonel George Papadopoulos and subsequently by Brigadier Dimitrios Ioannides. In 1974, a constitutional system was restored when Karamanlis was reinstated. In 1981, the Panhellenic Socialist Movement (PASOK) won the election under Andreas Papandreou. Even though PASOK was a socialist party, it did not resemble the Marxist socialist regimes in other Balkan states because of its divergent ideological base.[26]

Throughout the entire postwar period, Greek foreign policy retained a Western orientation, although it was constantly at odds with its allies. Despite the fact that Greece became a member of the NATO defense system in the eastern Mediterranean, the alliance weakened during the 1974 Cypriot Crisis because the Greek government felt the United States had betrayed Greek interests. As the Greek leaders disengaged from American association, they sought closer ties with the Western European countries by joining the European Economic Community (EEC). However, the Cyprus issue remained on the forefront of Greece's foreign policy.

Although Greece retained a Western constitutional government during the postwar period—with the exception of a seven-year period during which a military dictatorship prevailed—the country underwent tremendous change. Paralleling its neighbors, Greece experienced a demographic revolution. Not only was there a mass exodus from the countryside to the cities following the civil war, but the emigration which had begun prior to the war continued until 1975 when a reverse trend began. Adjustments were necessary as formerly rural populations experienced new conditions, including new technological advantages. Even though conscious efforts were made to improve the economic standards of the country, social and eco-

[26] For a brief analysis of PASOK, see generally Kevin Featherstone, "PASOK and the Left" in Kevin Featherstone and Dimitrios K. Katsoulas eds., *Political Change in Greece: Before and After the Colonels* (London: Croom Helm, 1987) 112–33.

nomic problems persisted through the first years of the 1980s. These problems were a reflection of the difficult world conditions of the time.[27]

III. CONCLUSION: TRANSNATIONAL NATIONALISM AND THE SEARCH FOR A THEORETICAL FRAMEWORK TO UNDERSTAND THE CYPRIOT CRISIS

Although a historical analysis reveals that tremendous advancements were made throughout the Balkan Peninsula by the close of the nineteenth century, many of the chief goals of the national leadership were not fully achieved. Territorial unification of the states had not been accomplished, particularly in regards to the Albanian national movement. In addition, the Habsburg empire, which retained its great-power status into the twentieth century, still housed many South Slav and Romanian nationals. The Ottoman Empire also managed to maintain its control over much of the peninsula. Furthermore, the dawn of the new century was accompanied by severe economic and social problems, including the tragedy of the two devastating world wars which only exacerbated an already difficult task.

The theme of a conflicting attraction and repulsion to foreign political, ideological, and economic influence remains an enduring element of Balkan history. However, even though Balkan societies have absorbed a great deal from the outside world either willingly or involuntarily, it must be stressed that where foreign institutions and ideas were implemented, they were subsequently shaped and altered to conform to national traditions and prejudices. Accompanying the difficulties that stemmed from rival external influences, compounded

[27] For more information regarding political developments in post-World War II Greece see generally Jelavich, *History of the Balkans* 400–38; Clogg, *A Short History of Modern Greece* 166–225; and Close, 'The Legacy," *The Greek Civil War, 1943–1950* 214–31. Additionally, for a detailed account of Balkan developments see Stavrianos, *The Balkans Since 1453* (New York: Rinehart & Company, Inc., 1959).

by significant internal pressures, the passion for liberation could not be extinguished. A close examination of the individual national revolutions reveals that although they were individually executed with relatively little cooperation among the Balkan nationalities, a common thread can be traced in each historical experience. Each movement was energized by the dream of a cultural revival where their language, consciousness, and institutions would reign superior. Cries from kinsmen, deep within the earth and long since buried, whose blood was spilled for the preservation of their cultural identity, could not and cannot be silenced. Thus, the war among the Balkan people in general, and between Greece and Turkey over Cyprus in particular, wages on even to this day.

What kind of theorizing is best suited for understanding the endless Cypriot dispute? Rather than attacking theories specifically directed at Cyprus, I have drawn from social science literature to formulate three paradigms; I then test their explanatory power when applied to the Cypriot case. For simplicity, I have chosen to test the accuracy of this tri-model explanation of stability in its application to the persistent dispute on Cyprus. Following the lead of Graham Allison, I examine a specific incident from three theoretical vantage points.

Allison's first model maintains that important events have equally important causes. The important and relevant determinants of an occurrence must be identified and the extent of their influence determined. Model one analysts assume that an individual player, or rational actor, makes choices and acts with reference to his or her plans and tactics.[28] The second model, an organizational process model, frames the determinants of an incident as the output of large, established organizations that behave in accordance with fixed procedures and regular patterns of behavior.[29] Lastly, the third model, a bureaucratic politics model, focuses on the politics of a government. Events are characterized as the result of numerous bargaining games

---

[28] Graham T. Allison, *Essence of Decision: Explaining the Cuban Missile Crisis* (New York: Harper Collins Publishers, 1971) 10–38.

[29] Allison, *Essence of Decision* 67–100.

among between a number of distinct players. Each player possesses distinct perceptions, motivations and positions, yet all players share power in the negotiating process.[30]

Allison shows how the rational actor, organizational process, and the bureaucratic politics paradigms each provide different explanations for the Cuban Missile Crisis. While each model provides insights to an incident, a comprehensive understanding of an event is found only in the interaction of the three models.

Like the Cuban Missile Crisis, the Cypriot dispute must be analyzed using several theoretical approaches in order to capture its logic. Only an explanation that borrows and combines elements from international relations and comparative approaches is effective. The problem with this approach, however, is that some degree of parsimony and novelty is lost; but this loss is better dealt with than an incorrect understanding of events.

Despite their limitations, international relations and comparative theories prove beneficial in that they help to explain the conditions and circumstances that caused the Cypriot Crisis. Specifically, international relations theories are applicable when evaluating the role of Cyprus's neighbors and their level of influence on the development of the crisis. Of equal importance is the comparative approach. This approach offers an explanatory framework for analyzing the domestic policies of a country. Together, these two theoretical approaches contribute to the formation of a hypothesis which incorporates the effects of interaction and the impact of culture.

The eclectic and interactive approach to theory I have applied has revealed a phenomenon I have labeled "transnational nationalism." This phenomenon occurs when a country attempts to extend its nationalistic ideology and culture across its boundaries. In order to understand the limits and potential effects of nationalism, it is beneficial to have a test case or an ideal model. One such case is a plural society, characterized by component cultures tied to other states. In this societal form, external politics may prove more influential than politics within the government, especially if cultural bonds

---

[30] Allison, *Essence of Decision* 144–84.

between the people and external governments resist alteration. The effect of transnational nationalism is enhanced when it is buttressed by the cultural institutions that bind and unify individuals from different nations.

While this theory is merely a suggested theoretical framework for analyzing the Cypriot Crisis, it is a starting point for understanding larger historical events and those that will confront the world in the years to come.

CHAPTER 2

APPLICATION OF INTERNATIONAL RELATIONS THEORIES TO THE CYPRIOT CASE: SEARCHING FOR AN UNDERSTANDING OF THE DETERMINANTS OF THE 1974 CYPRIOT CRISIS

> They have their liberty, and this means that it will be a long time before they begin to take precautions against us. We are more concerned about islanders like yourselves, who are still unsubdued, or subjects who have already become embittered by the constraint which our empire imposes on them. These are people who are most likely to act in a reckless manner and to bring themselves and us, too, into the most obvious danger.[1]
>
> —Thucydides

I. INTRODUCTION: AN OVERVIEW OF INTERNATIONAL RELATIONS THEORIES

The inhabitants of the island of Cyprus, predominantly of either Greek or Turkish descent, have been subjected to the intrusive behavior of their respective homelands since the island was colonized. Well aware that the Cypriots were embittered by the divisive nature of the interference, the motherlands feared that the Cypriot people might one day decide to take destiny into their own hands, and in so doing

[1] Thucydides, *History of the Peloponnesian War* 403.

produce irreparable harm to all parties involved. Did the conflicting noneconomic foreign policies of Greece and Turkey cause the 1974 Cypriot Crisis? Or were the domestic policies of Cyprus themselves the culprit? In order to answer these questions, it is helpful to examine international relations theories and apply them to the case of Cyprus.

Realists argue that to a large extent, social behavior is a product of the structure of power relations. In order to understand the behavior of social actors, not only must the role of the individual state be understood—socially, economically, and politically—but the state must also be considered in an international setting with respect to its relations with the community of states. Neorealists simplify the work of realists by arguing that the three major players, captured by three different levels of analysis, or "images of power," perform independently or conjunctively and determine the state of peace or war of their members.[2]

The first image of international relations looks to the nature and conduct of man. From this first-level perspective, "Wars result from selfishness, from misguided aggressive impulses, from stupidity.[3] If these human tendencies are the fundamental causes of war, then the logical solution for the elimination of war lies in the readjustment of the "psychic-social" character of man. According to the first-image analysts who link war to the imperfections inherent in society, sociopolitical institutions impel change. The first-image theorist recognizes the contribution of state actions, or, more accurately, "of man acting for states."[4]

The second image highlights the internal structure of states as a factor which determines human conduct. The complexity of any explanation reveals that human nature cannot possibly be a single determinant of war or peace. Peace with justice cannot occur without an organization that resembles a government in its qualities and structure, just as internal justice too requires a strong and active government.[5] Even though the second image of international relations

2 Kenneth N. Waltz, *Man, the State, and War: A Theoretical Analysis* (New York: Columbia University Press, 1959) 16.

3 Waltz, *Man, the State, and War* 16.

4 Waltz, *Man, the State, and War* 16 and 122.

5 Waltz, *Man, the State, and War* 120.

implies that "the internal structure of states determines . . . [e]xternal behavior,"[6] it encounters the same difficulty as the first image in that it is an incomplete theory. While the actions of states comprise the substance of international relations, the global political environment itself exerts tremendous influence over the behavior of states.[7]

Finally, the third image is that of international relations, where sovereign states are void of any universal law system and are bound by their inherently conflictual circumstances to eventually engage in war. Furthermore, there is no steadfast method of imposing harmony in an anarchic world; wars occur because there is nothing to prevent them. Thus, third-image analysts conclude that a world government, if possible to create, is the only solution.[8]

There are also problems, however, with a third-image analysis. First, in the event of war, a state must rely on its domestic policies and the efficient use of its own resources to achieve the upper hand and ultimately defeat its adversary. Secondly, the causes of war are determined as heavily by preconditions as they are by world events. Finally, politics are influenced, at least in part, by the notions which politicians entertain.

Consequently, the "three images" are fundamental to a credible understanding of international relations; an examination of all three levels of analysis and their interrelatedness is crucial. "[I]t has by now become apparent that there is a considerable interdependence among the three images."[9] For Cyprus, the three images—social actors, the internal dynamics of the state, and the world structure—are all interrelated. Therefore, a clear understanding of the 1974 Cypriot Crisis depends upon a consideration of the interdependence of the three images. In order to determine the role that each level of analysis played in the Cypriot dispute and its aftermath, I will examine each level as follows in reverse order: from third- to second- to first-image approaches.

---

6 Waltz, *Man, the State, and War* 125.

7 Waltz, *Man, the State, and War* 120 and 230.

8 Waltz, *Man, the State, and War* 238.

9 Waltz, *Man, the State, and War* 16.

II. THIRD-LEVEL THEORIES

Third-level theories hold that within the structure of the bipolar global system, the state is a representative of the dominant class, and the state's behavior as a unit is influenced by the structure in which it exists. The world systems theory is a third-level approach which postulates that international outcomes are just the aggregate of individual state behavior. In turn, state behavior is the product of the interplay of international characteristics. Upon examining the state unit, it becomes clear that various patterns and the recurrence of behavior are determined by the state's structure of the international system. Specifically, system structure influences the behavior of its agents through the socialization of its members and competition among them. Finally, system structure partially determines domestic political structures by specifying the roles and functions of the state's components. Hence, structure and political outcome are, in essence, the product of organization and order.[10]

According to the balance of power theory, another world system theory, national power is determined by three primary factors: population size, political efficiency, and economic development. The interplay and shifts of these factors lead to variations in the distribution of power. Modern times have been characterized by great changes and increases in power due to industrialization, as well as permanence of ties among nations. These two causes of change provide the framework for a recurring pattern of activity in recent international politics. In the context of international politics, several factors operate to make war more or less likely. War is more likely when the balance of power between the two nations is unequal. Other considerations also affect the potentiality of war: the power of a rising challenger, the speed with which the challenger gains power, the flexibility of the dominant nation, the degree of friendship between the dominant nation and the challenger, and the challenger's intentions regarding

[10] Kenneth Waltz, "Reductionist and Systemic Theories," in Robert O. Keohane ed., *Neorealism and Its Critics* (New York: Columbia University Press, 1986) 47–68; and Waltz, "Political Structure," *Neorealism and Its Critics* 74–94.

the existing international order. All of these factors operate together to promote or inhibit the development of war.[11]

Finally, the international capitalism theory maintains that the world should be viewed using a systems-down approach where the behavior of a state is described as a product of the capitalist world economy. As such, the state is not a completely distinct unit, but a partially independent representative of the dominant class that plays a structural role in the system. Structurally, the state is produced from the top down, and core states are strong because peripheral states are weak. The state in the core of the system is strong because the state in the periphery is weak. In essence, the world capitalist system structures the performance of individual states and their member classes, dominant and otherwise.[12]

A. Waltz's World Systems Theory

World systems theorists support the predominance of the third image over the other images. Their interpretation of the international sphere stems from a macro-level perspective where the focal considerations are the distribution of global power, world structures, and regimes. These theorists contend that the condition of international politics cannot be inferred from the internal composition of states, nor can an understanding of international politics be derived from a summation of foreign policies and the external behavior of states.[13]

According to a world systems perspective, global political structure dictates all international activity. Therefore, the bipolar power structure that prevailed in 1974 directed universal behavior. Under this theory, the logic of bipolarity influences all states at all levels, regardless of their domestic politics. From this viewpoint, the 1974

---

[11] A. F. K. Organski, *World Politics* 2nd edition (New York: Random House, Inc., 1968) 340–74.

[12] Immanuel Wallerstein, "The Rise and Future Demise of the World Capitalist System: Concepts for Comparative Analysis," *Comparative Studies in Society and History* vol 16, no. 4 (September 1974) 398–415.

[13] Waltz, "Reductionist and Systemic Theories" and "Anarchic Orders and Balance of Power," *Neorealism and Its Critics* 51, 52–60 and 129.

Cypriot Crisis can be understood in light of a bipolar world. Hence, the Cold War competition of the United States and Soviet Union helps to shed light on our understanding of the Cypriot situation.

From the onset of American involvement in the region, which commenced with Britain's request as a result of her economic exhaustion at the end of World War II, United States policy was the pursuit of security interests through the confinement of the perceived threat of Soviet expansionism. American interests, which were also held by Great Britain, can be identified along two dimensions: the inter-allied dispute which arose as Cyprus threatened the cohesion of the Western Alliance of NATO, and the undermining effect the "Cyprus Question" had on the broader security interests in the Eastern Mediterranean and the Middle East.

Despite United States urgings to approach the issue through quiet diplomatic negotiations with Britain, Greece made repeated efforts in the early 1950s to internationalize the "Cyprus Question." Quiet diplomacy triumphed in a series of covert negotiations that were codified in the Zurich Agreements. The American policy stance toward Cyprus evolved following the 1974 collapse of the Cypriot Republic. In 1964, the United States had supported the 1964 Acheson-Ball proposals calling for a partition of the island and an end to the independent existence of the republic, whereas by 1974, American policy reinforced the principle of a unitary independent Republic of Cyprus under the leadership of Archbishop Makarios.

The Acheson Plan grew out of American concern with the growth of Soviet political and military missions in the region, and the need to contain the fighting on Cyprus. This fighting represented the type of conditions which the Communist Party of Cyprus (AKEL) and the Russians could exploit. The first suggestion, to broaden the British peace-keeping force on Cyprus, was unacceptable to Makarios. However, the UNFICYP (United Nations Peacekeeping Force), an international force funded and manned by NATO, was an acceptable temporary solution. The objectives of the Acheson-Ball Plan were to safeguard American interests, provide enosis for the Greeks, and protect Turkish political and strategic interests.

As an independent state of strategic placement and Communist leanings, Cyprus was viewed as a threat to American interests and the United States urgently sought a permanent resolution to the Cypriot problem. Hence, dismemberment became the ideal. For the Cypriot case, the prevailing bipolar world system affected the behavior of the interested states. However, world systems advocates go awry in this context because they fail to recognize the role of small states like Greece and Turkey. These countries strive for self-determination and thus they often behave at the regional level in a manner more characteristic of a multipolar structure. Regional multipolarity is incompatible with international bipolarity of the point of view of world systems theory.[14]

The world systems theory's construction of a bipolar world system does not explain the Cypriot case. Conflicts between Greece and Turkey over ethnicity in Cyprus predate the Cold War era. It has been argued that "[t]he roots of the ethnic conflict in Cyprus go back to history and deep into the bicommunal structure of the Cypriot society . . . [where] the two communities remained separate, distinct, and self-contained ethnic groups . . . ."[15] Within this hostile arena, disputes over the occupation and political control of Cyprus have been a dominant issue. Although the distribution of international power has undergone numerous transformations over the last several centuries, both in the number of dominant powers and in the names and faces of the key players, possession of Cyprus has simply changed hands between Greece and Turkey. The continuing and consistent enmity over Cyprus, regardless of change in world systems, casts doubt on the argument that the world structure is the decisive factor. Other factors must be evaluated to determine the relevance of the third-image analysis to the Cypriot case.

---

[14] Van Coufoudakis, "United States Foreign Policy and the Cyprus Question: A Case Study in Cold War Diplomacy," in Michael Attalides ed., *Cyprus Reviewed* (Nicosia: The Jus Cypri Association, 1977) 101–02, 104, 107, 112, 114–15 and 121.

[15] Joseph S. Joseph, *Cyprus: Ethnic Conflict and International Concern* (New York: Peter Lang, 1985) 63.

The history of Cypriot colonization reveals that the behavior of the tripartite relationship between the island, Greece, and Turkey, has not been confined to the parameters established by the world power structure. Furthermore, the desirability of the island's strategic geographic location produced defiance to externally imposed limits, if any even existed. Ironically, Cyprus's location, a predestined characteristic, constituted the crux of the hostilities because it offered security for the controlling power, yet at the same time undermined the stability of the forfeiting opponent. Thus, both Greece and Turkey suspected their security would be jeopardized if their influence over Cypriot affairs was reduced. The intensification of the Cypriot dispute thrust the tripartite players into action that was indifferent to the global structure. These illustrations undermine the notion of a world "autocracy" because they reveal the behavioral liberties of both Greece and Turkey over time, irrespective of the global power structure in place at any particular time.[16]

However, reference must still be made to the specific bipolar power structure that prevailed at the time of the Cypriot Crisis. World systems theory advocates would maintain that, within the context of the bipolar world of that day, virtually all global conduct was the product of the greater conflict between the United States and the Soviet Union, often referred to as the Cold War. The nature of the order is contingent on the dispositions of the states which constitute it, and therefore a revision of international political outcomes will occur only subsequent to an alteration of the internal nature of the internationally important states.[17] However, some theorists believe the Cold War did not play an important role in the Cypriot Crisis because Cyprus was considered a nonaligned country and did not maintain any relations with the Soviet system.[18]

---

[16] Joseph, *Cyprus* 60.

[17] Waltz, "Reductionist and Systemic Theories," *Neorealism and Its Critics* 50.

[18] Interview with Efstathios Lagakos, Member of the European Parliament, Athens, December 24, 1992. From August 1972 to July 13, 1974, he was the Greek Ambassador to Cyprus. However, he resigned his post three days before the coup and held a position at the Ministry of Foreign Affairs.

The Cold War dichotomy of the United States versus the Soviet Union implies an acknowledgment that all international decision making is under the control of, or indirectly influenced by, the two superpowers. Considering this acknowledgement in light of Cyprus, it is important to note that during a meeting in 1957 when Turkish officials met with Lord Radcliffe of Britain to explore the possibility of an independent Cyprus, the Turks, who pressed for a federation, provided a map of Cyprus which displayed their proposal of an acceptable division. The present day partition of Cyprus duplicates that map. Again in 1964, Turkey presented a map to the United Nations mediator, and once again the line which serves as the current boundary of the land in Cyprus is the same line as was indicated on the 1957 map.[19]

In addition, "behind the scenes" covert conferences concerning the division of Cyprus transpired between Greek and Turkish officials. The first instance was the Paris Protocol initiated on December 17, 1966, by Greek Foreign Minister J. Toumbas and his Turkish counterpart, I. Caglayangil. The most important consensus, to move toward a final solution to the Cypriot problem, was reached in Lisbon on June 3–4, 1971, between Palamas of Greece and Olcay of Turkey. Even though Department of State analysts acknowledged and endorsed the consensus to unite Cyprus with Greece after relinquishing part of Cyprus to Turkey, Makarios did not. Therefore, it was decided during these surreptitious meetings that "'Makarios's problem must be left essentially to Greece."[20] In a letter to Makarios, Greek Prime Minister George Papadopoulos refuted the rumors that were circulating regarding the covert meetings 1 and their outcomes.

---

[19] Interview with Michalakis Triantafylides, Attorney General, Nicosia, June 24, 1992. In 1974, he was the president of the Supreme Court.

[20] Coufoudakis, "American Foreign Policy and the Cyprus Problem, 1974–1978: The Theory of Continuity Revisited," in Theodore A. Couloumbis and John O. Iatrides eds., *Greek American Relations: A Critical Review* (New York: Pella Publishing Company, 1980) 110–11. For additional information regarding what was discussed at the Lisbon meeting, see Glafkos Clerides, *Cyprus: My Deposition* vol. 3 (Nicosia: "Alithia" Publishing, 1990) 79–80.

Regardless of the covert conferences, with the support and understanding of Turkey, Greece developed a plan to eliminate Makarios.[21]

The independent acts of self-determination between Greece and Turkey are not acceptable under a bipolar world structure theory because this theory portrays international politics as a competitive system where its members don characteristics associated with competitors. Because the fate of a state depends on its responses to the actions of other states, states mimic one another in efforts to integrate into the world system that acts as a constraining and disposing force.[22] Greece and Turkey's behavior is characteristic of multipolarity, where sovereign nations fight among themselves in order to establish alliances that maximize their positions. A state cannot necessarily achieve its goal of security by increasing its power because the greater concern is to maintain its position in the system.[23] Cyprus has been caught in the midst of the antagonistic interests of Greece and Turkey, the superpowers in the region. Thus, an element of regional superpower rivalry was injected into an already unmanageable conflict. But more important, the combined blunders of Greece and Cyprus made them the weakest of all of the territories comprising Turkey's neighbors, both in political and military terms. Consequently, Cyprus rendered itself an attractive target for the implementation of Turkey's expansionistic policies.[24]

Greece and Turkey interacted with Cyprus in a manner characteristic of a multipolar world structure because they acted, in some respects, as independent agents rather than in a manner dictated by the United States or the Soviet Union. States within a multipolar framework conduct their own affairs in an independent manner because decisions originate and are implemented from within the state rather than from the outside. As Greece and Turkey intervened in Cyprus to pursue their conflicting national goals and to support

---

21 Clerides, *Cyprus* vol 3, 77.

22 Waltz, "Anarchic Orders," and "Reductionist and Systemic Theories," *Neorealism and Its Critics* 57 and 128.

23 Waltz, "Anarchic Orders," *Neorealism and Its Critics* 27.

24 Christos P. Ioannides, *In Turkev's Image: The Transformation of Occupied Cyprus into a Turkish Province* (New York: Aristide D. Caratzas, 1991) 193–94.

Even though it has been determined that the bipolar global system which prevailed at the time of the Cypriot conflict was not exclusively or even primarily responsible for the Crisis, still, the Cold War antagonists nevertheless had the capability to alter the final outcome. The structure of the world system in 1974 mirrored that which existed in 1964 and 1967 when the intervention of a superpower successfully averted a crisis. Therefore, although the global environment was the same, and the influencing capabilities of the superpowers had not waned over the course of the decade, one must deduce that intercommunal negotiations were exerted by choice. The Cold War rivals opted for an idle stance because the pending constitutional changes posed too serious a threat to their respective interests.

B. Organski's Balance of Power Theory

Balance of power theorists believe modern times are characterized by the permanence of ties among nations. Moreover, they argue that there are three determinants of national power: population size, political efficiency, and economic development. Shifts in these areas lead to changes in the distribution of power. In order to determine the relevancy of this balance of power theory when applied to the Cypriot Crisis, the elements which affect the distribution of power must be examined.[30]

Graph One illustrates the population of Cyprus, Greece, and Turkey from 1960 to 1965 to 1974. Statistics reveal that not one of these three countries underwent significant population change over the fourteen-year period prior to the 1974 Crisis. The population of Cyprus increased by 9.5 percent during this time frame, while Greece grew by 6.5 percent, and Turkey by 19.4 percent. Therefore, as Graph One indicates, the increase occurred within customarily expected numbers.[31] Would a substantial population shift occur if

[30] Organski, *World Politics* 338 and 351–54.

[31] For the 1960–65 figures, refer to the *Demographic Yearbook 1965* (New York: United Nations, 1966) 113, 115, and 117. Countries conduct population census in different years, which explains the variance in the years compared between Cyprus, Greece, and Turkey. Also, for the 1974 figures of Greece and

the numbers of the Greek-Cypriot and the Turkish-Cypriot populations were combined with those of their native homelands? The total population of Cyprus in 1974 was 639,000. Approximately 78 percent of this figure, or 498,420 individuals, were Greek-Cypriots, whereas 17 percent, or 115,020, were Turkish-Cypriots. By combining Cypriot figures with those of their mother countries, the Turkish figure of 39,055,020 still outnumbered the Greek population of 9,468,420 by four times.[32] (See appendix 1, graph 1.)

APPENDIX 1

GRAPH 1

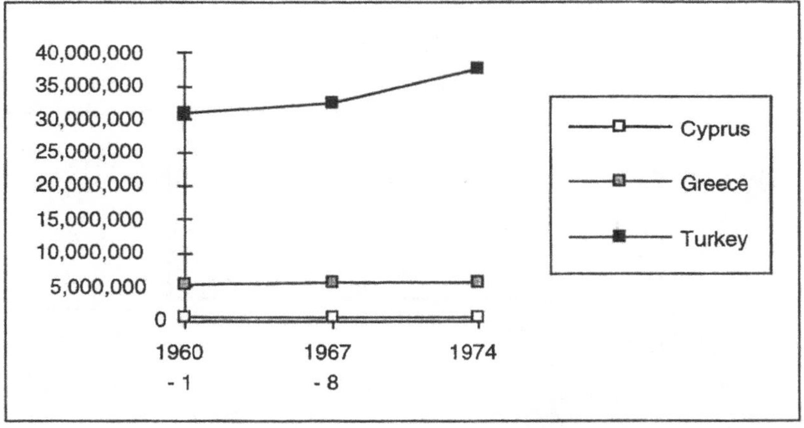

Balance of power theorists maintain that in addition to population size, political efficiency (ratio of civilian to soldiers) determines the distribution of power.[33] Graph 2 illustrates the extreme disproportionality between the total number of Greek and Turkish armed forces. Not only did Turkish numbers exceed Greek num-

Turkey, see *The Military Balance 1974–75* (London: The International Institute for Strategic Studies, 1974) 23 and 26.

32 For Cyprus' 1974 population size refer to the *Demographic Yearbook 1975* (New York: United Nations, 1976) 173.

33 Organski, *World Politics* 338.

bers in all branches of the military, but its army surpassed the Greek army three to one. Despite the obvious imbalance in numbers, it can be argued that Greece and Turkey were more equitable militarily than it appeared because of the effects of two military factors: first, the monies budgeted by each country for defense purposes, and second, the monies acquired from the United States to be channeled into the military. In 1968 Greece's defense expenditure was $318 million while Turkey's was $472 million.[34] Greece received $67.1 million in military assistance from the United States in comparison to the $172.3 million Turkey acquired. As can be noted, the gap in equitable political efficiency in 1968 was widened rather than narrowed by these economic disparities.[35] (See appendix 1, graph 2.)

GRAPH 2

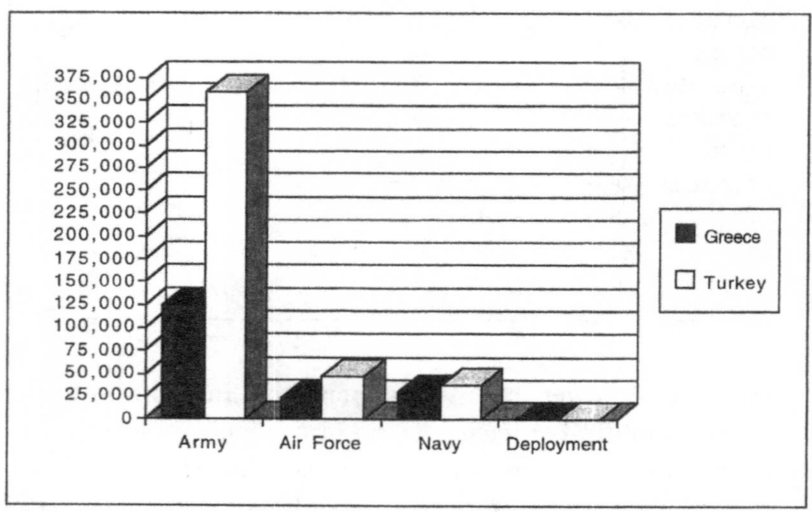

[34] *The Military Balance 1968–1969* (London: The Institute for Strategic Studies, 1968) 24 and 26.

[35] Couloumbis, *The United States, Greece, and Turkey* 178.

Did something revolutionary occur between 1968 and 1974 to cause these figures to change to such a degree that Greece drew closer to a position where a balance of power was perceived? To the contrary, over the course of these six years, Greece could never perceive her military position to be anything but significantly inferior to that of Turkey. In 1974, the defense budget of Greece had close to doubled and reached $602 million, but Turkey's had more than doubled, totaling $995 million.[36] United States military assistance to Greece in 1974 barely increased to $67.5 million, a 0.6 percent increase, while assistance to Turkey rose to $192.6 million, nearly a 12 percent increase. Thus, according to statistical data, if anything, Greece fell further behind Turkey during this six-year time frame in terms of military power.[37]

Balance of power theorists claim that war is far more likely when contenders hold comparable military power. Therefore, the fact that the Cypriot Crisis occurred should indicate the existence of comparable military power. However, an equitable power structure did not exist militarily. Hence, the balance of power theory directs us to the third determinant of national power, that of economic development.

Graph 3 illustrates that the gross national product (GNP) of Greece in 1967, as estimated by the Institute for Strategic Studies, was $6.7 billion. By 1973, this figure had more than doubled to an estimated $16.4 billion. Similarly, Turkey's GNP in 1967 was $10.1 billion and it, too, more than doubled to $21.5 billion by 1973. The figures representing the GNP of each country indicate that growth occurred in each country at approximately the same rate, and therefore Greece did not gain any economic advantage to boost it into a more suitable position than its competition.[38] (See appendix 1, graph 3.)

---

36 *The Military Balance 1974–1975* (London: The International Institute for Strategic Studies, 1974) 23 and 26.

37 *The Military Balance 1974–1975* 23 and 26.

38 *The Military Balance 1974–1975* 23 and 26.

GRAPH 3

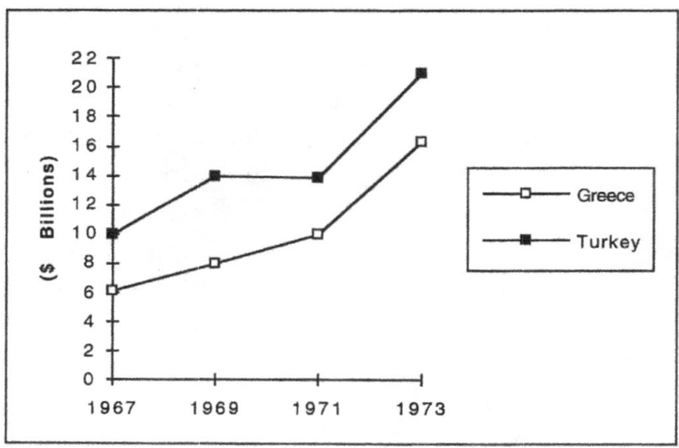

It has been maintained that, in modern times, industrialization brings the greatest power increase to a nation.[39] By examining the manufacturing industries of both Greece and Turkey, the degree of industrialization of each country should be recognizable. In 1970 the value of the gross output in Greek manufacturing was $102.43 million. By 1972, this value had risen to $132.11 million, and by 1973 it totaled $183.40 million.[40] Between 1970 and 1972 there was a 29 percent increase, and from 1972 to 1973 there was a 39 percent increase. Turkey's figures indicate an even greater growth rate. From 1970 to 1972, the gross output value jumped from $71.26 million to $104.94 million, a 47 percent increase. A 35 percent increase occurred between 1972 and 1973 as the value improved from $104.94 million to $141.22 million.[41] While manufacturing production increased in both countries, the figures reveal that neither country could boast about its industrialized status. To portray this point, Graph 4 illustrates the dramatic change in German automobile production between 1950 and 1965, an increase of 500 per-

[39] Organski, *World Politics* 340.

[40] *Statistical Yearbook 1976* 217.

[41] *Statistical Yearbook 1976* 216.

cent. Full industrialization is typically accompanied by growth which resembles that of Germany.[42] (See appendix 1, graph 4.)

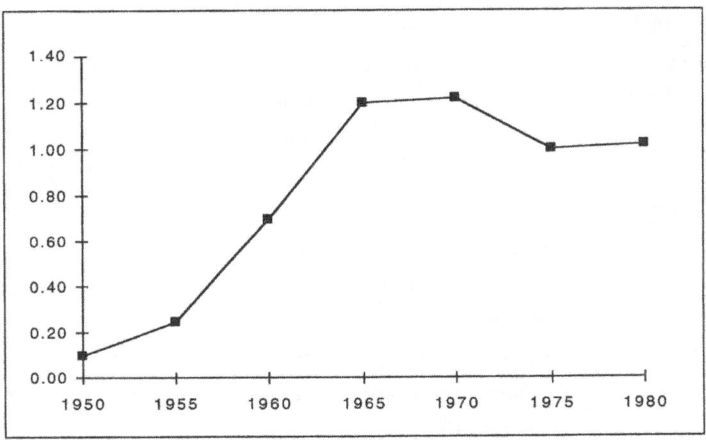

Two characteristics—alteration in power due to industrialization and the ties between nations in competing international orders—provide the framework for a recurring pattern which can be identified in recent international politics.[43] The balance of power theory and its effects on the probability of war rest on a shift in one or more of the three elements which influence the distribution of power: population size, political efficiency, and economic development. At least one of the three elements must undergo a transformation to propel a nation of insignificant strength into an equitable power position with a rival. Applying these three elements to Greece and Turkey and their effects on Cyprus, it is clear that neither Greece nor Turkey underwent any significant change in any one of the elements. Therefore, the 1974 Cypriot Crisis must have been the result of yet another influential factor.[44]

42 *Statistical Yearbook 1976* 216.
43 Organski, *World Politics* 376.
44 Organski, *World Politics* 376.

The new autonomous Cypriot state that would have emerged in 1974 and its accompanying signed arrangements would have proved too serious a threat to the unconstitutional government of Greece and Turkey. The 1974 constitutional proposals were much superior to the 1960 Constitution, and a settlement among the lines of the proposed arrangements would have constitutionally and politically favored Cypriots alike. The two communities on Cyprus recognized the need to abolish the zero-sum competitive consequences established by the structure of the 1960 Constitution. However, the state was unsuccessful at restoring external interference because the island was still bound by the 1960 constitutional provisions which granted Greece and Turkey the right to intervene when necessary to guarantee Cyprus's independent status. Paradoxically, true Cypriot sovereignty, possible only by barring the external interference guaranteed in the 1974 arrangements and abolishing the zero-sum competition, proved to be the catalyst of the crisis. The failure of the new constitutional arrangements was due to the external powers, motivated by factors external to the Cypriot question, principally fears that the current balance of power structure would be annihilated. Political expediency resulted in the destruction and division of Cyprus by way of an externally inspired coup and invasion.

C. Wallerstein and the International Capitalism Theory

Theorists who support the international capitalism theory for dependent relations assert that the capitalist world economy dictates the behavior of states.[45] To apply this approach to Cyprus, the countries with the greatest economic interaction with Cyprus must be identified. Table 1 identifies the principal countries of production and consignment with which Cyprus had dealings in 1973. During this year, the United Kingdom was Cyprus's major economic player in both imports and exports. Imported commodities from the United Kingdom accounted for 24.6 percent of Cyprus's total imports in comparison to 5.7 percent from Greece (a difference of

[45] Wallerstein, "The Rise and Future Demise of the World Capitalist System," *Comparative Studies in Society and History* 390.

more than four times) and 1.1 percent from Turkey. Similarly, Great Britain received 43 percent of all Cyprus's national exports, while Greece received 1.8 percent and Turkey 0.47 percent. Thus, as Table 1 reveals, the United Kingdom was clearly Cyprus's main trading partner in 1973.[46] (See appendix 1, table 1.)

TABLE 1

CYPRUS: TRADE BY PRINCIPAL COUNTRIES OF PRODUCTION AND CONSIGNMENT (1973)

(VALUE IN THOUSAND U.S. DOLLARS)

PRINCIPAL COUNTRIES	GENERAL IMPORTS	TOTAL	NATIONAL EXPORTS	TOTAL
UK	10, 432	24.6%	66, 346	0.43%
GREECE	25,628	5.7%	2,788	1.8%
TURKEY	4,984	1.1%	727	0.47%
ALL COUNTRIES	447, 810	100%	153, 954	100%

In addition to determining the country which had the greatest influence over Cypriot economy, an examination of Greece and Turkey's economic roles should be evaluated. Tables 2 and 3 represent these economic roles. Economically, Greece and Turkey interacted to a greater extent between themselves than with Cyprus. Table 2 demonstrates that Greece imported about six times as much from Turkey (5.9 percent) in 1973 than it did from Cyprus (.98 percent). The disparity in Greek exports was not nearly as significant. Greece's exports to Cyprus (1.75 percent) were about two- thirds larger than those directed to Turkey (1.16 percent). These statistics clearly demonstrate that Greece's interest in the Cypriot dispute was

[46] Department of Economic and Social Affairs Statistical Office, *Yearbook of International Trade Statistics 1972–1973* (New York: United Nations, 1974) 202.

based on more than mere economic consequences. Because Greece's imports from Turkey far outnumbered those from Cyprus, it is evident that Greece had much to sacrifice economically if it entered a war with Turkey, such as the potential loss of a significant portion of its total imports.[47] (See appendix 1, table 2.)

TABLE 2

GREECE: TRADE BY PRINCIPAL COUNTRIES OF FIRST CONSIGNMENT AND CONSUMPTION (1973)

(VALUE IN THOUSAND U.S. DOLLARS)

PRINCIPAL COUNTRIES	SPECIAL IMPORTS	TOTAL	SPECIAL EXPORTS	TOTAL
CYPRUS	3, 412	0.98%	25, 485	1.75%
TURKEY	20, 428	5.9%	16, 854	1.6%
ALL COUNTRIES	3, 473, 049	100%	1, 454, 055	100%

Although Turkey's import statistics pertaining to Cyprus and Greece were nearly equivalent, its exports to Greece far surpassed those to Cyprus. Table 3 demonstrates this fact. Table 3 shows that Turkey imported more than six times as much from Greece (3.3 percent) in 1973 than it did from Cyprus (.49 percent). Moreover, Turkey exported more than four times as much to Greece (1.48 percent) than it did to Cyprus (.34 percent). Although these numbers represent a small portion of total imports and exports, they reveal that Turkey would face economic loss to imports and exports should it enter a military confrontation with Greece over the Cyprus question. These figures are especially significant because they demonstrate that mere economics was not the primary motivating factor behind Greece and Turkey's efforts to secure Cyprus. If trade was the sole determining factor, Great Britain would be the most likely power to

[47] *Yearbook of International Trade Statistics 1972–1973* 318.

intervene militarily in Cyprus since British imports from and exports to Cyprus far outweighed those of Greece and Turkey, as Table 1 clearly demonstrates. (See appendix 1, table 3.)

TABLE 3

TURKEY: TRADE PRINCIPAL COUNTRIES OF PRODUCTION AND CONSUMPTION (1973)

(VALUE IN THOUSAND U.S. DOLLARS)

PRINCIPAL COUNTRIES	SPECIAL IMPORTS	TOTAL	SPECIAL EXPORTS	TOTAL
CYPRUS	1, 029	0.49%	4, 611	0.34%
GREECE	7, 003	3.3%	19, 525	1.48%
ALL COUNTRIES	2, 098, 565	100%	1, 318, 044	100%

Since Greece and Turkey interacted economically more with each other than either did with Cyprus, as Tables 2 and 3 reveal, other significant forces must have induced these important trading partners to alienate each other over Cyprus.[48] Considering that Cyprus's imports far outnumbered its exports, it is fortunate that the tourist industry functioned to offset the trade deficit. In the case of Cyprus, "tourism is one of the mainstays of . . . [its] economy."[49] Table 4 reveals that the United Kingdom provided the bulk (39.6 percent) of Cyprus's tourist industry in 1973. In contrast, Greece provided a smaller portion of the tourist industry (5.3 percent). Turkey's representation (1.7 percent) was negligible. These statistics further demonstrate that Cyprus conducted most of its commerce with Britain. For Greece and Turkey to potentially engage in conflict over Cyprus points to motivating factors other than those which were commercial and economic in

48 *Yearbook of International Trade Statistics 1972–1973* 834.

49 *Cyprus: Republic of Cyprus 30 Years 1960–1990* (Nicosia: Press and Information Office, 1990) 107.

nature. These tourism statistics aptly demonstrate that Greece and Turkey's degree of economic interaction with Cyprus during this period was, at best, minimal.[50] Additionally, Cyprus was a debtor nation prior to the Crisis (and still is), borrowing money from the World Bank and other countries.[51] (See appendix 1, table 4).

TABLE 4

TOURIST ARRIVALS IN CYPRUS DURING 1973

CONTRY OF USUAL RESIDENCE	NUMBER OF ARRIVALS	PROPORTION OF TOTAL ARRIVALS
UK	43, 984	39.6%
GREECE	5, 834	5.3%
TURKEY	1, 902	1.7%
TOTAL	110, 953	100%

In order for the world capitalism theory to work in this context, it must be determined that the dominant player, the United Kingdom, was in fact controlling Cyprus's political fate. If the international capitalist economy was the major motivating factor, Cyprus's key trading partner would strive out of interest to defend its dependent relationship with Cyprus from anyone who might attempt to interfere for economic benefit. (See appendix 1, table 1). Interestingly enough, Britain did not feel compelled to utilize either Greece or Turkey, who were devising plans to divide the island. The Turkish Prime Minister, Bulent Ecevit, traveled to London on July 18, 1974, to talk about the possibility of British/Turkish intervention in Cyprus to restore the antebellum status. Great Britain did not accept the coercive options that Turkey offered, but hoped instead

[50] Cyprus, Annual Report of Cyprus Tourism Organization *1974–1975*: Printing Office of the Republic of Cyprus, 1975.

[51] Interview with Michael Sarris, Division Chief at World Bank in Washington D.C., February 11, 1993. This interview was conducted over the telephone.

for a diplomatic resolution. Recognizing that British cooperation was unattainable, Ecevit returned to Ankara so he could supervise the final preparations for the invasion.[52]

In addition to assuming a hands-off stance during the preinvasion period, Great Britain neglected its role as the controller of Cyprus's political destiny during the initial intervention. Britain shouldered its obligatory role as protectorate of Cyprus upon implementation of the 1959 Zurich Agreements that granted Greece, Britain, and Turkey guarantor status over the independent, territorial integrity and the constitution of the new state of Cyprus.[53] Great Britain's role in the 1974 Crisis has been described as aggressive by default because, although British troops were stationed on the island and had retaliatory capability, they "stood at the sidelines" and repudiated their responsibility.[54]

Why did Britain refrain from intervening on behalf of Cyprus? Throughout Cyprus's history, she has played a valuable role not only for Turkey and Greece, but for Britain as well. The island served as a central element of Britain's military position from the time of its acquisition in 1878 until well after World War II. Even after Cyprus gained its independence, Britain retained two key base areas, one at Dhekelia and another at Akrotiri. Although Britain's interest in Cyprus was worth defending, when given a second opportunity to affect the 1974 outcome, she still failed to effect a change in her two partners. After the first invasion, but prior to the second, a committee of representatives from each of the three guarantors, including Great Britain, met in Geneva to devise and implement a solution for Cyprus. Only after the Geneva conference failed to agree on a solution did Turkish forces seize approximately 40 percent of the territory of the republic. Thus, British efforts to mediate failed because Greece and Turkey were incapable of surmounting their ethnic pas-

---

52 Stavros Panteli, *A New History of Cyprus: From the Earliest Times to the Present Day* (London: East-West Publications, 1984) 382.

53 Stanley Kyriakides, *Cyprus: Constitutionalism and Crisis Government* (Philadelphia: University of Pennsylvania Press, 1968) 176.

54 Interview with Marios Evriviades, Press and Information Officer, Nicosia, June 23, 1992.

sions and deeply entrenched hatred; they could not settle their differences through compromise.[55]

Britain's repeated passivity toward Cypriot affairs undermines the macro-level dependency argument that conflict results from economically dependent relations which have developed with dominant economic partners. Cyprus's interdependency on other nations was not only economic, but was military and political in nature. This interdependency was solidified by the Zurich Agreements which accorded rights of special relationship to Great Britain, Greece, and Turkey for all types of agreements.[56]

The Cypriot conflict was not the result of deepening hostilities over inequitable monetary relationships, nor was there even an attempt on the part of the key economic player to intervene in order to safeguard its economic interests when problems arose. Cyprus's major military and political players, Greece and Turkey, ignited the conflict over politically dependent relations. The Treaty of Alliance under the 1960 Constitution outlined Cypriot military dependency on Greece and Turkey by granting the contracting parties the power to resist any aggressive behavior directed against the independence or territorial integrity of Cyprus. For this purpose, it was further provided that a tripartite headquarters be established and that military contingents consisting of 950 Greek officers and men and 650 Turkish officers and soldiers be stationed on the island. Consequently, Cypriot dependency on Greece and Turkey was clearly military rather than economic in nature.[57]

International capitalism theory purports that the international capitalist economy is a source of conflict because it directs the behavior of states. An analysis of economic census statistics provides irrefutable evidence of Cyprus's globally inconsequential economic value and that its leading trading partner stayed uninvolved; the world market economy virtually had no bearing on the Cypriot Crisis.

---

[55] Interview with Glafkos Clerides, President of Cyprus, Nicosia, June 27, 1992. When I interviewed Mr. Clerides, he held the position of party leader. See also Joseph, *Cyprus* 106.

[56] Clerides, *Cyprus*, vol. 1, 391.

[57] Clerides. *Cyprus*, vol. 1, 395.

Rather than contentions deepening over inequitable economic matters with Britain, tensions stemmed from dependency on Greece and Turkey in the military and political realms. Political and military ties between the homelands and Cyprus would soon be severed if the 1974 constitutional proposals were implemented, a thought too threatening for Greece and Turkey to entertain. In order to avert the likelihood of such an occurrence, Greece staged the 1974 coup which was followed by Turkey's invasion of Cyprus. Despite the fact that the island had served Great Britain's military from the time of its acquisition in 1878, and although Britain had a legal right to intervene in the Crisis (as was done in 1964 and 1967) through the Treaty of Guarantee, she did not intervene. For strategic reasons rather than economic ones, Britain had more to gain from a divided Cyprus than from an autonomous one.

D. Conclusion of Third-Level Theories

In conclusion, third level analysts maintain that the behavior of all states, whether independent or interdependent in nature, is influenced by the structure of the bipolar global system. The two competing international orders provide the framework within which permanent ties between nations are established and the interstate expropriation of wealth has played the most significant role in determining the likelihood of war. The international capitalist economy creates conflicts because it directs the behavior of states.

After testing these third-level theories, we find that they do not provide a comprehensive explanation of the factors that caused the Cypriot Crisis. Small countries may practice multipolar behavior at the regional level despite the global existence of a bipolar structure. Greece and Turkey's balancing behavior was of a micro- not macro-nature. A shift in the distribution of power did not occur, nor was the balance disrupted, and yet the Crisis erupted. The key players, Greece and Turkey, did not dispute over inequitable economic matters, but over dependency in the political-military realm. As prospects of exclusion from Cypriot affairs drew closer to reality, as would have occurred with the implementation of the 1974 constitutional solution, fear of isolation from their respective ethnic communities drove Greece and Turkey to interfere in order to eradicate such a possibility. Even though Great Britain, the third guarantor, intervened both in 1963 and 1967 as she was entitled, she chose, as did the United States, to remain silent in 1974 because a partitioned island was more to her advantage than an autonomous one.

III. SECOND-LEVEL THEORIES

Second-level theories view international conflict as the product of domestic politics. Whether it is domestic political stability, internal class struggle, or imperialist conflict exportations, all of these theories place culpability for war with individual countries. Domestic political stability theories contend that intractable wars are the product of domestic instability.[58]

Yet another second-level theory deals with class struggle, postulating a triple alliance of three independent partners comprising the dominant class is interested in the subordination of the general population and capital accumulation. At the same time, the three interdependent partners have conflicting interests. Even though it is accepted that the interests of protecting dependent development are addressed in the triple alliance of multinational, state, and local capital, the alliance itself is an ambivalent one. Consequently, internal class struggle is the result of the ever-widening unequal distribution of newly acquired industrialized wealth that is controlled by the alliance.[59]

Finally, we turn to the theory of imperialism, which holds that one facet affecting the harmony of interest between the center of the Periphery and that of the Core. Under this model, an imperialistic

---

[58] Henry A. Kissinger, "The Domestic Structure and Foreign Policy," in James N. Resenau ed., *International Politics and Foreign Policy: A Reader in Research and Theory* (New York: Free Press of Glencoe, 1961) 261–75; and Henry A. Kissinger, *A World Restored: Mettemich. Gastlereaqh and the Problems of Peace 1812–1822* (Boston: Houghton Mifflin, 1979) 312–32.

[59] Peter Evans, *Dependent Development: The Alliance of Multinational, State, and Local Capital in Brazil* (Princeton: Princeton University Press, 1979) 5–51.

relationship promotes greater inequality or disharmony of interest with the Periphery nation than with the Center nation. Lastly, imperialism creates disharmony of interest between the periphery of the Center nation and the periphery of the Periphery nation. The asymmetric economic exchange accounts for the conflict between imperialist nations. In essence, imperialistic relationships produce both harmony and disharmony of interest among nations; this dynamic system ultimately determines the environment of the state.[60]

A. Kissinger's Domestic Political Stability Theory

Domestic political stability theorists argue that the stability of a state's domestic structure and ideology determines the amount of social effort which can be devoted to foreign policy, affects the interpretation of other states actions, and is decisive in the elaboration of positive goals. In short, domestic structure has a tremendous impact on the conduct of international affairs. The very nature of the governmental structure introduces an element of rigidity, thereby complicating the decision-making and negotiating process. The planning and research elements of an administrative machine may encourage paralysis while a degree of ideological persuasion may exacerbate the tendency toward rigidity. In addition to the impact of a state's administrative structure, foreign policy is also affected by the formative experience of leadership groups which may be of a bureaucratic-pragmatic, ideological, or revolutionary-charismatic type. In summary, domestic ideology and structure plays a determinative role in world affairs. Stable governments with stable ideologies pursue policies that are peaceful or incremental in demands for change. Governments without this stability account for instability and unpredictability in international relations.[61]

An examination of domestic political structure theory in terms of Cyprus indicates that the governmental structures of Greece and

---

60 Johan Galtung, "A Structural Theory of Imperialism," *Journal of Peace Research* vol. 8 (1971) 81–85.

61 Kissinger, "The Domestic Structure and Foreign Policy," *International Politics and Foreign Policy* 262–67 and 274; and Kissinger, *A World Restored* 325–30.

Turkey in 1974 as with their respective decision makers, impacted both their own countries' foreign policies and the stability of Cyprus. Greece's political structure underwent a series of changes beginning in 1967 which greatly affected the country's stability. On April 21, 1967, the Greek junta seized power under the leadership of three army officers: Colonel George Papadopoulos, Brigadier General Stylianos Pattakos, and Colonel Nicholas Makarezos. Papadopoulos named himself prime minister and minister of defense. Yet again Greece's stability was threatened on November 17, 1973, when General Dimitrios Ioannides, head of the military police (ESA), in opposition to Papadopoulos's overcentralization of powers and ineffective efforts against Makarios, led a coup against Papadopoulos from within the military junta. Although Lieutenant General Phaidon Gizikis took office after Papadopoulos' regime was overthrown, it was Ioannides who held the real power on the sidelines. In order to carry out his fanatically anti-Communist, anti-Makarios and pro-enosis plan, he had no inhibitions against using large-scale military force especially to remove his bitter rival Makarios from power.

Ioannides' power became completely uninhibited by the death of General Grivas in January 1974; Grivas had acted as a relatively reactionary influence on EOKA-B. This, in addition to a failing Greek economy and an ongoing dispute with Turkey over the disposition of Aegean Sea, drove Ioannides to implement his plan to assassinate Makarios and thereby fulfill enosis once and for all with the hope of preserving his position in power.[62]

In Turkey, too, the environment was hardly a model of predictability and harmony. The October 1973 general elections did not yield an autonomous majority for any single party. The Bulent Ecevit–led Republican People's Party secured a legislative plurality and was therefore forced to form a coalition government with fundamentalist rightist, Necmettin Erbakan. The new government's program pledged to safeguard the interests of the Turkish community on Cyprus. Being a minority premier in parliament, and fully aware

---

[62] Couloumbis, *The United States, Greece, and Turkey* 79–80; and interview with Evriviades.

of the frailty of his condition, Ecevit seized his golden opportunity for a great diplomatic victory and a chance of altering the social, geographic and political position of Cyprus's Turkish minority by responding aggressively to the Greek coup. Because of Ecevit's success in partitioning Cyprus, he counted on winning the next general election, which came to pass as he had predicted.[63]

Thus, the domestic structure does provide some insight into the Cypriot case. Clearly, the instability of Greek and Turkish domestic politics gave their leaders little leeway in their policy-making efforts regarding Cyprus. However, let us look at whether they were irrational or behaved any differently than a stable government would have. First, leaders must deal with their security of tenure. Faced by militant ideologies of Panhellenism and Pan-Turkism held by their domestic populations, each could not allow its rival to achieve its goals in Cyprus. Second, leaders must consider the strategic significance of events they face, regardless of other distractions. Neither Greece nor Turkey could afford to lose Cyprus to each other, because of the security implications.

Because the intercommunal negotiations were almost complete, threatening the formation of an autonomous Cyprus, both Ecevit and Ioannides had to act with dispatch to avoid losing everything, both at home and abroad. Even if Ecevit and Ioannides had occupied the most legitimate position imaginable, they would have had to address the threat of a sovereign Cyprus as they did. Greece's solution under Ioannides' lead may seem irrational, but we must consider the inferiority of his military force and strategic position; he had no other choice, and neither did Ecevit.

B. Evans and Class Struggle Theory

In a way, second-level dependency theories resemble third-level models. The ultimate determinant is, after all, the world capitalist economy, as Wallerstein argued. However, Evans and his colleagues

---

[63] Taki Theodoracopulos, *The Greek Upheaval: Kings, Demagogues, and Bayonets* (London: Stacey International, 1976) 58.

accord independent significance to the way that domestic political actors respond. Their reactions are not automatic, but mediated by contingent state-level factors. Moreover, the internal class struggle produced by economic disparity drives both civil war and aggressive external behavior. Because domestic politics do matter, we have classified class struggle theory as a second-level approach.[64]

According to this view, Cyprus's economic benefit to dominant nations like Greece and Turkey is the foundation of Cypriot hostilities. The effects of imperialism on the internal social structures of peripheral countries, narrowly defined as class struggle, ultimately instigate a crisis. Internal class struggles intensify as a result of the ever-widening unequal distribution of newly acquired industrialized wealth, which is manipulated by an alliance of multinational, state, and local capital.[65] The economy is therefore considered to be the independent variable in dependency situations. As such, one would expect economics to be the driving force behind the 1974 Cypriot Crisis. Unmistakably, Cyprus experienced greater prosperity in the years immediately preceding the 1974 Crisis than ever before.[66] Would not heightened harmony accompany this flourishing economy?

It has been argued that a thriving economy is not necessarily synonymous with compatibility; in fact, many theorists readily argue that tensions rise as inequitable conditions among classes become more pronounced. It is important to note that for Cyprus, the economic class system is not one in which ethnicity and stratification coincide. Cyprus's atypical system has been defined as follows: "Communal division has not been identical with class or status, but ethnic differentiation is horizontal, not vertical, encompassing two parallel social structures, each with its own stratification."[67] The "classes" which are inequitably defined in Cyprus do not refer solely

64 Evans, *Dependent Development* 4.

65 Evans, *Dependent Development* 4 and 50.

66 *The New York Times*, August 15, 1973.

67 Paschalis M. Kitromilides, "From Coexistence to Confrontation: The Dynamics of Ethnic Conflict in Cyprus," in Michael Attalides ed., *Cyprus Reviewed* (Nicosia: The Jus Cypri Association, 1977) 52.

to divisions based on economic status; rather, to make matters worse, communal divisions are based on ethnicity as well.

Economic disparity between the Greeks and Turks on Cyprus has always been a critical issue. For as long as these communities have shared the island, the Greeks have had a far greater share of the national income than the Turks because "[e]conomic production in most sectors was largely in the hands of the Greek Cypriots . . . [which] means that the Cypriot bourgeoisie was Greek Cypriot rather than Turkish Cypriot."[68] While the Greek Cypriots lived comfortably in a Greek-dominated economy, Turkish Cypriot workers were reduced to the status of exploited proletariat dependent on their mother country for survival. An order to the Turkish Cypriots in Paphos issued by Sancaktar Ferit Cengit, a Turkish Cypriot official, revealed the Turkish Cypriot community's dependency on Turkey. Cengit reprimanded the Turkish Cypriots for wasting food supplies provided to them by Turkey. Cengit stated he was aware frozen meat was being thrown away and other food stuffs such as chick peas and cracked wheat were being fed to the livestock. He admonished his compatriots for their ingratitude, and reminded them of the sacrifice being made on their behalf by children and orphans in the motherland, who were deprived so that they could be assisted. In conclusion, Cengit outlined the new rationing guidelines and forewarned his people of the consequences of an infraction. This situation existed in the late nineteenth century under the Ottoman Empire and persisted throughout the period of British rule.[69]

The disproportionality between Greek and Turkish Cypriots grew more apparent with Cypriot independence from Britain in 1960 as the island experienced "[a]n annual growth rate of 7 per cent, a rise in per capita income to more than $900 a year."[70] As the inequitable distribution of wealth became more acute with a dramatic rise in the national per capita income, it can be argued that hostilities

---

68 Michael Attalides, "The Turkish Cypriots: Their Relations to the Greek Cypriots in Perspective," *Cyprus Reviewed* 87.

69 Ioannides, *In Turkey's Image* 211.

70 *The New York Times*, February 12, 1973.

intensified. On Cyprus, the gap widened considerably after 1963, and by 1971 a United Nations economist estimated that the average per capita income of Turkish Cypriots was 50 percent lower than that of Greek Cypriots. Consequently, Turkish Cypriot farmers, businessmen, and entire villages suffered from underdeveloped projects including inadequate streets, rural roads, and water supplies. In order for the government to provide these necessities to villages, the villages could not be in debt to the government and were required to finance half of the projects. Since villagers could not afford to be taxed more heavily in order to finance their 50 percent, they were forced to forfeit government subsidies.[71]

Accusations surfaced and tempers flared as the Turkish Cypriot leadership charged the Cypriot government with discrimination because it withheld services from the Turkish Cypriot community; thus, the theoretical diagnosis proved to be accurate for Cyprus. But even though contention over economic factors rose prior to the 1974 Crisis and undoubtedly aggravated the tension, economic strife did not spark the combustible situation. Rather, as I will explain below, external organizations instead of internal ones acted as the catalyst.[72]

Now that economic factors have been refuted, it is helpful to address the contributions of theorists from a political perspective to gain an understanding of the Cypriot situation. Some theorists maintain that conflict is the product of class struggle in the form of a derivative of dependency relations.[73] In Cyprus, it was not class contention which generated the ultimate conflict, but the desire of both Greek and Turkish Cypriots to enjoy nationalistic solidarity by reuniting with their respective homelands. These passions were inevitably disharmonious with each other and consequently led to conflict.[74]

Nationalistic ideologies, conceived and encouraged by the individual homelands, were fundamental to the domestic dis-

---

[71] Attalides, "The Turkish Cypriots," *Cyprus Reviewed* 87–88.

[72] Attalides, "The Turkish Cypriots," *Cyprus Reviewed* 88.

[73] Evans, *Dependent Development* 4.

[74] Alexander G. Xydis, "Cyprus: What Kind of Problem?" *Cyprus Reviewed* 21.

putes—they were one of the most influential sources of divisiveness on the island. The Greek movement of Megali Idea (Great Idea), which was aimed at the reconstruction of the Byzantine Empire under Greek hegemony, captured the allegiance of the Greek population on Cyprus. As was the case with Megali Idea, Kibris Turktur (Cyprus is Turkish), the Turkish counterpart, evoked yearnings among its people for union with their homeland. This ideology exemplified Turkey's fundamental belief that Cyprus was historically and ideologically a Turkish island. Although Turkish irredentism favored territorial and political union of Cyprus with Turkey, the Turks were willing to accept *taksim* as a satisfactory alternative. The character of Kibris Turktur outlined the organization's objectives as the advancement of Turkey's nationalism by familiarizing the world with the notion that Cyprus is Turkish, and conditioning the public to defend the rights and privileges of Turks in regards to their stake in Cyprus.[75]

It cannot be denied that ethnic fragmentation and political division, initially instituted through the British colonial policy of "divide and rule," had a horrendous impact on Cyprus. Despite the damaging nature of fragmentation and division, the element which proved the most catastrophic was permanence of the contrary ideological goals of enosis and taksim. It has been argued:

> [T]he most destructive element in biethnic relations was the fact that the two communities failed to abandon their old conflicting goals of enosis and partition. This was manifested in the attitudes of the communal elites who missed no opportunity to deliver intense patriotic speeches reaffirming their continuing commitment to the achievement of those goals. In effect, the creation of an independent state was viewed by the two sides as an interim phase for materialization of enosis or partition.[76]

Domestic confrontations were bound to occur as each of these ethnically diverse populations strove to actualize their plans.

---

[75] Ioannides, *In Turkey's Image* 77.

[76] Joseph, *Cyprus* 55–56.

Once nationalistic skirmishes broke out in Cyprus, Greece became an advocate for its ethnic community, while Turkey advocated the position of the Turkish Cypriots. Instead of resolving the conflict, Greek and Turkish actions exported it to their respective homelands. The conflicting ideologies created internal disturbances that culminated in a division of the island, and promoted organizations designed to fulfill the goal of union with their respective homelands.[77]

An inevitable outgrowth of the intensifying enosis and taksim ideologies was heightened political division, which was strongly supported by the homelands. Attachment to these conflicting goals "led to a political polarization of the two ethnic groups."[78] Intrinsic to the amplification of ethno-political divisiveness was the proliferation of conflict, which ultimately culminated in the 1974 Cypriot Crisis.

The glaring flaw in the class struggle theory, even when tested from a political rather than economic perspective, is that class contention was insufficient, if not irrelevant, to the Cypriot Crisis. But ethnic conflicts did exist. Nationalist ideologies, kept alive to polarize politics and maintain an elevated passion for homeland solidarity among Greek and Turkish Cypriot compatriots, encouraged domestic divisiveness and incited violence. Eventually, to further aggravate hostilities, each homeland established organizations as agents for the advancement of ideological goals. Conflicts escalated and were ultimately the apex of the 1974 Cypriot Crisis. Under the 1974 constitutional agreements, the nationalist identities and agent organizations that had been woven into the fabric of the ethnic communities by their respective homelands might have been unraveled and replaced by a new Cypriot identity fortified by new cultural institutions. Outraged by the very idea that their respective communities would consider abandoning and, in so doing, desecrating their cultural roots, Greece and Turkey intervened via the 1974 coup and invasion.

---

77 Interview with Clerides.

78 Joseph, *Cyprus* 29.

C. Galtung's Theory of Imperialism

Most imperialist theories are third-level, but Galtung's theory is essentially second-level because he borrows a page from Schumpeter's argument. That is he argues that imperialism is the exportation of conflict between classes in dominant states to their dependent client states.[79] Thus, class conflict between the center of their Center and the periphery of the Center is shunted off onto the periphery of the Periphery. The center of the Center, periphery of the Center, and center of the Periphery gang up on the periphery of the Periphery. Thus, imperialist conflict exportation is a second-level theory; the domestic politics of the dominant country is the causative factor, rather than the capitalist world system. This portion of Galtung (Schumpeter) is also refuted by Cyprus because the peripheries and centers of the Periphery unite with the peripheries and centers of the Center, based on ethnicity and not on class. The peripheries of the Peripheries are harmoniously linked to all three other players for both the Turkish and Greek factions in the case of Cyprus. (See appendix 1, figure 1).

Figure 1: Imperialism Modeled

Dominant (center) country Dominated (periphery) county

Harmony between C_c and C_p

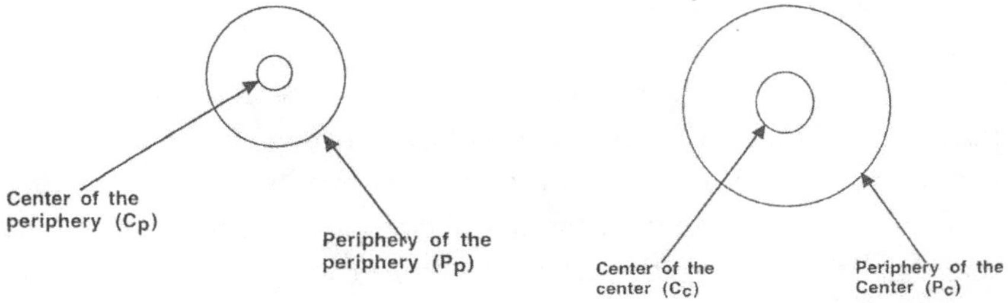

Center of the periphery (C_p)

Periphery of the periphery (P_p)

Center of the center (C_c)

Periphery of the Center (P_c)

Disharmony between P_c and P_p

[79] Joseph Schumpeter, *Capitalism, Socialism, and Democracy* (New York: Harper Torchbooks, 1950).

Although many second-level theorists adhere to dependency theory's contention that the economics dictates the behavior of states, some identify imperialistic relations as contingent on political and cultural motives. Under the latter approach, conflict is certain to occur when the connection of two parties produces an increasing disparity in the quality of life.[80] The Cypriot conflict was not formed from a gaping distinction in lifestyles between the Cypriot population and a dominant power, but rather on a tripartite relationship where two antagonistic controlling powers—Turkey and Greece—interfaced with one dependent power, Cyprus. Blame for the 1974 conflict has been placed on the different objectives of the core countries: Greek interests uniting Cyprus with Greece, and Turkey's goal of partitioning the island and uniting one part with Turkey.[81]

Regardless of the number of players, asymmetric economic exchange created conflict among imperialistic (or Center) and Periphery nations. Some theoretical models still assume that economic power accompanies political power.[82] As previously argued regarding the Cypriot situation, if inequitable economic exchange was to blame for Cypriot hostilities, contention would exist with Cyprus's prominent trading partner, Great Britain, rather than the two powers that had negligible economic interaction on the island. Therefore, the Cypriot case undermines both capitalist economic theory and the economic elements of this approach. The remainder of this theory must therefore be tested for its cultural and political application.

This capitalist economic model holds that dependency relationships promote interest compatibility between the center of the Center nation and the center of the Periphery nation, while creating dissonant interests between the periphery of the Center nation and the periphery of the Periphery nation.[83] To test this principle in the context of Cyprus, the elements of the model can be substituted with

80 Galtung, "A Structural Theory of Imperialism," *Journal of Peace Research* 81–110.

81 Interview with Clerides.

82 Galtung, "A Structural Theory of Imperialism," *Journal of Peace Research* 85.

83 Galtung, "A Structural Theory of Imperialism," *Journal of Peace Research* 83.

the actual players of the 1974 Crisis. For example, the center of the Center nation refers to the elites within Greece and Turkey. The center of the Periphery is represented by the decision makers on Cyprus. The periphery of the Center nation represents the general population of Greece and/or Turkey, and the periphery of the Periphery signifies the Greek and Turkish Cypriots. According to this theory, then, the dependency relationship which characterizes Cyprus enhances the symmetry of interests between the leaders in Greece and Cyprus and between those in Turkey and Cyprus.

A discrepancy in this model as applied to Cyprus is already visible. During the intercommunal talks of October 1972, the leaders of Greece and Turkey met with Archbishop Makarios to attempt to resolve the hostilities within Cyprus that were caused by a divisive constitution. Makarios, who had been previously labeled a traitor to enosis for accepting the Zurich and London Agreements, knew that any workable solution must bar both enosis, the ideal of the Greek contingency, and the Turkish goal of partition. Similarly, Rauf Denktash (the Turkish Cypriot representative) demonstrated his opposition to the rigid position of Turkish officials concerning the Cypriot Constitution when he accepted Makarios's Thirteen Amendments in 1972.[84]

This theory of harmonizing interests among leaders becomes yet weaker in light of the outcome of the 1968–74 negotiations. As a result of the negotiations, the Greek Cypriot representative, Glafkos Clerides, and Denktash, reached common ground on nearly all of their differences. The two communities essentially arrived at a global resolution.[85] These incidents reveal that, although Cyprus was a dependent nation, interests among the leaders of the interacting countries were not always harmonious. The prominent leaders of Cyprus cooperated with one another in order to reach a compromise which would benefit Cyprus instead of aligning themselves with the position of the elite within Greece and Turkey. Therefore, the inter-

---

84 Interview with Clerides; and Clerides, *Cyprus*, vol. 3, 213.

85 Interview with Polyviou; and Polyvios Polyviou, *Cyprus: Conflict and Negotiation 1960–1980* (New York: Holmes and Meier Publishers, 1980) 109–10.

ests of the centers of Center nations are not necessarily harmonious with those held by the centers of Periphery nations.

Also implicit in this analysis is that the interests of the Cypriot people must be incompatible with the interests of the Greek and Turkish population. Once again, the Cypriot case fails to meet this criterion. Interestingly enough, for Cyprus, the antithesis was true. Greek Cypriots yearned to be united with their homeland compatriots. When Clerides spoke in a declaration to the House of Representatives on January 10, 1971, he remarked that nationalism to the Greek Cypriots meant only one thing: enosis. At the same time, Turkish Cypriots longed for partition of the island in order to be integrated with Turkey, or in other words, to become Turks living in a Turkish province.[86]

Theorists of imperialism point to the increasing gap in the quality of life, which is the inevitable product of dependency relationships, as the cause of conflict in imperialist relationships. Proponents of this approach maintain that asymmetric economic interchange results from imperialist relationships, which cause congenial interests between the centers of the interacting states, while simultaneously creating disharmony of interests among the peripheries. More specifically, the Periphery nation traditionally has a center—its leaders, that is—that benefits from the relationship, and at the same time, one periphery—the masses, or general public—which finds the imposed relationship deleterious.[87]

This model is ineffective when applied to Cyprus. The condition which describes dependency relationships between two states fails altogether because dependency for Cyprus involved a tripartite relationship. The second point, place blame on economic inequities, is flawed because Cyprus's key trading partner, Great Britain, was disinterested. Greece and Turkey, on the other hand, had virtually nothing to gain economically, but were the antagonistic countries.

---

[86] Rauf R. Denktash, *The Cyprus Triangle* (London: K. Rustem and Brothers and George Allen and Unwin, 1982) 62–63; Kyriakides, *Cyprus* 136; and Ioannides, *In Turkey's Image* 49.

[87] Galtung, "A Structural Theory of Imperialism," *Journal of Peace Research* 81.

The third and fourth points, that dependency results in harmony of interest between centers and disharmony of interest between peripheries, are moot because the antithesis of these conditions characterized Cyprus. The final point, that the Periphery is comprised of one center and one periphery, is invalid for Cyprus because two distinct centers govern two distinct populations, and each center, and its periphery, desires to unite with its native homeland. (See appendix 1, figure 2.)

Figure 2: Cyprus

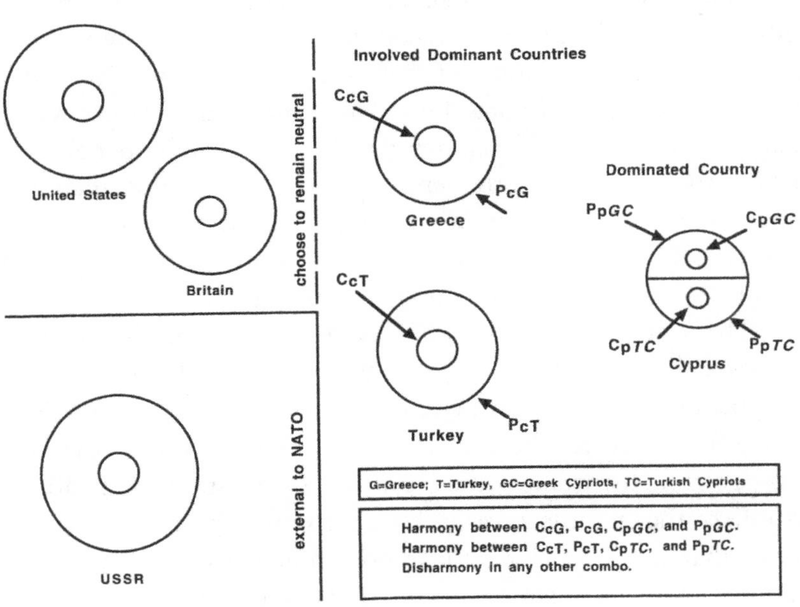

Thus, the various aspects of this approach shed no light on the case of Cyprus. Under the 1974 arrangements, the two Cypriot centers and the two Cypriot peripheries, which had been established and fostered by the 1960 constitutional provisions, were to be eliminated. The two centers would be united as one, as would the two peripheries. Additionally, as a true independent state, Cyprus's destiny would no longer be in the hands of Greece and Turkey, but determined by a democratically elected Cypriot government. To avoid being ousted from their supervisory positions, Greece implemented the coup while Turkey waged war on Cyprus.

D. Conclusion of Second-Level Theories

In sum, second-level theorists tend to categorize all conflict as the product of domestic politics and economics. For example, domestic stability theory argues that unstable states behave in ways that cause intractable conflicts, whereas stable countries are either peaceful or make war only incrementally or defensively. Yet another second-level theory focuses on class conflict: divergent levels of economic achievement cause tension and eventually internal war. This conflict can expand beyond national boundaries and lead to larger wars. A final iteration of second-level theory takes the form of imperialist conflict exportation. Elites in the center countries both export their internal conflict with their own periphery and thwart potential alliances between workers in first- and third-world countries, as well as those that might have united leaders and masses within peripheral states.

The Cypriot Crisis of 1974 demonstrates the limits of second-level theory. First, of all, the domestic stability theory would place blame on the tenuous circumstances that faced the leaders of Turkey and Greece. The former was constrained by a weak coalition government, whereas the latter was of questionable legitimacy because of the circumstances of his ascension to power. But we have shown that any Greek or Turkish government would have acted as Ioannides and Ecevit's regimes did. The stakes were too great, both domestic and strategic, to allow Cyprus to secure its sovereignty.

Secondly, internal class conflicts derived from economic dependencies cannot be blamed; instead, ethnic conflicts resulting from political dependencies with the mother countries are responsible. In addition, several characteristics of the Cyprus case clash with theories of Center-Periphery relations. Unlike traditional imperialist relationships, the Greek center and periphery on Cyprus made cooperative efforts, and so did the Turkish center and periphery of the island. The antagonistic forces in this case were the elites in Greece and Turkey as they strove to actualize their contrasting ideologies. Another atypical factor is that Cyprus's two centers and two peripheries corresponded with their respective Greek and Turkish ethnic groups. Therefore, the 1974 Crisis and its aftermath can be attributed in part to the ties that bound the ethnic centers and peripheries on the island to their native homelands.

The 1974 constitutional proposals proved to be far too threatening to Greece and Turkey. Settled comfortably in their central roles with power over the importation and implementation of their contrasting ideologies as well, the homelands would not tolerate disruption. Facing the reality that if the agreements were institutionalized they would no longer determine Cyprus's course in world politics, nor be able to preserve the unique cultural identities and institutions on the island, Greece and Turkey had no alternative but to unleash the prearranged coup and invade.

IV. FIRST-LEVEL THEORIES

First-level theories maintain that state alliance formation allows states to maximize security and minimize risk within an anarchic environment characterized by conflicts and pressures. In forming such alliances, states tend to establish an ideology to guide the behavior of its policy makers. According to offensive ideology theory, policy makers can assume either an offensive or defensive military strategy, depending upon various factors. Such factors include policy goals, technology or geopolitics, and the military balance between powers. These factors do not act in isolation; they are influenced by bias resulting from motivations and interests, the need to see the necessary as possible, and the need to simplify doctrine. While this is a short list of biases, an examination of strategic planning reveals others as well. Finally, in addition to rational calculations and motivational biases, the selection of an offensive or defensive strategy is affected by organizational, cognitive, and strategic variables.[88]

---

[88] Jack Snyder, *The Ideology of the Offensive: Military Decision Making and the Disasters of 1914* (Ithaca: Cornell University Press, 1984) 19–24.

The security dilemma theory holds that state formation is designed to protect the state against the threat of the international environment. In a security dilemma, two issues are paramount: whether the offense or defense has the upper-hand, and whether the opposing stances of offense and defense can actually be differentiated. In evaluating the former, technology and geography are primary in determining whether a strategy will be offensive or defensive. As to the latter, weapons and policies dictate which states are adequately protected, and which are vulnerable to attack. However, in addition to the role of such variables, misperception can intensify the security dilemma in that if a state misperceives a threat, that state will intensify its strategy in order to protect itself. In turn, the state perceived as the threat or aggressor will respond to the other state's fortification. Hence, several variables and circumstances affect security, and further application of the security dilemma theory reveals recognizable types of security environments that can develop.[89]

The misperception theory is another first level theory; this theory focuses on the ways in which images of reality, which are often misperceived, restrain bureaucratic politics in terms of perception and understanding, the choice of reactions, and efforts to influence other bureaucrats and other nations. With its concentration on misperception, this theory identifies fourteen common misperceptions that result when policy makers try to interpret another state's intentions. These misperceptions have in common the processing of, and reactions to, new information: more specifically, how a state receives, reacts to, incorporates, and processes new information in light of its existing and established images, directly impacts whether a state accurately interprets or mischaracterizes another state's intentions. Finally, whether diplomatic and military leaders correctly interpret another state's intentions affects these policy makers images of "reality" and in turn influences international relations.[90]

---

[89] Robert Jervis, "Offensive, Defensive, and the Security Dilemma," in Robert Art and Robert Jervis eds., *International Politics: Enduring Concepts and Contemporary Issues* 3rd edition (New York: Harper Collins Publishers, 1992) 146–66.

[90] Robert Jervis, "Hypotheses on Misperception," in H. Halperin and Arnold Kanter eds., *Readings in American Foreign Policy: A Bureaucratic Perspective*

A. Snyder's Offensive Ideology Theory

An offensive ideology is adopted when a state's military interests and strategic needs deem it necessary. The decision to adopt an offensive or defensive strategy is based on foreign policy goals, technological and geopolitical considerations, military balance, and an offensive ideology.[91] In order for Turkey to accomplish partition and Greece to achieve union, each country had to maintain an offensive ideology. Cypriot policy, shared by Turkey and Greece, was to control the island of Cyprus through partition or union because of the unique geographic position it held. Even though Turkey's original plan advocated territorial and political union of Cyprus with Turkey, Turkey later became agreeable to taksim, despite the fact that taksim was considered a significant concession. Nevertheless, the Turkish Cypriot community was to be integrated with and absorbed by Turkey, so that Turks would simply become "Turks living in a Turkish province."[92] Similarly, Megali Idea was the goal of the Greek nationalist movement to liberate the Greeks still subject to Ottoman Turkish rule, including the Greeks of Cyprus. Pursuit of this dream intensified in the 1950s when Greek involvement in the enosis movement increased.[93]

Even though Greece and Turkey's common, and yet antagonistic, goals regarding Cyprus were of tremendous significance to strategic decisions, other factors must be considered. Military balance is another important consideration. When an obvious military advantage is held, an offensive position is usually assumed; in contrast, when a state is in a disadvantageous militarily position, a defensive stand is most often taken.[94]

As Graph 5 illustrates, Turkey's conscripted army in 1973 consisted of 365,000 men in contrast to the 85,000 members of the Greek army. Turkey's numerical advantage in deployed forces was equaled in reserve strength. The Greek army reserves totaled about

(Boston: Little, Brown and Company, 1973) 113–37.

91 Snyder, *The Ideology of the Offensive* 19–20.

92 Ioannides, *In Turkey's Image* 49.

93 Ioannides, *In Turkey's Image* 51; and Kyriakides, *Cyprus* 36.

94 Snyder, *The Ideology of the Offensive* 22–24.

230,000 men, while those of Turkey consisted of about 17,500 men. The Turkish navy had about 40,000 men, and 25,000 reserves. The Greeks had a smaller, yet more experienced navy with a personnel strength of about 17,500 men and 20,000 in reserve. Similarly, the Turkish air force had the advantage because it had a personnel strength of 48,000, in comparison to the 22,700 members of the Greek air force. As has been documented, Turkey clearly enjoyed a quantitative military advantage at this time. This advantage existed in the years prior to 1973, which indicates an offensive stance, if offensive ideology theory holds true. Because Greece was the weaker power, it assumed the defensive position.[95] (See appendix 1, graph 5.)

GRAPH 5

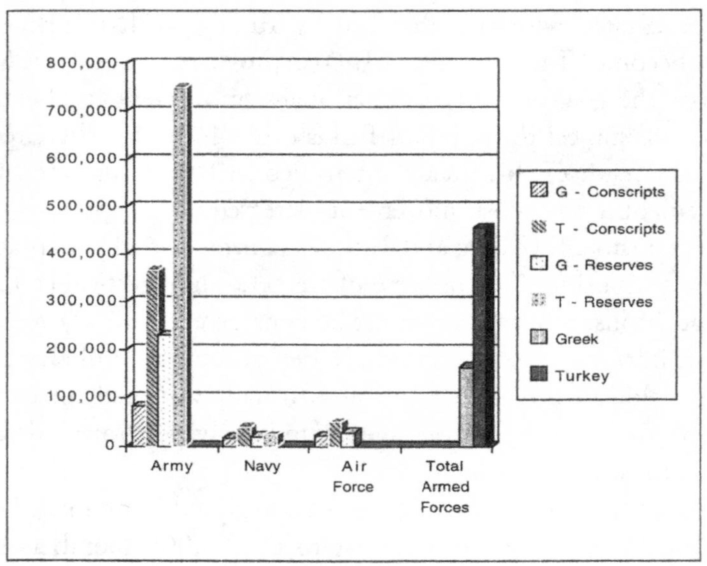

Geotechnical factors also influence the particular strategy, offensive or defensive, a country chooses to implement.[96] Geographically,

[95] United Nations, *The Military Balance 1974–1975* 23 and 26; and The New York Times. July 20, 1974.

[96] Snyder, *The Ideology of the Offensive* 20–22.

Turkey had an advantageous location because its borders lie a mere forty miles from those of Cyprus. This close proximity assured Turkey greater rapidity in the deployment of its forces in comparison to the Greek military, which had to travel approximately five hundred miles from the mainland of Greece.[97] From a technical perspective, Greece and Turkey were comparable because "[b]oth military establishments are equipped almost entirely with United States weapons systems."[98] Additionally, both Greece and Turkey shared boundaries with Warsaw Pact countries. Therefore, even though they were equipped with military weaponry that was technologically equivalent, the disparity in their geographic proximity to the island of Cyprus placed Greece at a disadvantage.[99]

In applying to Greece and Turkey the offensive ideology elements which are claimed to be influential in military strategy selection, one can presume that Turkey would adopt an offensive plan because of its numerous advantages, and that Greece, being the underdog, would assume a defensive stance. Ironically, Greece, the handicapped country in virtually all of the theory's elements, triggered the Cypriot Crisis. The Cypriot coup was launched on Monday, July 15, 1974, when units of the National Guard, commanded by officers of the Greek army and reinforced by tanks and artillery, stormed chief police stations around the island. The troops met little resistance in Nicosia as they seized communications ports such as the radio station, post office, and airport. But the troops were not as successful with the Presidential Palace, President Makarios's private residence, and the archbishop's religious headquarters at Kyko Monastery. These establishments were defended by members of a tactical police reserve which Makarios had established as a counterforce to the National Guard and its Greek army officers.[100]

Even though Greece took an offensive position in striking first, Turkey assumed an aggressive role in bringing its military to bear

---

[97] *The New York Times*, July 16, 1974.
[98] *The New York Times*, July 20,1974.
[99] *The New York Times*, July 20, 1974.
[100] *The New York Times*, July 20, 1974.

first. Turkey invaded Cyprus by land, sea and air on July 20, 1974. Bombs were strategically dropped on locations such as the capital city of Nicosia, a Cypriot National Guard camp south of the capital, the Northern part of Kyrenia, and on the Nicosia airport. Machine gun fire, rockets, and napalm blasted Greek Cypriot defenders as two thousand Turkish troops stormed ashore along the northern section of Kyrenia. Even after the cease-fire went into effect on July 23, naval landing crafts continued to pour troops and equipment onto Cypriot shores, thus enabling the Turks to expand their lines by a mile or two each day.[101]

Despite the pretexts Turkey offers for its dutiful invasion of the island, namely its responsibility under the Treaty of Guarantee, many contend that the offensive attack was an outright breach of the law. They argue that the Treaty of Guarantee did not give such rights to Turkey, which was never motivated by a desire to reestablish constitutional legitimacy under the expressly declared purpose of the Treaty. It has been further argued that Turkish military operations were in direct and flagrant violation of the principles of international law.

Shortly after the Turkish invasion of Cyprus, the Greek junta and its Cypriot appendage fell from power and the president of the House of Representatives, the constitutionally prescribed presidential successor, assumed the position of president of Cyprus. A cease-fire was negotiated between the two sides under United Nations auspices, but Turkish military forces ignored it and persisted with their operations. When it came time to negotiate at the July 25–30 Geneva Conference, Turkey would not cooperate because of its preconceived decisions and dissatisfaction with its gains from the July 20 invasion. Turkey struck again on August 14, 1974, this time confiscating approximately 40 percent of the island. Hence, application of the offensive ideology theory to the Cypriot case reveals that the Crisis erupted as a result of Greece's offensive coup and Turkey's offensive invasions.[102]

---

[101] *The New York Times*, July 20, 1974.

[102] Polyviou, *Cyprus* 85 and 157.

The unconventional aspect of the Cypriot case which remains a puzzle is that Greece, the undisputed underdog in all three of the theory's strategic elements, initiated a confrontation with Turkey when the possibility of a victory was remote. Offensive ideology theory maintains that, almost invariably, some degree of bias will influence the assessment of the three theoretical factors. The theory holds that institutional interests of the military and the need to see the necessary as possible ultimately cause biases.[103] In Greece, the 1967 military takeover signaled the beginning of new problems. Although General Ioannides faced problems on many sides and saw the need for drastic action, he did not recognize the Turks as his primary enemy. Instead, Ioannides perceived his archenemy to be Makarios. Despite Greece's glaring disadvantage, Ioannides anticipated the attempt to eliminate Makarios as one which would be successfully executed, void of any negative consequences, because he perceived the attempt as necessary.[104]

As previously noted, both Turkey and Greece desired to achieve their individual goals of partition and union. Militant ethnic group movements that were established to assist in the realization of these goals, exerted pressure and fueled Greece's nonmilitary offensive and military defensive positions. Offensive ideology theorists maintain that the possibility of war can be greatly reduced by shifting to a defensive strategic approach from an offensive one. Indisputably, both Greece and Turkey, in addition to the militant movements which influenced them, held offensive ideologies to fulfill their goals. Analysis of this case, however, reveals that even though an offensive ideology was a necessary condition and colored the perception of events, it was not sufficient in itself to drive the Cypriot Crisis.[105]

What propelled Greek and Turkish leaders to take offensive positions, regardless of whether the elements conducive for such a stand existed, was the paramount responsibility to safeguard their

---

[103] Snyder, *The Ideology of the Offensive* 24.

[104] C. M. Woodhouse, *The Rise and Fall of the Greek Colonels* (London: Granada, 1985) 149–50.

[105] Snyder, *The Ideology of the Offensive* 15.

respective ideologies of enosis and taksim, which were about to be jeopardized by the 1974 constitutional provisions. If these provisions were implemented, the channels through which cultural influences had so freely flowed since 1960 would dry up, thus curtailing the importation of ethnicity. Out of desperation, Greece staged the coup, and Turkey divided Cyprus using military means.

B. Jervis's Security Dilemma Theory

Security dilemma theorists claim that the condition which determines the degree of a state's security is the perceived advantage, if one exists, of an offensive or defensive military position. This theory maintains that a second variable, whether one combative stand can be differentiated from another, plays a key role in the security dilemma as well.[106] The ideology of the offensive and defensive, militarily speaking, is applicable to Cyprus in the conflicts of 1964 and 1967. By the middle of 1964, Cyprus had been infiltrated by military troops from Greece and Turkey in excess of those allotted by the 1960 Constitution. Turkey dispatched more than six hundred men, claiming that the additional troops were needed to protect Turkish Cypriots who were outnumbered on the island by four to one. Likewise, Greece increased its numbers on the island by at least five thousand men, claiming that Cypriot defense needed to be strengthened to deter any notions of invasion that Turkey might entertain. Even though both Greece and Turkey excused their actions as defensive, they were in flagrant violation of their rights under the treaty of alliance and were perceived by each other as offensive. Consequently, as security dilemma theorists assert, the security of the island was shaken as the Turkish government prepared to mount an invasion because of a misperceived combative stand.[107]

Again, by 1967 Greece and Turkey exceeded their allotment of military troops on Cyprus. And again, because offensive and defensive motives could not be differentiated, Turkey "[threatened

---

[106] Jervis, "Offensive, Defense, and the Security Dilemma," *International Politics* 146.
[107] Kyriakides, *Cyprus* 157.

to invade the island, but it held its hand when Greece agreed to withdraw all its soldiers on Cyprus in excess of the contingent authorized under the 1960 settlement."[108] In both cases, without the forthright intervention of the United States, a crisis would likely have occurred.

The narrowly averted crisis situations of 1964 and 1967 clearly exemplify the role that perceptions of another's military position played in Cyprus's security dilemma. However, a close evaluation of the events also discloses that application of the offensive and defensive ideologies must be broadened to introduce political alliances. Apparently, because small countries face a more threatening security dilemma than dominant powers, and because alliances are their principal method of security, alliances are a greater concern than any technological threat.

From the time when enosis was conceived, Greece desired to establish an alliance with Cyprus for the fulfillment of this idyllic union. Greek Cypriots favored enosis and strove to insure its fruition with movements. Unfortunately, for small countries any move is typically regarded as offensive to one party, while appearing defensive to another. Turkey and the Turkish Cypriots perceived the idea of enosis as an offensive ideology on the part of Greece because the movement entailed Greece's absorption of the Turkish Cypriot community. This would jeopardize Turkish security since Turkish Cypriots would subsequently be considered an insignificant minority. Likewise, Greece viewed the Turkish ideology of taksim, and its accompanying movements as a menacing force, capable of undermining its security. Since all interested parties in 1959 were aware of the dangerous consequences of the fruition of either antagonistic ideology, the 1960 Treaty of Guarantee provided for the exclusion of total or partial union of Cyprus with any other state or the separatist independence of Cyprus. Despite this institutionalized exclusion, and Archbishop Makarios's efforts to dissuade support of these ideological movements because of their disastrous capabilities, there were increasing

[108] Thomas Ehrlich, *Cyprus 1958–1967: The International Crisis and the Role of Law* (New York: Oxford University Press, 1974) 3.

attempts to fulfill these opposing ideologies by fortifying the bridges between the homelands and their respective communities.[109]

Did the menacing notions of enosis and taksim spark the crisis in Cyprus? Granted, irreconcilable desires for union with Greece and Turkey increased the tensions, but if enosis and taksim alone were to blame, why was there no Greek or Turkish assault at the time enosis and taksim were conceived? Is it possible that at the time of their inception, neither enosis nor taksim had the support and intensity to threaten Greece and Turkey, but as they gained momentum the potency of these ideologies increased? Could this ideological intensification have brought the tensions to the point of crisis?

If the numbers in support of these causes actually multiplied over time and ideological momentum increased, we can understand why the mother countries would be concerned about the safety of their respective communities on Cyprus. Greece, aware of its subordinate military position, undoubtedly had legitimate concerns for the safety of its people on Cyprus. It seems logical to assume that each decision and every action on the part of Greece was intended to ensure Greek Cypriot security and promote a harmonious solution rather than instigate military intervention. In order to eliminate the possibility of inciting a conflict, Greece tried to steer away from any plan that could be even remotely construed as offensive. In contrast, Turkey had a "large army" with "greater power" than the forces in Greece.[110] Because Turkey had geographic advantages to supplement its extensive military, the chance of offensive tactics founded exclusively on elevated security fears were slim. Therefore, while alliances among small countries pose security problems that may culminate in war, the Cypriot Crisis cannot be attributed solely to heightened security fears.

Does the security dilemma theory which holds that the determinant of war is the offensive or defensive stance of a party, and the opposition's perception of that position, hold true for Cyprus? This theory explains the background of the Crisis, but not what sparked

---

[109] Interview of Archbishop Makarios, President of the Republic of Cyprus, with Michael Cacoyannis, Attila 1974.

[110] Interview with Lagakos.

it. Both Greece and Turkey's dispatch of excessive military troops onto the island and their attempts to fortify political alliances for the fulfillment of enosis and taksim created friction over the definition and perception of the offensive- defensive ideology, so to that extent the theory is correct. However, the tensions existed much earlier, and although they increased again before the 1974 Crisis, and actually forced the two communities to acknowledge that negotiations were imminent, they did not solely cause it.

Upon entering the 1968–1974 negotiations, the two communities were well aware of the nearly impossible task that lay ahead. They acknowledged that a prospective solution must necessarily exclude both enosis and taksim, and a form of independence where the majority's rules and the minority's rights were guaranteed, because of the tendency toward self-determination. The two communities were also conscious of the fact that a workable constitutional formula must promote the growth of Cypriot communal cooperation, thereby encouraging allegiance to Cyprus. After nearly six years of negotiations, the two communities produced a set of constitutional proposals which they believed would pave the way for intercommunal trust and cooperation. Because Greece and Turkey perceived the 1974 proposals as sabotage to their respective plans for Cyprus, they had no alternative but to disrupt the intercommunal talks by launching a coup and waging war on Cyprus.

C. Jervis's Misperception Theory

The misperception theory suggests that, in addition to alliances which agitate stability, rigid paradigms are ingrained in the minds of decision makers and generate misperceptions which provoke conflicts. Advocates of this theory claim that images of reality inflict restraints on the business of bureaucratic politics in two principle ways. First, a bureaucrat's images limit perceptions, how they are understood, and the choice of a proper reaction. Second, because a group of actors shares the same rigid images, any bureaucrat who supports a policy must persuade the others to believe these images whether or not he or she agrees with them.[111]

The Greco-Turkish relationship, consisting of thousands of years of combative, recalcitrant interaction, has irrefutably produced images that have become well entrenched in the hearts and minds of all its members. Rigid opinions regarding territorial possession have been an issue of conflict dating as far back as ancient times. This ageless dispute resurfaced in February of 1974 with the sizeable discovery of oil near the Greek island of Thasos that lies in an area of the eastern Aegean which is claimed by both Greece and Turkey. It has been argued that "[o]il is only the latest source of discord between the two countries, which have been allies in the North Atlantic Treaty Organization for 22 years but enemies for centuries."[112] Enmity over the island of Cyprus is at the forefront of the conflict. Clearly, each country regarded Cyprus as its rightful possession. In order to transform the island from its independent status into one united with Greece or partitioned with Turkey, the ideologies of enosis and taksim were conceived. Thus, it is apparent that the Greek and Turkish communities established and rigidly preserved antagonistic ideologies.

Misperception theorists claim that insistence upon these paradigms creates misperception. Some misperceptions develop because data is often influenced by the concerns of the person at the time the new information is received, and by the person's own beliefs and personal cognitive structure.[113] An examination of the years prior to the 1974 Crisis reveals that the governments of both Greece and Turkey were in a constant state of flux and upheaval as power was seized and confiscated. The Cyprus issue took on new meaning with heightened stakes for Greek and Turkish individuals who strove to secure a stable position of authority during this erratic period.

Not only are perceptions influenced by personal concerns, according to the misperception theory, but errors may be made as

---

[111] Jervis, "Hypotheses on Misperception," *International Politics* 113.

[112] *The New York Times*, April 16, 1974.

[113] Jervis, "Hypothesis on Misperception." *International Politics* 132–33.

policy makers attempt to interpret the intentions of other states.[114] An examination of the Cyprus case reveals that critical errors in judgment were made on the part of both the leadership in Greece and that in Cyprus. Testing the misperception theory on the Cyprus case first reveals that the Crisis occurred as a result of an actual, not misperceived, security threat. Even though Makarios was initially concerned about the serious security threats to Cyprus, he assuaged these fears by implementing several precautionary measures. Secondly, analysis discloses that Cypriot perceptions were less important than Greek and Turkish perceptions of the conflict. Misperception theorists claim that, in order to determine how an actor will behave, that actor must attempt to predict how others will behave and how that behavior will influence his or her intentions. This claim holds true in the case of Cyprus. If the Greek junta had accurately perceived the potency of the Turkish threat, he certainly would have taken a different course. However, because both the leaders of the Turkish government and the Greek junta sensed the vulnerability of their positions of power, they made decisions they hoped their respective communities would support and thus enhanced their individual chances for political survival.[115]

The culprit behind the 1974 Cypriot Crisis, then, was not misperception on the part of the interested leaders, but securing the threats to both Greece and Turkey as they stood ready to lose their control over Cypriot affairs should the 1974 constitutional proposals be implemented. If Greece and Turkey were stripped of their means of preserving their cultural identities and ideologies on Cyprus during their terms in power, both leaders would unquestionably be replaced with others who would promise to restore the status quo conditions. In order to avoid such a risk and to chance a victory, Ioannides' government launched the coup and Ecevit's government commandeered partition of Cyprus.

---

114 Jervis, "Hypotheses on Misperception," *International Politics* 115–25.

115 Theodoracopulos, *The Greek Upheaval* 26–55.

D. Conclusion of First-Level Theories

In summary, first-level analysts claim that policy makers form alliances to minimize risk and maximize security within the anarchic environment in which they reside. Although security would appear to be endemic to alliances, in reality a competitiveness among states frequently occurs. In an effort to become effective competitors, allied states must establish an ideology and strategy, either offensive or defensive, to enhance the attainment of their goals. Conflicts arise because motives for the formation of alliances, and even the opposing offensive or defensive ideologies they uphold, are frequently indistinguishable. Potentially defensive alliances and ideologies are misperceived as offensive in nature, and this misperception incites hostilities.

Application of first level theories to Cyprus shows that, although they illuminate some of the key antagonists, the theories do not provide a thorough understanding of the factors which spurred the Cypriot Crisis. Neither Greece nor Turkey assumed an offensive stance in Cyprus because they conformed to the military characteristics conducive to their positions. In fact, the alliances which agitated the Cypriot problem were not formed in order to minimize risk in a military sense, but to secure the political means by which to safeguard their respective cultural identities and institutions on Cyprus. Even though both Greece and Turkey chose to violate their military privileges by exceeding their entitlement to presence on Cyprus numerous times between 1960 and 1974, their individual motives in 1974 were not misperceived by each other, but were more accurately understood to be strategic moves on the part of both to avert a true security threat. The 1974 constitutional proposals signaled the forthcoming of an upheaval that Greece and Turkey perceived as fatal to their ideological designs for Cyprus. Because the homelands envisioned themselves stripped of their cultural identities and institutions on Cyprus, Greece implemented the coup and Turkey stormed the island to effect a partition.

V. OVERALL CONCLUSIONS OF INTERNATIONAL RELATIONS THEORIES

An overall study of international relations theory reveals that each of the three images lends an understanding to the determinants of a crisis. While a consideration of the interaction of the three images is important, state conduct is attributable more to the third level of analysis applied at the regional level than any other. A neorealist might claim that small countries practice behavior at the regional level characteristic of a multipolar structure, even though a bipolar structure prevails globally. Furthermore, a micro-level balancing act for political-military matters may be as harmful to regional powers as economic dependency can be at the macro-level. Therefore, if one applies world systems, balance of power and international capitalism explanations to the Cypriot dispute, the deficiencies are obvious. A regionally generated construct therefore serves as the critical dynamic for understanding the Cypriot Crisis.

Second-level theorists attribute international events to the domestic politics and economics of individual states. From domestic stability to class struggle and imperialist conflict exportation, second-level theories provide a number of explanations for war. Contrary to the expectations of those who valorize stability, we have found that unstable states may behave no differently than they would under less volatile conditions. In addition, the volatility of class struggle is not alone in dividing states, lest we forget ethnic conflict. Finally, in contrast to the contentions of imperialist theories, there may be multiple centers and peripheries within the borders of one country. For Cyprus, these theories are deficient and cannot completely explain the Cypriot Crisis of 1974.

Finally, first-level analysis reveals that while it is possible for a state to assume a military stance, offensive or defensive, this stance may conflict with the positions for which states are best suited. Even though security is considered to be an indicator of alliances, it may actually produce conflict, particularly when an alliance is politically established to preserve cultural identities. Motives for the formation of alliances and the military position that must necessarily accompany them may be misperceived by others, thus producing conflict and resulting in a true security threat. If one applies offensive ideology, security dilemma, and misperception analysis with respect to the Cypriot case in the strict sense of policy makers forming alliances in order to minimize security risks, then much is lost. Standing alone, these theories fail to acknowledge that the impetus for Greek and Turkish alliance formation with their respective diasporas on Cyprus was to protect Greek and Turkish cultural identities and institutions on the island.

Although international relations theories fall short with respect to the Cypriot Crisis, they demonstrate that the Cypriot case must be examined within the international context because of the influential capabilities of Cyprus's neighbors. For Cyprus, the 1974 Crisis can be better understood by international relations theory if it is applied to local regions rather than at the aggregate level of hegemony, multipolarity, or bipolarity. Because Cyprus is only relatively autonomous and appears to be directed by events which occur within or are initiated by its two closest dominant neighbors, a second-level version of international relations theory is more applicable. The domestic stability model undervalues the continuity of raison d'état, regardless of superficial changes in governments. The dependency imperialist models also become problematic for Cyprus because they tend to favor purely economic cases. Cyprus's dependency is clearly an ethnic one in that the military and political actions of Greece and Turkey cannot be understood as being merely economically motivated. Instead, the overriding rationale for actions of both Greece and Turkey with respect to Cyprus is best understood in terms of their shared and separate desires to secure the political means with which to safeguard their cultural identities and institutions on the island. Ultimately, these motives entailed the strong desire of each of these two countries to effect enosis and taksim.

Looking back at Greece and Turkey's intervention in Cyprus, one can conclude that the threats and issues which existed until the point of the coup and invasion evolved into a "real" and not misperceived confrontation. Thus, it is clear that the history and cultural background of a crisis interjects unique political factors into the international relations formula. In terms of the Cypriot Crisis, the dynamic and politically charged background of the dispute influenced the Cypriot people and fueled their battle for independence.

As Thucydides observed so long ago, a nation at the helm of an empire is cognizant that a conquered people can act in a manner that threatens them (the imperialist power). In the case of Greece and Turkey with respect to Cyprus, however, such a danger can be felt even in the case of countries, or "motherlands," that have an obvious cultural affinity to the "subject" country. Thus, while international relations theories are enlightening, the Cypriot Crisis is likely to remain an enigma to those who rely exclusively on international relations insights.

CHAPTER 3

UNDERSTANDING THE 1974 CYPRIOT CRISIS WITH COMPARATIVE THEORIES: AN EXAMINATION OF THE CYPRIOT CONSTITUTION

> Despite the fact that a Cypriot 'nation' did not in fact exist in Cyprus the Turkish and Greek national communities had reached an agreement to establish a Cyprus state in partnership. It had been hoped that out of this Cypriot State a Cypriot 'nation' would eventually emerge. This of course, requires time, goodwill, and cooperation between the two communities. It was with this understanding that the two communities had come together on the basis of equality and prepared the Constitution of this bi-communal state. [1]
>
> — Denktash

I. INTRODUCTION: AN OVERVIEW OF COMPARATIVE THEORIES

Aspirations toward one day becoming citizens of a united nation-state drove the Greek and Turkish Cypriot communities to abandon their historically conflicting ideologies in favor of those that were not only mutually compatible, but had cohesive tendencies as well. It was the hope of the Cypriot people that concessions and sacrifice on

---

[1] Denktash quoted in Joseph, *Cyprus* 63.

their part would ultimately bring stability to the island. Was Cyprus's constitutional structure exclusively to blame for the 1974 Cypriot Crisis? Or were Greek and Turkish influence a determinant? In order for these questions to be addressed, it is important to evaluate the comparative approach in relation to Cyprus.

Comparative theories originally delineated internal role structure and a homogeneous political culture as the two preconditions for stability, but eventually extended these conditions to include heterogeneous culture in certain governmental structures. Later on, comparativists instead turned to study of the relationship between civil society and the state. A fully developed civil society with polycentric traditions, integrated politics, military restriction, and adaptive politicians—permits stability. The possibility of stability, however, can be diminished by ethnic divisions in the society. But group entitlement may allow this issue to be dealt with and restore stability in plural societies. Another group of comparativists theories focused on state structure rather than civil society. Some have pointed to an institutionalized control system as essential to stability, while others have contended that a triangular power structure is crucial. This triangular structure rests on a combination of central executive leadership at the state level with links to strong leaders at the regional and local levels. Yet another theory argues that conscociational democracy can provide stability in conditions of fragmentation. Finally, these theorists argue that without party depolarization and the implementation of a grand coalition, proportionality, segmented autonomy, and a mutual veto, democracy will ultimately fail because of political disunity.

This cursory survey of comparative theories should make it clear that comparativists focus on domestic politics and ignore international factors. Because of this domestic focus, comparativists attribute the relative stability of a country to either structural or social causes. Structural theorists highlight the role of institutions, whereas social theorists claim that groups are central. More specifically, both social and structural approaches operate at either the micro or macro level.[2]

2 The divisions of theories along lines of social/structural and micro/macro have the unfortunate byproduct of decontextualizing debate. Gabriel A. Almond,

Macrosocial theories emphasize the general nature of society at the large level, in terms of degree of homogeneity or autonomy of civil society. Microsocial theories instead stress the way that specific groups like classes, parties, or sub-cultures behave in a country. Both sets of theories focus on the society rather than the state; social variables cause outcomes. At the macro level, social theories look at the general character of society, whereas at the micro level, social theories examine the specific workings of groups.

Macrostructural theories highlight the overall structure of the state and the credibility of institutions. Microstructural theories, rather, point to the rules of the game and the way they constrain or empower different people. Both sets of theories focus on the state rather than society; structural variables cause events. At the macro level, structural theories look at the general structure of a country, but at the micro level, structural theories claim a central role for specific political institutions.

The following paragraphs will present two versions of each of the four varieties of comparative theory. We will begin with macrosocial and then turn to microsocial theories. Next we will examine macrostructural, and end ultimately with microstructural approaches. After presenting each model we will place it into the context of the 1974 Cypriot Crisis and test its validity for this particular case.

II. MACROSOCIAL THEORIES

Macrosocial theories focus on the larger system that faces societal groups and state agents. The preconditions-for-stable-democracy theory holds that patterns of political structure and culture, as well as the psychological dimension, or role structure, in a society, determine the political stability of a country. The first component, that

---

Arend Lijphart, and Brian Barry are part of one debate, but offer different approaches. Almond offered a macrosocial theory, Lijphart criticized Almond with the microstructural approach, and Barry criticized Lijphart with a micro social model. This chapter for convenience separates these theories, although they are part of the same dialogue in the literature.

of political structure, focuses on a society's political system, as well as the attitudes, mores, and beliefs which influence and shape a particular culture. The second component addresses role structure and entails the various political and social institutions, organizations, and groups within a society. Role structure also involves role differentiation, which refers to the development and alteration of social roles over time. In essence, the two components of political and role structures overlap and operate within a system to determine the interests of various groups within a society and the degree of segregation or fragmentation of such groups, which ultimately determines the level of stability or instability of a particular country.[3]

Another macrosocial theory is the civil society theory. This theory stresses the importance of social values and institutions for political transition and for the consolidation and institutionalization of a new regime. Economics, social change, rural transitions, demographic patterns, and the development of social segments are endemic to institutional changes which stem from political and cultural conflicts within society. An understanding of conflict is necessary to trace the appearance of liberal democratic societal traditions. Such democratic traditions are significant in that they shape rules and institutions which, in turn guide decision makers and form civil societies.[4]

A. Almond's Preconditions for Stable Democracy

A country's stability or lack thereof is determined by its homogeneous political culture.[5] A multicommunal character has character-

---

3 Gabriel A. Almond and Bringham Powell Jr., *Comparative Politics: A Development Approach.* (Boston: Little Brown, 1966) 11, 21–23, 122 and 259; and Almond, "Comparative Political System," *Journal of Politics* vol. 18, no. 3 (August 1956) 397–407.

4 Victor M. Perez-Dias, *The Return of Civil Society: The Emergence of Democratic Spain* (Cambridge: Harvard University Press, 1993) 56–58, 78–79,186–190 and 280.

5 Almond, "Comparative Political System." *Journal of Politics* 398–99; Arend Lijphart, *Democracy in Plural Societies: A Comparative Exploration* (New Haven:

ized Cyprus throughout its history. The 1960 bicommunal society, composed of Greek and Turkish Cypriots, was delineated by religious, linguistic, and cultural disparities, and divergent political aspirations. The Greek national character of the Greek Cypriots has been preserved and fortified by the Greek Orthodox Church of Cyprus while the Turkish national character has been retained and nourished by the Turkish Cypriots.[6] These divisions penetrated the organizational structures on the island as well. Each community passionately preserved its ethnicity by means of "[i]ts own system of education conducted in its own language and there is no intermarriage between the two communities who have maintained and jealously guarded their respective cultural and national heritages over four centuries of coexistence in the island."[7]

It has been argued that the degree of stability of a country depends upon the homogeneity of its political culture. Indubitably, Cyprus is far from a homogeneous island. As the theory would predict, its heterogeneous composition provoked conflict and instability; intercommunal disputes erupted, first in 1963–64 and again in 1967. Even though these violent incidents did not culminate in war, greater distance developed between the Greek and Turkish Cypriot communities, not intrinsically due to the conflicting cultural composition, but primarily due to the emergence of nationalism.[8]

In addition to ethnic divisions in Cyprus's heterogeneous population, linguistic, religious, and cultural cleavages existed. However, despite the extensively divided nature of the country, relative peace and security was maintained on the island from the inception of its independent status in 1960 to its dissolution in 1974. Therefore, in spite of its heterogeneous composition, a sufficient degree of internal cohesiveness was preserved on the island until the constitutional revisions proposed during the 1968–1974 intercommunal negotiations threatened the persistently divisive cultural ideologies of

---

Yale University Press, 1977) 6–7.

6 Kyriakides, *Cyprus* 56 and 163.

7 Denktash, *The Cyprus Triangle* 17; and Kyriakides, *Cyprus* 67–68 and 163–64.

8 Kyriakides, *Cyprus* 11; Denktash, *The Cyprus Triangle* 118; and Panteli, *Cyprus* 354 and 373.

Greece and Turkey. Traditional identities were no longer nourished via a cross-boundary umbilical cord; rather, a new identity emerged, nurtured by an autonomous Cypriot state.

In 1974 the environment of Cyprus was rocked with instability because of its heterogeneous composition. The near solution of the Cypriot problem, as indicated in a statement made to the Turkish Cypriot delegation on June 11, 1974, was based on the concept of "an independent, sovereign and unitary state with complete autonomy" over all matters of state. Threatened by its exclusionary character, Greece and Turkey felt compelled to intervene. Interference of the two external powers in Cypriot affairs culminated in the direct use of force for the preservation of its culture and identities; thus, the Crisis erupted.[9]

B. Perez-Dias's Civil Society Theory

Civil society, where the persistence or recreation of traditions is confined, guarantees a successful transition to democracy. With a civil society, defined by its polycentric traditions, integrative politics, military restriction, and adaptive politicians, comes a smooth transition to democracy and consequently the avoidance of a crisis.[10] Cyprus severed its colonial ties with Britain in 1960 after serving under her tutelage since 1878. Cyprus broke free from Britain's persistent traditions and created a new independent identity, one based on a constitutional government. Cyprus's civil society, characterized by polycentric traditions, integrative politics, military restrictions, and adaptive politicians, eased the transition to democracy as the

---

9 Polyviou, "The Problem of Cyprus and Constitutional Solution," *Cyprus Reviewed* 216. Although Almond is somewhat dated and has been critiqued powerfully by scholars like Lijphart, it is still worth putting out his argument. The reason is that the general premise that homogeneity allows political stability and especially democratic stability is still accepted in various ways throughout the literature. The point is that heterogeneity alone is not the cause for Cyprus' woes. Had there not been external influence, the consociational constitution might have worked in spite of Cyprus' heterogeneity.

10 Perez-Dias, *The Return of Civil Society* 39–40.

theory purports. Polycentric traditions were not only deemed worthy of respect, but served as the backbone of the 1960 Constitution which acknowledges and enacts bicommunalism.[11]

A civil society capable of securing stability must consist of integrative politics in addition to polycentric traditions. Without a doubt, this element is constitutionally sanctioned and readily practiced in Cyprus. It is apparent that: "In all spheres of government regardless of whether the character is national or local, the Constitution recognizes the Turks and Greeks of Cyprus primarily as members of their respective communities with political and constitutional rights, that is not as citizens of Cyprus but as members of one or the other community."[12]

The third element of civil society, a restricted military, was also constitutionalized on Cyprus. Military restrictions are provided for both in directorship and in numerical distribution. First, the Constitution designates the president and vice president as the heads of the armed forces, and thus the military is restricted. But the Constitution is simultaneously vague in that the position of commander-in-chief is not restricted to any particular leaders; this makes the military less restricted than it would ideally be. This element proved to be problematic despite its institutionalization. The source of the numerical and formation difficulties lies in the veto power provisions which severely hampered the leadership's decision-making capabilities.[13]

After finding three of the four criteria for a stable civil society established to some extent on Cyprus, though not without problems, we must now determine whether the final measure, adaptive politicians, were present and functioning. By the very structure of the Constitution, Cypriot leadership in all branches at all levels were forced 1 to accommodate other power sources. More specifically, the Cypriot executive branch of government—the president and vice president—had to cooperate in order to function. President

---

11 Kyriakides, *Cyprus* 56.

12 Kyriakides, *Cyprus* 57.

13 Kyriakides, *Cyprus* 57 and 94.

Makarios and Vice President Kutchuk and Denktash strove to exemplify adaptive behavior during their fourteen-year history together, but because of constitutional defects, particularly the veto provision, deadlocks resulted. Consequently, dormant fears and mistrust surfaced thus producing governmental paralysis.

In an attempt to resolve the impasse, Makarios proposed a series of major alterations in the Constitution which were promptly rejected by the Turkish vice president. The December 1963 intercommunal strife was the culmination of these negative forces. Tensions over the Constitution vented again in 1967, but were cooled by the intervention of the United States, as was the case in 1964. Since all four characteristics of a civil society were manifested at least to a limited degree in Cyprus, a crisis should have been avoided, but as history reveals, anarchism erupted in 1974.

After two close encounters with what could have escalated into a crisis situation, the two communities opted to try to settle their differences through negotiation. The product of these cooperative efforts was the 1974 constitutional settlement, which, if enacted, would have greatly improved Cypriot civil society. Had the settlement been implemented, the first of a civil society's components, polycentric traditions, would have been instituted as with the 1960 Constitution. The practice of integrative politics would have been enhanced as the officers of the House of Representatives increased to three (the president and two vice presidents, one of whom would be Turkish), the communal character would be abolished, and the 'separate-majorities' provisions would be eliminated. Additional revisions would have improved both the restricted military and adaptive politician elements as well. The abandonment of the presidential and vice presidential vetoes would have eradicated all chances of a deadlock, and simultaneously fostered adaptive behavior between the leaderships.[14]

Cypriot leadership recognized that the 1960 constitutional shortcomings were impairing Cyprus's civil society, and that in order

[14] Polyviou, "The Problem of Cyprus and Constitutional Solutions," *Cyprus Reviewed* 214 and 218–19.

to preserve stability on the island, it was necessary to implement revisions, thus the 1974 constitutional arrangements ensued. Tragically, the 1974 constitutional provisions were never finalized because of Greek and Turkish interference. As word of the negotiated conditions reached the homelands, plans for a coup and invasion were developed in order to exterminate the possibility of an autonomous island which was perceived as an obstacle to their respective designs. Civil society adherents correctly assess the central role of a healthy civil society for stability, yet they fall short when they neglect to consider the capabilities of neighbors whose interests run counter to those of the civil society.

C. Conclusion of Macrosocial Theories

The consensus of the macrosocial theorists that have been examined is that the stability of a state can only endure when the society is unified or controlled. States become powerful when they are homogeneous and conducive to a democratic political system. The civil society must be characterized by polycentric traditions, integrative politics, military restriction, and adaptive politicians. If the system is void of even one of these elements, a smooth transition to democracy, and therefore the preservation of stability, will be disrupted. Therefore, macrosocial theory contends that a crisis can be avoided only if the state consists of a homogeneous culture which has successfully incorporated local and societal elites into the state structure. However, an examination of the Cypriot case shows us that it is possible to maintain stability despite heterogeneity. Furthermore, Cyprus had manifested all four characteristics of civil society to one degree or another. The problem was that interference from other countries could not allow the continuation of peace and stability.

III. MICROSOCIAL THEORIES

Microsocial theories focus on micro-level group behavior within the society. According to one theory that provides a domestic-level critique of the consociational model, a consociational democracy cannot successfully prevail in any fragmented setting. While consociationalism can prevail in religiously and ideologically fragmented settings, it cannot flourish in societies that are ethnically divided. There are three reasons for the destabilizing phenomenon of ethnic fragmentation: first, a shunned ethnic group is more inclined to support inhumane behavior; second, ethnic conflicts occur among solidary groups, which are prone to riots and violence; and finally, policies that favor ethnic groups are more visible than those that favor religious groups. As a result of these social cleavages, ethnic identity is less likely to conform to consociational management.[15]

Additionally, according to group entitlement theory, ethnicity is the key determinant of a society's cohesiveness or level of internal conflict. As a factor relevant to both mass and elite behavior, ethnicity is a source of state instability. Because ethnic conflict is perceived as an issue of entitlement, it is necessary to consider group entitlement, the product of comparative worth and legitimacy, to understand the role of ethnicity. Specifically, group entitlement accounts for group behavior, the degree of influence a group wields over its members, and group reaction. Group entitlement remains significant because the internal political arrangements that govern group structure are conducive to policy intervention. The role of policy is critical within the spectrum of group entitlement because with the careful implementation of measures designed to inhibit ethnic allegiance at levels prone to bifurcation, democracies can prevail in divided societies.[16]

A. Barry's Domestic-Level Critique of the Consociational Model

A constitutional government is doomed to fail in ethnically divided societies because conflicts arise among solidary groups that

15 Brian Barry, "Political Accommodation and Consociational Democracy," *British Journal of Political Science* vol. 5, no. 4 (October 1975) 500–03.

16 Donald Horowitz, *Ethnic Groups in Conflict* (Berkeley: University of California Press, 1985) 141–84, 226–90 and 563–652.

are not defined by a particular leadership.[17] Cyprus is, without a doubt, an ethnically divided island. Moreover, two distinct solidary groups—Greeks Cypriots and Turkish Cypriots—are not characterized by their homage to specific leadership but by their allegiance to their respective homelands. The solidarity and allegiance of these groups have been a source of conflict for the several centuries of their coexistence.

During the 1950s, serious dissension arose among the solidary groups on Cyprus and Britain. British control of Cyprus persisted until the late 1950s when Greek and Turkish Cypriots incited rebellions in attempts to sever ties with Britain and establish an independent island. The large Greek population on Cyprus organized a revolutionary movement called EOKA (National Organization Fighters), while the Volkan group, later referred to as TMT (Turkish Resistance Organization), became identified as the Turkish counterpart.[18]

The ferocity with which EOKA members pursued their goal of liberation is exemplified in the words of their oath: "I swear in the name of the Holy Trinity that I shall work with all my power for the liberation of Cyprus from British rule, sacrificing for this even my life . . . ."[19] And lives were sacrificed between April 1955 and July 1956. Upon achieving independence in 1960, thus fulfilling the liberation objective of both EOKA (later to become EOKA-B) and TMT, the groups transferred their allegiance to their homelands. EOKA revitalized its mother country's steadfast goal of enosis, while TMT focused on furthering its "irredentist" nationalism within Cyprus, or at least implementing taksim.

Thus, the 1955–58 hostilities, as well as the 1963–64 and 1967 conflicts, reveal that ethnically divided states undergo conflicts because solidary groups do not adhere to a particular leadership. Although the diverse ideologies of solidary groups are known to incite problems, further evidence demonstrates they were not solely

---

[17] Barry, "Political Accommodation and Consociational Democracy," *British Journal of Political Science* 502.

[18] Ioannides, *In Turkey's Image* 49–149.

[19] Panteli, *Cyprus* 265.

responsible for sparking the 1974 Cypriot Crisis. The roots of the ethnic conflict in Cyprus are in its history and embodied within the bicommunal structure of Cypriot society. Ethnic bonds and loyalties between the Cypriots and their motherland were maintained and reinforced by the cross-boundary educational integration which was a major instrument for ethnic propaganda and the transference of Greek-Turkish antagonism.[20]

In addition to education, religious ties and practices contributed to the maintenance and reinforcement of cultural bonds between the two Cypriot ethnic groups and their homelands. The churches functioned as centers of national indoctrination that stressed the indivisibility of religion and ethnicity, and the necessity of union with Greece and partition with Turkey. To further solidify the national bonds of the two Cypriot communities with their homelands, national holidays were commemorated and nationalistic symbols employed. Additionally, in the military field, close ties that extended across state boundaries began to develop along ethnic lines as Greek and Turkish troops were dispatched to the island under the 1960 Treaty of Guarantee.[21]

It is evident that the absence of cross-cutting ethnic, social, or political cleavages prevented the establishment of common Cypriot patriotic bonds and the bridging of national loyalties between the two communities. Proponents of this theory assert that pervasive mass-level differences, as opposed to elite-level differences, created the breakdown of the Constitution.[22] Irrefutably, the existence of cross-boundary ethnic, linguistic, educational, religious, cultural, and military bonds between the Cypriots and their respective homelands had a devastating impact on inter- communal relations. These solidary groups, however, even with their diametrically opposed ideologies, were not in and of themselves the primary cause of the constitutional crisis.

---

[20] Kyriakides. *Cyprus* 26–52 and 104–34.

[21] Joseph, *Cyprus* 63 and 83–84.

[22] Kyriakides, *Cyprus* 53–71.

What, then, were the overriding forces? To help answer this question, it is helpful to examine the historical interest other nations had in Cyprus, and how this interest was acted upon to affect Cyprus's political status. Greece's interest in Cyprus developed because of the historical and cultural traditions it shared with Cyprus. Makarios explained this relationship: "Cyprus is Greek. Cyprus was Greek since the dawn of its history, and will remain Greek."[23] In a way, the Cypriot issue became enmeshed in Greece's Panhellenic movement of Megali Idea. Greece's claim to Cyprus was fortified by the persistent Greek Cypriot drive for enosis.[24]

Like Greece, Turkey's interest in Cyprus stemmed from its unremitting belief in the cultural interconnectedness of Cyprus to the homeland. Advocates revealed their enthusiasm for this belief when they passionately proclaimed in a pamphlet: "It is our sacred duty to resist any action which will disturb the tranquility of the island which is an inseparable part of our own country and a sacred legacy of our grandfathers."[25] Turkey further justified its claim to Cyprus by emphasizing its geographic proximity, military security, and cultural affinity to the Turkish Cypriot population.

The deeply ingrained interests of Greece and Turkey had disastrous effects on the constitutional and inter-communal well-being of Cyprus. Continued friction prevented the Cypriots from establishing their own political consciousness. This prevention reinforced Cypriot dependency on its respective homelands for direction and support in solving domestic problems. Cyprus's neighbors were aware that any possible constitutional agreement on Cyprus, which would certainly entail a bicommunal compromise, would require debarring Greece and Turkey from intervening in Cyprus's business, thus extinguishing enosis and partition.[26]

---

[23] Ertekun, *The Cyprus Dispute* 27.

[24] Joseph, *Cyprus* 29.

[25] Ioannides, *In Turkey's Image* 76.

[26] Kyriakides, *Cyprus* 168; Kyriakos C. Markides, *The Rise and Fall of the Cyprus Republic* (New Haven: Yale University Press, 1977) 154; and Kitromilides, "From Coexistence to Confrontation." *Cyprus Reviewed* 60.

Enosis was thoroughly unacceptable to the Turkish Cypriots and Turkey because the Turks objected to Greek expansionism and refused to assimilate to Greece. If the Greek Cypriot majority desired a compromise with the Turkish Cypriot minority in order to establish stability on the island, the Greek Cypriots and Greece had to abandon enosis. Likewise, taksim, which was completely unacceptable to the Greek Cypriots and Greece, was necessarily excluded as a solution. Obsessed with sheer devotion to their nationalistic aspirations, neither Greece nor Turkey could accept a denial of their ideologies. Therefore, Greece and Turkey, through their grassroots movements embodied in EOKA-B and TMT respectively, set to work to insure the demise of the Constitution. They did so by not only preserving but also strengthening their political and cultural causes. Ultimately, Greece and Turkey were successful, but their actions heightened hostile ethnic sentiments and impeded cooperation.

In addition to the belief that mass-level differences destroy a constitutional government, it has been asserted that solidary ethnicity is to blame.[27] Although mutually hostile ethnic sentiments exacerbated the existing Cypriot problems, it was not the dissimilarity of the two ethnic populations that ultimately triggered the disaster. Rather, the 1974 Crisis was instigated by the underground EOKA-B and TMT movements thriving within Cyprus, which were financially supported and ideologically inspired by their ethnically connected homelands.

Although the 1960 Constitution granted both mother countries the right to foster the cultural identities of their respective communities, this privilege was severely bridled in the treaty of guarantee by the strict prohibition of enosis and taksim. On two separate occasions, in 1963–64 and again in 1967, the externally propelled underground movements incited violence between the two communities as the mother countries transgressed their constitutional privileges. Fortunately, war was averted on both occasions because the intervention of international forces. Shortly after the 1967 hostile

[27] Barry, "Political Accommodation and Consociational Democracy," *British Journal of Political Science* 502.

outbreak, constitutional negotiations between the two Cypriot communities commenced and ultimately produced the constitutional arrangements. Although the negotiators successfully clarified most of the questionable elements in the 1960 Constitution, they recognized that nationalistic issues would be the most problematic.[28]

In summary, it is believed that ethnic segregation among solidary groups, which develops because of mass-level differences rather than elite-level differences, was the cause for the failure of the Cypriot Constitution. The contradictions emanating from distinct and conflicting cultures widened the gap between the bicommunal Cypriot population, as evidenced by the 1963–64 and 1967 Constitutional uprisings. However, the cultural contradictions in themselves were not extensive enough to cause the 1974 Crisis. Under the provisions of the 1960 Constitution, despite the explicit exclusion of enosis and taksim, Greece and Turkey were granted the authority to exert influence over their respective communities. These concessions pacified the mother countries into submission. However, from the perspective of the new leadership in Greece and Turkey, the proposed 1974 constitutional arrangements appeared to occlude all avenues of external involvement, including influence over EOKA-B and TMT agendas. Therefore, Greece and Turkey were compelled to intervene in order to prevent constitutional settlement. For Cyprus, the divisiveness between the two ethnically bound populations only exacerbated the difficulties. The roots of the 1974 Crisis were therefore contained in the proposed provisions of the 1974 settlement that prevented Greece and Turkey from achieving their policies, namely enosis for Greece and taksim for Turkey.

B. Horowitz's Group Entitlement Theory

Group entitlement theorists argue that ethnicity, a powerful obstacle to the consolidation of states and a source of global friction,

---

[28] Bureau of Intelligence and Research, "Intelligence Report No. 8047: Analysis of the Cyprus Agreements, July 14, 1959," in *Journal of Hellenic Diaspora: A Quarterly Review* vol. XI, no. 4 (Winter 1994) 25.

is at the core of politics in virtually every country. A comprehensive theory of ethnic conflict should be able to justify both elite and mass behavior. Therefore, the answer to the Cypriot Crisis lies in group entitlement, which exists as a dual function of comparative worth and legitimacy.[29]

The Cypriot population as a whole recognized that group entitlement was imperative to the formulation and preservation of autonomy. Even prior to signing and implementing the 1960 Constitution, the government of Cyprus was a recognized democracy, as was evidenced by the electoral process of 1959. The suffrage procedure exercised on Cyprus clearly revealed group entitlement at the level of the masses. With the selection of President Makarios and Vice President Kutchuk to employ the democratic electoral system, decisions regarding group entitlement were made at the elite-level. Like the masses, the leaders of Cyprus acknowledged that group entitlement was critical and came to an understanding regarding the distribution of power. Indubitably, group entitlement exists and is readily exercised by Cyprus's democratic system.

In addition, some theorists claim the maintenance of democracy and the ability to limit ethnic conflict are dependent upon avoiding bifurcation along ethnic lines. For Cyprus, not only was group entitlement a consideration for the masses through the electoral process and for the elites through power apportionment, but the consideration was made possible for the two communities through the 1960 Constitution. Although many considered George Grivas to be the biggest potential obstacle to acceptance of the Agreements when he initially voiced his doubts and hesitations concerning them, in time he grew to personally support them and elicited EOKA members to "[r]ally united round the Ethnarch."[30] The 1960 Constitutional Agreements, which ensured group entitlement at all levels, ultimately met with unanimous approval. The Agreements were actively practiced and upheld throughout the first three years of Cypriot indepen-

29 Horowitz, *The Return of Civil Society* 89 and 226.

30 Evangelos Averoff-Tossizza, *Lost Opportunities: The Cyprus Question 1950–1963* (New York: Aristide D. Caratzas, 1986) 363–89.

dence, but were only practiced in a limited sense after meeting with resistance that culminated in the 1963–64 and 1967 hostilities.

Group entitlement theory asserts that the origins of bifurcation lie in the inclination of group comparison and are sustained by the critical nature of established electoral majorities.[31] For Cyprus, bifurcation resulting from the constitutional articles that stressed ethnic differences and the establishment of electoral majorities created problems of division, as demonstrated in the 1963–64 and 1967 hostilities. However, as disuniting as these elements were, they were not strong enough to disrupt the prevailing democracy. The results of the 1968 presidential elections in which Archbishop Makarios won 97 percent of the votes, an increase in excess of 30 percent from the previous election, and the uncontested election of 1973 disclosed mounting support for the President and his proposed group entitlement policies. Simultaneously, the unity of the Turkish community was reflected in the results of the 1968 election where Vice President Kutchuk was proclaimed the winner because there was no opposition, and in 1973 when Denktash secured his position as Vice President. As a result, bifurcation became more pronounced as the two communities became more geographically segregated.[32]

Despite the existence of bifurcation, group entitlement theory resorts to internal political arrangements when they find a strong case for policy intervention. These theorists believe that democracies can prevail in deeply divided societies through the careful planning of electoral and territorial arrangements, and by implementing measures which prevent ethnic allegiances at levels inclined to bifurcation. For Cyprus, because of the constitutional crises of 1963–64 and 1967, both communities realized that constitutional revisions were necessary to minimize their differences. Consequently, the intercommunal constitutional negotiations of 1968–1974 were initiated.[33]

Why, then, did the major crisis of 1974 occur when group entitlement was guaranteed in the 1960 Cypriot Constitution, practiced

[31] Horowitz, *Ethnic Groups in Conflict* 141–84.

[32] Kyriakides, *Cyprus* 119.

[33] Horowitz, *Ethnic Groups in Conflict* 601–52.

to a limited degree by the elites and masses of Cyprus in 1960–1974, and improved upon in the 1974 constitutional arrangements? Since it has been previously shown that major internal elements on Cyprus assisted in preserving group entitlement, it is necessary to examine any and all interference that emanated from Greece and Turkey in order to understand the nature of the 1974 Crisis.

Just two months prior to the signing of the 1960 Agreements, neither the Greek Parliament nor Greek public opinion favored the proposed Cypriot Constitution controversy over the Agreements was widespread. It was anticipated that: "[public opinion was going to tip against the Agreements."[34] Controversy over the Agreements was widespread. After five days of parliamentary deliberations, "[a] role-call vote was taken on the motion of no confidence. It was defeated by 170 votes to 118, with twelve absentees."[35] Appeased by the Cypriot response to the Agreements, Greece agreed to patronize the Cypriot position. The official texts of the Agreements were signed by the Greek and Turkish delegates from Cyprus, Greece, and Turkey. The Agreements were endorsed not only by the Greek and Turkish elites, but by the Greek church as well. It has been documented that both Greece and Turkey ultimately validated the principle of group entitlement by signing the 1960 Constitutional Agreements.[36]

The significance of group entitlement was acknowledged at both the elite and mass levels, and externally by Greece and Turkey with the origin of Cypriot independence in 1960. Its value never domestically depreciated; in fact, it appeared to appreciate, exemplified by the intercommunal constitutional negotiations of 1968–1974 which were encouraged by Archbishop Makarios and the governments of Greece and Turkey. Where, then, did the problem lie?

During the latter part of 1973 and early 1974, the names and faces of the influential decision makers in Greece and Turkey changed, in addition to the key players in Cyprus itself. As could be expected, the transition in leadership ushered in agenda alterations that caused

---

[34] Averoff-Tossizza, *Lost Opportunities* 373.

[35] Averoff-Tossizza, *Lost Opportunities* 343 and 361.

[36] Averoff-Tossizza, *Lost Opportunities* 343 and 361.

an interruption in the intercommunal constitutional negotiations scheduled to occur between April and June 1974. Group entitlement was no longer considered of value within the minds of the interested parties, but rather as an obstacle to the implementation of their own nationalistic plans. The revisions contained in the 1974 constitutional proposals posed a threat to Greece and Turkey in that they strengthened group entitlement, while, at the same time, eliminating their right to preserve their identities through the control of cultural matters such as religion, education, and the like. Thus, the leadership of Greece and Turkey, and also the Greek church, opposed the provisions of the new constitutional arrangements.

Throughout history, cultural identity has been determined and perpetuated via church pedagogy. This has also been the case in Cyprus. The vitalization and preservation of nationalistic pride and Greek culture has always been an integral responsibility of the church. Perceiving they were about to be stripped of this life support system should the proposed agreements be enacted, three bishops—Gennadios of Paphos, Anthimos of Kitium, and Kyprianos of Kyriania—attempted to defrock Archbishop Makarios with charges that he violated canon law by holding both a state and church office. After months of debate, Archbishop Makarios emerged victorious.[37]

Shortly thereafter, additional opposition was encountered because of the proposed 1974 constitutional revisions. A successful conclusion to the intercommunal discussions was reached, in part, due to "insufficient encouragement and support from abroad . . . [and] had it not been for the Greek coup and the Turkish invasion of July 1974 a complete agreement would have been concluded before long."[38] Only with Greece and Turkey's endorsement could group entitlement be preserved. Therefore, group entitlement was guaranteed by the constitution, and was implemented and revised to a certain extent through governmental policies from 1960 to 1974, though finalization was not allowed during the intercommunal talks. However, these measures were not sufficient to maintain stability on

[37] *The New York Times*, March 8 and October 10, 1973.

[38] Polyviou, *Cyprus* 153.

Cyprus because of the unwillingness of the unconstitutional leadership in Greece and the weak coalition government in Turkey to accept group entitlement, which would undermine their respective cultural ideologies.

C. Conclusion of Microsocial Theories

The microsocial theorists who have been analyzed conclude that stability, the product of a functional constitution, can only persist if mass-level solidary groups are not ethnically divided. These theorists contend that ethnically divided societies cannot establish common patriotic bonds and national loyalties because of their opposing ideologies which are preserved culturally, politically, economically, and militarily through the maintenance of cross-boundary relations with their respective homelands. Inevitably, the gap between the solidary groups widens because of conflicting cultures that ultimately cause the failure of the constitution. However, if group entitlement—which limits the impact of ethnic affiliations—is institutionalized and exercised, a successful stable democracy will prevail.

Applying this principle to Cyprus reveals that states comprised of ethnically divided solidary groups, like the Greek and Turkish communities on Cyprus, experience hostilities that emanate from the two distinct and conflicting cultures. It was also discovered that as long as group entitlement is provided for in the constitution and implemented to some degree, a crisis can be avoided, as evidenced by the 1963–64 and 1967 contentions. For Cyprus, it was not the ethnically divided solidary groups nor the internal failure to uphold group entitlement that caused the 1974 Cypriot Crisis. Instead, the crisis arose when the provisions of the 1960 Constitution, which granted Greece and Turkey the right to limit Cypriot autonomy to promote their respective identities, were eliminated in the 1974 constitutional arrangements. Had these arrangements been implemented, stability would probably have been maintained, but at the expense of Greece and Turkey.

IV. MACROSTRUCTURAL THEORIES

Macrostructural theories focus on state structure as a macro-level constraint on group behavior. According to the control system theory, "consociationalism" and "control" are two approaches for understanding continued political stability in societies that are characterized by deep vertical cleavages. On the one hand, consociationalism focuses on the mutual cooperation of elites in a society, while acknowledging the presence of divisions or vertical cleavages within that society. The second approach examines the relationship of control in a society whereby the dominant segment mobilizes stability by restricting and suppressing the weaker segment. There are several important distinctions between consociationalism and control in areas such as the allocation of resources, political and material exchanges, bargaining, the role of the official regime, perpetuation of the political order, the central strategic problem, and the optimum condition for each system. Examination of the factors within each system aids in the derivation of a functional understanding of control within political and economic contexts.[39]

Another macrostructural approach is the theory of the triangle of accommodation. This theory examines the issue of social control within a state, particularly the operative rules which function to structure a population's behavioral patterns, resources, and distribution of control. This approach postulates that one must look to factors such as established institutions, land ownership and taxation patterns, economic and market conditions, a state's internal structure, and the political mobilization process in order to understand the mechanisms of control within a state. Focusing on political mobilization as a facet of social control, the triangle of accommodation theory posits that three levels of state organization determine state-society relations, and thus, social control. The three levels that must be examined are central executive leadership, leadership in the central agencies of the

[39] Ian Lustick, "Stability in Deeply Divided Societies: Consociationalism Versus Control," *World Politics* vol. 31, no. 3 (April 1979) 326–28, 330–33 and 342–44.

state, and state leaders at regional and local levels. These levels are significant in that they interrelate to form patterns of both continuity and change, as well as patterns of distribution of societal control. While these patterns are complex and require individual examination for a complete understanding of social structure, they ultimately determine whether a state is strong or weak.[40]

A. Lustick's Control System Theory

A control system theory entails the notion that stability can be guaranteed by confining the political actions and opportunities of rival groups.[41] Although the 1960 Cypriot Constitution was supported by the Cypriot people as was evidenced by their support of the Cypriot leadership, many of the provisions were found to be problematic and thus objectionable. Within a short time, it would become apparent whether an adequate control system existed on Cyprus. Within the Cypriot context, testing the validity of the control system theory would entail a determination that a superordinate elite failed to institute dominance through political, economic, legal and sociocultural methods, resulting in the Cypriot Crisis. The theory holds that if a superordinate elite is successful in dominating all cultural and material resources, stability is ensured.

Application of the control theory to the Cypriot case first requires an examination of the 1960 Cypriot Constitution to ascertain whether its structure grants dominance to the elite, coupled with political, economic, legal, and sociocultural means of social administration. As previously discussed, many of the constitutional provisions are regulatory in nature. They establish and regulate bicommunal interests which are then directed by a limited dual executive system as well as legislative and judicial branches of government. The force behind this established control system is described within the

---

[40] Joel Migdal, *Strong Societies, and Weak States: State-Society Relations and State Capabilities in the Third World* (Princeton University Press, 1988) 4–9, 51–90, 180 and 207–69.

[41] Lustick, "Stability in Deeply Divided Societies," *World Politics* 332–33.

Treaty of Alliance. Evidence reveals that a control system was institutionalized and administered by a superordinate elite on Cyprus; therefore, the first criterion of this theory has been satisfied.[42]

Additionally, it has been argued that a properly implemented control system ensures confinement of the political opportunities and activities of rival groups. For the first three years of Cypriot independence, the activities of rival groups were successfully impeded by Cyprus's control system. However, difficulties were encountered in 1963 as the rival groups began rearing their heads. Recognizing that the general state of the Greek and Turkish Cypriot relationship was deteriorating, Makarios attempted to repair the Constitution's structural defects in his thirteen constitutional amendments. However, the amendments were rejected by the Turkish leadership, thus provoking an eruption of intercommunal violence. Many believe the "artificial and rigid structure" of the 1960 Constitution could not absorb the intercommunal tensions, and therefore existing differences intensified. In 1967 an outbreak over a constitutional breach of privilege on the part of Greece again shook the system. In both instances the National Guard rose to the occasion and was able to quell the disturbances, fulfilling their regulatory function. This was not the case in 1974, and so the question we must address is why the Crisis was not suppressed.[43]

In order to answer this question we must examine what transpired between 1967 and 1974 to erode the effectiveness of the Cypriot control system. Upon discovering in 1967 that the number of the Greek and Turkish contingencies on the island exceeded the two thousand officers allotted by the Treaty of Alliance, war was threatened unless the excess numbers were immediately retracted. Both Greece and Turkey complied. This violation of external privilege, in addition to mounting internal rivalries between the two Cypriot communities, propelled Cypriot elites to begin settlement negotiations.

The outcome of nearly seven years of talks was the 1974 constitutional agreements which, if signed and implemented, would

42 Kyriakides, *Cyprus* 54–56.

43 Polyviou, *Cyprus* 8.

have guaranteed Cypriot sovereignty by confiscating all means of direct influence granted to Greece and Turkey under the 1960 Constitution. No longer would officers of the National Guard and its decision makers be primarily from Greece and Turkey, but from the Greek and Turkish communities on Cyprus. The proposed exclusions proved to be too great a threat to Greece and Turkey because each relied upon these accessible avenues for the preservation of their cultural identities and the achievement of their objectives, enosis for Greece and taksim for Turkey.

The control system theory is correct, then, in that stability is maintained when a state's control system is in place and operable. But what the theory fails to consider is that in some circumstances, a state's control system becomes undermined and is rendered ineffective because of the permitted involvement of external forces that desire conflicting goals. This situation is exemplified in the fact that, acting under the 1960 constitutional allowances, Greece staged a coup and Turkey executed an invasion in order to thwart the institutionalization of the 1974 agreements.

B. Migdal's Triangle of Accommodation Theory

A proper bled of central executive leadership, state organized central agency leadership, and regional and local state leaders employed for the implementation of state rules lends strength to the state. In turn, a strong state produces stability, which reduces the chance of crisis. An analysis of the Cypriot Constitution of 1960 reveals a pervasive bicommunal character, but the bicommunal element was particularly acute in the communal participation within the executive, legislative, and judicial branches.[44]

The Cypriot Constitution of 1960 provides for a presidential system with a Greek president and Turkish vice president directly elected by their respective communities for five-year terms. The nature of the roles and executive powers of the president and vice president are exhaustively defined in the Constitution. Among these

---

[44] Migdal, *Strong Societies and Weak States* 263.

powers is the right of final veto on decision of the council of ministers regarding foreign affairs, defense, or security. Provisions of various articles also guaranteed the president and vice president assistance in fulfilling their individual responsibilities. The council of ministers appears to be entrusted with a great deal of executive power. However, a different power structure emerges when we take into consideration the fact that council meetings are convened by the president and vice president, and the agenda is prepared by the president and suggested by the vice president. Moreover, the president and vice president retain a final veto on foreign affairs, defense, and security. Essentially, the council's structure is exclusively bicommunal.

Having established that a central executive branch of government existed and was functional on Cyprus, we turn our focus to state-organized central agency leadership, the second element of the triangle of accommodation. The House of Representatives is compositionally and functionally bicommunal. Even though the Constitution recognizes the independence of the House by prohibiting the president and vice president from dissolving it, the absolute veto power of the president and vice president prescribes executive limitations on the House. In addition to an established legislative branch, the Cypriot government consists of an operable judicial branch which institutionalizes the segregation of the two communities in the administration of justice. The Supreme Constitutional Court has exclusive jurisdiction and authority over the allocation of powers to the various bodies of the republic and over the constitutionality of legislation, while the function of the High Court is primarily appellate review of civil and criminal offenses.[45]

In addition to the second component, that of the legislative and judicial branches of government, we must examine the third and final ingredient, operable regional and local state leaders, to see whether they pass the test of accommodation. The Cypriot Constitution provides for communal minority rights through the communal chambers which hold exclusive authority in all matters concerning religion, education, culture, instruction, and personal status. Jurisdiction is

[45] Kyriakides, *Cyprus* 57–63 and 69.

provided for where interests or institutions are purely communal in nature and for the promotion of welfare.[46]

By the very nature of the communal chambers and the existence of these provisions, the political allegiance of the two communities became fragmented. The independent judicial power given to the communal chambers in all matters exacerbated fragmentation. Separate communal chambers were established to perform judicial functions. Each communal chamber could receive direct assistance from Greece and Turkey, which not only strengthened the ties between the two communities and their mother countries, but tended to undermine the authority of the Cypriot government. Despite the fact that a triangular power structure consisting of central executive leadership, leadership of state-organized central agencies, and regional and local state leaders existed in Cyprus, "[t]he unalterable nature of the basic articles made the constitutional life of the Republic extremely rigid," and therefore problematic. The rigid structure of the new state and the codification of community rights tended to perpetuate rather than eliminate communal cleavages, which ultimately prevented the implementation of state rules.[47]

In addition, the triangle of accommodation theory holds that a state gains social control by means of cooptation, absorption and coercion, and it is through social control that stability is achieved and endures.[48] In Cyprus, social control was not accomplished because friction regarding the validity of the basic provisions of the Constitution became an obstacle to compromise. The problems did not revolve around executive-legislative relations, but stemmed from bicommunalism in all spheres of governmental activity. Thus, "[t]here developed an intricate system of frictional crisis, which set the two communities in constitutional factionalism."[49]

A major area of friction that resulted in bicommunal constitutional deadlock was the separate majority vote and the income

[46] Bureau of Intelligence and Research, "Intelligence Report No. 8047," *Journal of Hellenic Diaspora* 19.

[47] Kyriakides, *Cyprus* 71.

[48] Migdal, *Strong Societies and Weak States* 219–27.

[49] Kyriakides, *Cyprus* 76.

tax legislation. The Constitution provides that "[a]ny law imposing duties or taxes shall require a separate simple majority of the representatives elected by the Greek and Turkish communities respectively taking part in the vote." Through the eyes of the Greek Cypriots, the separate majority right gave the Turkish community "a privilege position" in governmental affairs that far surpassed its proportional strength in Cyprus. The Turkish community's rebuttal was that only through provisions such as the '"separate majority right" could it withstand complete domination by the Greek Cypriot majority. Both communities reverted to their communal chambers for income tax legislation, which caused a greater rift between the communities and greatly limited the prospects of constitutional governments.[50]

The constitutional provision of the final veto and the army deadlock was another major area of contention. The problem emanated from the provision that the presidential and vice presidential final veto could be applied to the formation of the army. A solution to the army deadlock was never reached. It remained a dormant source of tension between the two communities and reflected the leadership's inability to agree upon basic constitutional provisions.[51]

In an attempt to establish a more unified state, Makarios proposed to amend the Constitution through his "thirteen points" which attempted to remove the "negative elements" of the Constitution, a prerequisite to the "smooth functioning of the state."[52] The first of the thirteen points was abandonment of the right of veto of the president and vice president of the republic. The fifth point abolished the constitutional provision regarding separate majorities for the enactment of certain laws, including military decisions. Seven of the thirteen proposals were aimed at rectifying the constitutional provisions that the Greek Cypriot community believed contributed to the bicommunal deadlocks. The Turkish Cypriots were culpable for the deadlocks because they were unwilling to cooperate within the framework of the 1960 Constitution. Therefore, they rejected

50 Kyriakides, *Cyprus* 83.
51 Kyriakides, *Cyprus* 94.
52 Kyriakides, *Cyprus* 104.

the thirteen points. The constitutional conflict entered a new stage in 1968 when the two communities, attempting to restore a spirit of cooperation, embarked on the intercommunal negotiations which continued until 1974. After considerable hard bargaining and multitude of difficulties, a greatly improved constitutional settlement was nearly reached by 1974.[53]

It has been argued that if the triangle of accommodation theory was applied to Cyprus, Cyprus would pass the test if a proper mixture of the executive, state, and local leaders successfully in gained social control and thus produced stability, or if a Cypriot triangle of accommodation was not achieved and a crisis surfaced. By examining Cypriot history, it can be concluded that a triangle of accommodation was in place in a limited capacity from the inception of the island's independent status. The triangle was greatly improved upon by the 1974 arrangements which had not yet been signed and implemented. Although the two communities on Cyprus set out to abolish the zero- sum competitive consequences established by the structure of the 1960 Constitution, the state was unsuccessful at retaining social control. The island was still bound by the 1960 constitutional provisions that granted Greece and Turkey the right to intervene when necessary to guarantee Cyprus's independent status.[54]

Ironically, the catalyst of the Crisis was true Cypriot sovereignty, possible only by barring external interference all together and which was guaranteed in the 1974 constitutional provisions along with the abolition of zero-sum competition. The new autonomous Cypriot state, structured upon an improved triangle of accommodation, proved to be too serious a threat to the unconstitutional government of Greece and the shaky Turkish coalition. The failure of the new constitutional arrangements resulted in a crisis. The Crisis was not an internal one involving governmental instability, but was due to external powers and motivated by factors external to the Cyprus question

53 Kyriakides, *Cyprus* 108; *The New York Times*. February 20, 1974; and Polyviou, "The Problem of Cyprus and Constitutional Solutions," *Cyprus Reviewed* 221.

54 Kyriakides, *Cyprus* 53–71.

and political expediency. The destruction and division of Cyprus was pursued by way of an externally inspired coup and invasion.[55]

C. Conclusion for Macrostructural Theories

The macrostructural perspective of the theorists that were previously analyzed regarding the stability of the state is that in order to avert a crisis, one of two scenarios must exist. The first possibility is that constitutionalized dominance socioculturally, politically, economically, and legally must be strictly enforced by a superordinate elite so that the seditious behavior of rival groups can be impeded and a control system established. Alternatively, the prevailing democracy must consist of a proper mix of central executive leadership, leadership of state-organized central agencies, and regional and local state leaders in order to succeed at institutionalizing the rules of the state. The degree to which a state is able to control society is dependent upon its ability to blend its cooptive, absorptive, and coercive tactics.

Application of this concept to Cyprus reveals that an institutionalized control system was enforced and all three institutional elements of a triangle of accommodation were manifested in Cyprus. Despite these conditions—which should have guaranteed harmony—violence broke out in 1974. Evidence reveals that because concessions were made by the two communities during the 1968–1974 constitutional negotiations, a greatly improved control system and accommodation triangle were about to emerge on Cyprus. The domestic elements which once had been problematic were improved, and the provisions which had once granted Greece and Turkey the right to intervene were removed. These changes became problematic because, even though the new constitution was beneficial to Cyprus, it was perceived as detrimental to Greece and Turkey whose ideologies and expansionistic policies conflicted with those of a Cypriot nation-state.

---

55 Coufoudakis, "The Dynamics of Political Partition and Division in Multiethnic and Multireligious Societies: The Cyprus case," in Van Coufoudakis ed., *Essays on the Cyprus Conflict* (New York: Pella Publishing Company, 1976) 43.

V. MICROSTRUCTURAL THEORIES

Microstructural theories focus on micro-level behavior which is influenced by the rules of the game. The consociational democracy theory is a microstructural theory that considers the elements behind a stable democratic society, and posits that a stable democracy is possible even if it is characterized by social division, political differences, or other types of conflict. To comprehend the equation behind a stable system, consociational democracy theory addresses three variables: political culture, role structure, and the behavior of political elites. A consociational democracy is the best formula for a stable society because the leaders of different segments of the population balance the tensions inherent in a plural society via a system of compromise, accommodation, and commitment to cohesion and stability.[56]

In contrast, the party depolarization and operational code theory purports that economic interdependence and the destabilization of international economic equilibrium, combined with social, economic, and political pressures, lead to the syndrome of political ineffectiveness. With the presence of this syndrome, decision makers are often influenced by political institutions and rules that may not represent the current social conditions. As a result of decisional ineffectiveness, conflict over the rules that control the formation of agreement may surface. In turn, cultural conflict is reinforced by various parliamentary systems, particularly the system that rewards centrifugal forces and punishes cooperation. Moreover, the structure of the parliamentary system can foster ideology polarization because a parliament encourages the expression of partisan beliefs, while enabling legislators to set aside divisive issues and focus on administration.[57]

---

[56] Arend Lijphart, "Conscotiational Democracy," *World Politics* vol. XXI, no. 2 (January 1969) 211–18 and Lijphart, *Democracy in Plural Societies* 5, 25, and 213.

[57] Giuseppe Di Palma, *Surviving Without Governing: The Italian Parties in Parliament* (Berkeley: The Regents of the University of California, 1977) 2–5, 22–46, 65–98, 130–99, and 216–22.

A. Lijphart's Consociational Democracy Theory

A consociational structure of government comprised of a grand coalition, proportionality, segmental autonomy, and a mutual veto is the most promising method for achieving democracy and a significant degree of political unity. The most important characteristic of consociational democracy is that the political leaders of all communities which constitute the plural society cooperate in a grand coalition to govern the country.[58]

Cypriot history reveals that even prior to the implementation of the 1960 Constitution, cooperative efforts between the elite of the two communities were made in the development and enactment of the consociational constitution. Therefore, the assertion that "[e]lite cooperation is the primary distinguishing feature of consociational democracy" was acknowledged and exercised by the leaders in Cyprus.[59] Throughout the fourteen year period Makarios served as the President of Cyprus, he exercised discretion and diplomacy on numerous occasions and strove to preserve Cypriot independence. It cannot be denied that Makarios persistently employed finely honed diplomatic skills to preserve peace on Cyprus.[60]

Additionally in Cyprus, a grand coalition composed of a Greek president, Turkish vice president, and other top officers in a presidential system was embodied in the 1960 Constitution. Cypriot democracy was not characterized by leaders who had been elected to office with bare majority support and a significant opposition. As previously documented, President Makarios won the election of 1960 with 66.85 percent of the votes—a clear majority—and even gained support over time, and Kutchuk ran unopposed.[61]

The second element of a consociational democracy is proportionality as the primary standard of political representation, civil service appointments, and distribution of public funds.[62] For Cyprus,

---

58 Lijphart, *Democracy in Plural Societies* 5.

59 Lijphart, *Democracy in Plural Societies* 1.

60 Clerides, *Cyprus* vol. 1, 80; and Polyviou, *Cyprus*. 42.

61 Polyviou, *Cyprus* 18; and Averoff-Tossizza, *Lost Opportunities* 383.

62 Lijphart, *Democracy in Plural Societies* 38–41.

the principle of proportionality involved deliberate overrepresentation of the significantly smaller Turkish community in order to provide added protection and security. The Cypriot coalition pattern was evidenced by the provision that the cabinet be comprised of seven Greek ministers selected by the president and three Turkish ministers chosen by the vice president. The seven-to-three ratio was not a proportional representation. The legislature composed of thirty-five Greek members and fifteen Turkish members adhered to the same ratio. An even greater deviation from proportionality was seen within the army and police, where the Greeks held a majority by a six-to-four ratio.[63]

A constitution must guarantee segmented autonomy that provides for minority rule in areas which are of exclusive concern to the minority.[64] The Cypriot Constitution of 1960 does in fact provide for bi-communal autonomy in two primary ways. First, each community separately elects a communal chamber that holds exclusive legislative power over cultural, educational, religious, and personal status matters. Second, separate municipal councils are established in each of the five largest towns of the island. This third criterion, a high degree of bi-communal autonomy, is firmly established on Cyprus.[65]

The final principle which must be embodied in a constitution is the mutual veto, which serves as additional protection for important minority interests. As with the other three principles, the mutual veto is provided for in the Cypriot Constitution of 1960, to be exercised either separately or jointly by the president and the vice president as a method of "checking and balancing" the two communities in relation to the major affairs of the state.[66]

As previously discussed, each of the four basic elements of consociational democracy were embodied in the Cypriot Constitution. In addition, a constitutional system was operative on Cyprus. The constitutional system was not without its problems, however, as inter-

---

[63] Lijphart, *Democracy in Plural Societies* 159; and Kyriakides, *Cyprus* 57.

[64] Lijphart, *Democracy in Plural Societies* 41.

[65] Lijphart, *Democracy in Plural Societies* 159; and Kyriakides. *Cyprus* 66–68.

[66] Polyviou, *Cyprus* 19; and Kyriakides, *Cyprus*. 59–60.

communal violence broke out from 1963 until 1964. Even though the efforts of a United Nations peace-keeping force, dispatched for purposes of subduing the disturbances, were successful, the Cypriot government began to operate as two separate systems. Some blame the failure of the consociational constitution on the Greek majority's reluctance to fully accept and implement its main provisions, and the Turkish minority for insisting on strict adherence of every provision and abusing its veto power. These theorists believe that the constitutional failure can be understood when examining who arranged the Constitution, as well as the conditions of the London Zurich meetings at the time of its endorsement. Clerides claimed the Constitution was endorsed by Greece and Turkey in Zurich without input from the Cypriot population.[67] Consociationalism failed primarily because it could not be imposed against the wishes of any segment of the heterogeneous society, and particularly not against the resistance of the major segment. Therefore, the first strike against the successful implementation of the consociational constitution lay in the fact that the Cypriot people did not even consent to adhere to its structure. Cyprus's small population was an unfavorable factor as well. Additionally, intervention on the part of Greece and Turkey "hurt rather than helped internal unity" and undermined any development of Cypriot nationalism.[68]

Many of the conditions in Cyprus that were distinctly less favorable to a successful consociational constitution have been identified, but the list is inconclusive. External influence emanating from Greece and Turkey had a crippling effect on Cypriot affairs, but traditional ideologies also played a significant role. The problems encountered over the constitutional provisions in 1963 and again in 1967 were initiated and encouraged by Greece and Turkey in efforts to stir up trouble between the Cypriot communities and strengthen their ties with their respective communities as they called for help. Under the 1960 Treaty of Guarantee, Greece and Turkey were empowered with the right to act either collectively or individu-

67 Interview with Clerides.

68 Lijphart, *Democracy in Plural Societies* 160–61.

ally toward "reestablishing the state of affairs created by the present treaty" if any development in Cyprus was interpreted as detrimental to their interests. Greece and Turkey benefitted from the structure of the 1960 Constitution because it made allowances for the perpetuation of their traditions. Therefore, Greece and Turkey took advantage of every opportunity, and even created opportunities, to necessitate intervention on their part.[69]

The Cypriot trend toward increasing physical separation following the 1963 civil unrest prompted the two communities to commence the constitutional negotiations of 1968–1974. These talks produced a revised constitution that, if institutionalized, could have established true Cypriot autonomy. In lieu of the 1960 Constitutional elements which housed consociational principles and provided for external intervention were articles that strengthened Cypriot sovereignty. Herein lies the problem because although it has been claimed that Greek and Turkish threats and interventions counteracted the success of consociationalism, it is clear that external forces were a decisive factor behind the failure of consociationalism. The leaders in Greece and Turkey interpreted the proposed constitutional arrangements as a direct threat to the preservation of their respective ideologies and the implementation of their expansionist policies. Therefore, acting under the 1960 allowances, the leaders staged the 1974 coup and invasion.

B. Di Palma's Party Depolarization and Operational Code Theory

The key to a successful democratic government and stability rests in party depolarization and an operational code. It is only through successful party depolarization and the establishment of an appropriate operational code that cooperative legislation on all issues can develop. The true test for Cypriot stability is whether Cypriot parties were responsive to one another and an operational code was implemented.[70]

---

69 Kyriakides, *Cyprus* 55.

70 Di Palma, *Surviving Without Governing* 221–84.

Evidence indicates that the leadership of each community on Cyprus was not inclined to hold rigid party positions but instead repeatedly strove to resolve differences to insure independence through political and constitutional negotiations. Cypriot leaders first demonstrated compromise with the signing of the 1960 Agreements. Even though the leaders of Cyprus were aware of the antagonistic consequences that would inevitably ensue from signing the document, they felt pressured to do so in order to prevent the occurrence of a harsher reality.[71]

Party depolarization and operational code theory claims that a stable environment can exist and be maintained when leaders who hold sovereignty as their supreme objective are willing to cooperate.[72] Within Cyprus, Makarios more than satisfied this requirement; therefore, we must direct our attention to the second condition, an appropriate operational code. As previously addressed, a constitutional government was established on Cyprus in 1960 and functioned until civil strife broke out in 1963. Again in 1967 problems arose over defective constitutional provisions and continuing mistrust between the two communities. Despite the fact that the two Cypriot communities found themselves grouped against each other as they strove to safeguard their respective interests within the framework of the Constitution, relative stability was maintained. Therefore, even though the Cypriot party system was depolarized and an appropriate operational code was in place, these conditions were not adequate to create cooperative legislation between ethnically comprised governing bodies. The insufficiency was not due to sharply contrasting ideological images and an inappropriate operational code, but because agitated interest groups stirred up dissatisfaction with the compromising arrangements.

Serious negotiations between the two communities commenced in 1968 to eliminate the defective constitutional provisions, particularly the power of mutual veto, which had hindered attempts to enact

---

[71] P. N. Vanezis, *Makarios: Faith and Power* (London: Abelard-Schuman, 1974) 138; and Polyviou, *Cyprus* 59.

[72] Di Palma, *Surviving Without Governing* 145–55.

cooperative legislation in the past. Once again the cooperative efforts met resistance. Turkish representatives stated:

Six years of negotiations were wasted because the Greek side was determined to impose its own solution. The Greek responsibility for the failure of the talks during this period was later admitted by Mr. Clerides. In a public statement in August 1978, he referred to a 'near agreement' during the intercommunal talks between 1971 and 1972. He claimed that he had recommended the acceptance of the Agreement but the Greek Cypriot Council of Ministers had not shared his view.[73]

By 1974, intercommunal agreements had been drafted, but were not signed. The agreements removed the most offensive elements of the 1960 Constitution, thereby rendering a significantly improved operational code and fully depolarized party system. Presuming that the proposed revisions would ultimately debar Greece and Turkey from fulfilling their objectives, the leadership of the homeland intervened for the final time via the 1974 coup and invasion.

C. Conclusion for Microstructural Theories

According to the microstructural theories that have been analyzed, a state's stability, regardless of its ethnic composition, can be guaranteed if a significant level of political cohesiveness is maintained through democratic governing. The single most important determinant of political unity is party depolarization or cooperation among the leaders of all the communities that constitute the heterogeneous society. The Cypriot leadership was practiced in the art of compromise even before the inception of Cypriot independence, and became more adept during the 1968–1974 negotiations, despite the negative effects of the mutual veto.

Microstructural theorists claim that, in addition to responsive leadership, a successful operational code or consociational constitution must be characterized by four additional principles: a grand coa-

[73] Denktash, *The Cyprus Triangle* 58.

lition, proportionality, segmented autonomy, and a mutual veto. The Cypriot operational code permitted the existence and operability of these four principles, despite some limitations which incited the outbreaks of 1963 and 1967. Although the 1974 Crisis is blamed, for the most part, on the imposed status of the consociational constitution and to a smaller degree the external interference from Greece and Turkey, it was discovered the intrusive acts emanating from the homelands triggered the Crisis. When revisions to the 1960 Constitution were proposed during the intercommunal negotiations of 1968–1974, the real problem began. It is believed that Greece and Turkey perceived a more effective Cypriot operational code as a threat to their cultural identities and the fulfillment of their respective policies. Therefore, in order to eliminate any such threat, Greece and Turkey intervened under the 1960 Treaty of Guarantee by way of the 1974 coup and invasion.

VI. OVERALL CONCLUSIONS OF COMPARATIVE THEORIES

A sweeping comparative analysis of the variables that determine the stable climate of a state identify the internal state politics as the primary cause of the crisis. Macrosocial theorists originally believed that a harmonious environment could only prevail in homogeneous states. After a more comprehensive study, however, the comparative boundaries for stability were broadened to embrace designated heterogeneous cultures as well. Other stabilizing preconditions include the four characteristics of civil society: traditions that have conditioned the population to polycentric forms of order; a cultural idiom that stresses the integrative role of politics and directs people away from absolute politics; the military's consent to accept a restricted role for itself; and the ability of politicians to learn from and adapt to the former factors by creating the institutions, initiating policies, and appropriately performing their symbolic role. For Cyprus, although the constitutionally designated National Guard and police force contained the seditionists, for the most part, and Cyprus exemplified the four elements of a civil society in somewhat of a marred fashion, the Cypriot Crisis of 1974 exploded.

Additionally, microsocial theorists argue that stability can be maintained in fragmented environments when the social cleavages are of a religious or ideological nature, but democracy has a difficult time surviving in the face of serious ethnic divisions. By its very essence, ethnicity constitutes ideologies and affiliations sustained culturally, politically, economically, and militarily via cross-boundary dealings with the motherlands. As such, ethnicity prevents the development of common nationalistic bonds and loyalties. A stable democracy can only prevail with the institutionalization and implementation of group entitlement. This foundation is obtained by the careful planning of electoral and territorial arrangements and measures, which hinder the ability of ethnic affiliations to bifurcate. Cypriot group entitlement, which debilitates the bifurcating capabilities of ethnic affiliations sustained culturally, politically, economically, and militarily via cross-boundary dealings with the homelands, are imperative to the preservation of a stable democracy. Cypriot group entitlement was sanctioned and internally upheld to a degree which tempered the potency of the ethnically divided solidary groups. Nevertheless, violence erupted on Cyprus in 1974.

Macrostructural theorists further maintain that one precondition for stability is an institutionalized control system that is focused on the appearance and endurance of a relationship in which the dominant power of one segment is mobilized to support stability by confining the political actions and opportunities of rival groups. In addition to coercive tactics, effective control can be based on a variety of political and economic mechanisms, institutional arrangements, legal frameworks, and sociocultural circumstances. Strong states, conducive to a democratic political system, become such by maintaining a proper blend of central executive leadership, along with leadership at the state, regional, and local levels. This triangular power structure is capable of maintaining social control by implementing the rules of the state in a cooperative, all-encompassing, and coercive manner. The Cypriot triangle of accommodation, as framed in the 1960 Constitution, functioned adequately enough to prevent governmental collapse and restrain domestic unrest. Nevertheless, the 1974 Cypriot Crisis occurred.

Finally, microstructural theorists argue that a democracy will ultimately fail because of political disunity unless the four characteristics of consociational democracy are institutionalized. The four characteristics are: grand coalition of the representatives from each of the important segments of the political society; a mutual veto for added protection of minority interests; proportionality in all representation; and a high level of segmental autonomy in internal affairs. Additionally, microstructural theorists maintain that political ineffectiveness, due to the polarizing pull of parties, is the heart of the "malaise." The consociational constitution provided these four principles, and in spite of the vitiating effect of the mutual veto, the leadership of Cyprus was well adept at compromise. Nevertheless, the 1974 Crisis occurred.

Although a comparative framework elucidates the Cypriot dispute by emphasizing the necessity of examining the domestic policies of a country, it sometimes neglects international relations and cultural institutions. Unfortunately, much of the comparative tradition stresses only the constitutional structure, compromising capacity of elites, and homogeneous aspect of a state. Because of this comparative theory excludes external interference as well as cultural institutions which emerge from the grass roots. The comparative tradition often assumes that states are completely autonomous and are therefore unaffected by the behavior of others. Small states like Cyprus, however, have partial rather than absolute sovereignty, and as a result they are influenced by external forces.

Thus, as helpful as comparative theories are, they overestimate the importance of structure and underestimate the importance of culture. The role of culture is especially relevant when one considers that a fundamental hope of both the Turkish and Greek national communities in establishing a Cypriot state in partnership was for a Cypriot "national identity" to eventually emerge out of such a Cypriot state. While comparative theories lend a hand in understanding the Crisis of 1974, the history, culture, and traditions imbedded in Cyprus remain too complex to be reduced to a single explanatory theory or formula.

CHAPTER 4

UNDERSTANDING THE ORIGINS OF THE 1974 CYPRIOT CRISIS AND ITS AFTERMATH: AN EXAMINATION OF THE ROLE AND IMPACT OF A BICOMMUNAL SOCIETY

> Under these hallowed vaults let us take this loyal oath. We shall remain faithful to the national cause even unto death: unyielding, inflexible, uncompromising! We shall treat force and tyranny with contempt. By blood actions we shall uplift our moral stature, with one sole aim and object in view: Enosis and only Enosis!
>
> —Phaneromeni Oath

> O Turkish Youth!
>
> The day is near when you will be called upon to sacrifice your life and blood in the PARTITION struggle—the struggle for freedom.
>
> You are a brave Turk. You are faithful to your country and nation and are entrusted with the task of demonstrating Turkish might. Be ready to break the chains of slavery with your determination and will-power and with your love of freedom.
>
> All Turkdom, right and justice and God are with you.
>
> PARTITION OR DEATH.
>
> —T.M.T. Slogan

I. INTRODUCTION: AN OVERVIEW OF CULTURE AND GAME THEORIES

The Greek Cypriot goal of enosis expressed in the first passage runs counter to the Turkish Cypriot goal of taksim stated in the second quotation.[1] With divergent goals for the future, the stage was set for a showdown between these two groups. Why was Greek nationalism so strong among Greek Cypriots? Why was Turkish nationalism so salient for Turkish Cypriots? Why did not a Cypriot nationalism form to unite the two ethnic groups? In order to answer these questions, it is necessary to consider the role and impact of culture within the bicommunal Cypriot society.

Culture is defined by symbols and values which embody a collective sense of justice, power, authority, love, and change. The values embedded in the principal or hegemonic subsystem of a society supply information as to how a particular cultural division becomes "a privileged institutional locus of the symbolic process" perceived as common sense. As such, these values help to shape practical life and over time they develop enduring patterns of political cleavage which subsequently direct political action. Once enduring patterns of political cleavage are established by reifying traditional culture so that culture serves as the dominant symbolic framework patterning group activity, neither the hegemon nor the dominated society can easily escape from the political consequences of the subsequent nature and style of collective political action.[2]

In addition, culture orders political priorities and creates common identities which promote collective action. In this capacity, cultural identity is a political resource for attracting a following. Political saliency not only conditions the orientation of ordinary citizens but that of decision makers as well. When confronted with a series of choices, actors may sometimes appear to an observer to make irratio-

---

1 For the Phaneromeni Oath, see Averoff-Tossizza, *Lost Opportunities* 29; and for TMT's slogan, see Panteli, *Cyprus* 303–04.

2 David D. Laitin, *Hegemony and Culture: Politics and Religious Change Among the Yoruba* (Chicago: The University of Chicago Press, 1986) 11–19, 168–69 and 171.

nal decisions that lead to suboptimal outcomes. This perception may be fueled by insufficient information or the observer's limited perspective since the focus is on one situation rather than the complex tangle of circumstances that all actors face. Game theorists draw an analogy between decisions and games: when an actor/player makes a seemingly irrational decision, it may be that she or he is driven by the logic of a different game. The term "nested games" describes the situation when games in multiple arenas have variable payoffs that are affected by the prevailing circumstances of other arenas. Actors within nested games must consider games that are simultaneously being played in different arenas, all with varying advantages and disadvantages contingent upon the circumstances of the other games. Therefore, what may appear as irrational or mistaken behavior from the perspective of only one game is in fact optimizing behavior when the whole network of games is considered.[3]

International relations games can be identified at both regional and systemic levels. Regional games display the uncertainty and risk factors that are inherent in systemic games. These games are further complicated by the role of domestic politics. Concurrent with regional games, domestic political games are played between elites and masses regarding the distribution of power and wealth, especially along cultural lines. The games played by elites at the second and third levels—i.e., those games internal and external to their country—place elites in a double bind. The measures that elites take in order to win internal games hurt them vis-a-vis external interests and vice versa.

Because internal and external games are contradictory for the Greek and Turkish governments and for the leaders of Greek and Turkish Cypriots, all parties are engaged in a no-win situation. What each force must do in order to win the domestic politics game ultimately creates a loss in the international game. More specifically, while the Greek and Turkish governments and the Greek and Turkish Cypriot leaders engage in behavior that is acceptable to their constit-

---

3 George Tsebelis, *Nested Games: Rational Choice in Comparative Politics* (Berkeley: University of California Press, 1990) 1, 52–86, and 235–48.

uencies, such behavior remains unacceptable to each other. In order to understand the forces which led to the Cypriot dispute and its aftermath, I will address the dynamics of this no-win, "nested game" situation in the context of Cypriot politics.

II. HISTORY BEHIND THE CYPRIOT CONFLICT

Cypriot identity is not the major political divide; the identity of the people of Cyprus as either Greek Cypriots or Turkish Cypriots is the politically salient cleavage. Firmly affixed cultural bonds between both ethnic communities on Cyprus and their respective homelands, Greece and Turkey, are the core of the conflict, because these very ties were the justification for constitutionally granted interference. Hostilities intensified as Greco-Turkish political aspirations—historically centered on the fundamental opposition of the two incompatible nationalist ideas of enosis and taksim—were actively promoted by Greece and Turkey through legal means, and then professed and pursued by Greek and Turkish Cypriots. Because political violence within the Cypriot communities rose to an alarming degree, and conflicts between the governments of Greece and Turkey mounted, intercommunal negotiations were begun. These talks continued on Cyprus until a comprehensive settlement of the internal constitutional arguments had nearly been reached. The new constitution which seemed imminent in 1974 posed a severe threat to Greece and Turkey because it might slam and forever bolt the door of influence. Consequently, Greece and Turkey were forced to crush any possibility of such an occurrence by interfering in the internal affairs of Cyprus. Despite the West's negotiating capabilities which had been demonstrated both in 1963–64 and again in 1967, a laissez-faire position was assumed in 1974 because Western strategic interests could be better served with a divided island.[4]

[4] Polyviou, *Cyprus* 1–12.

A. The Effects of Cypriot Identity and Locale

Cyprus as a new nation did not have the advantage of a long standing tradition. Neither its ideology nor its institutions could protect its existence. The establishment of consociational constitution was a perfect recipe for weak national institutions because the aim of consociationalism is to ensure that the state poses no threat to the groups which form its plural society. But pluralism itself thwarted a national ideology; Cypriots identified themselves as either Greek or Turkish, not primarily as Cypriots. Without a strong national ideology or institutions, Cyprus was vulnerable to both internal and external attack. (See appendix 2, table 1.)

APPENDIX 2

TABLE 1: NATIONALISM, INSTITUTIONS, AND VULNERABILITY

PRESENCE OF A STRONG NATIONAL IDEOLOGY	PRESENCE OF STRONG STATE INSTITUTIONS	
	YES	NO
YES		
NO		CYPRUS

Table 1 exemplifies the vulnerability Cyprus faced because it lacked the strong national ideology and state institutions that we typically associate with the modern nation-state.

Cyprus's advantageous geographic, strategic, and commercial location has caused her to be coveted and conquered by different maritime powers throughout history. Unquestionably, conquerors left their mark on the culture of the island in social, political, religious, and economic ways. The Phoenicians contributed to the island's economic prosperity with their trading ability in 800 BC and again in 8 BC.

Cyprus fell prey to the conquest of Assyria and was subsequently dominated by one power after another, including the Egyptians, Persians, Romans, Lusignans, and Venetians. The Cypriot vantage point was also sought after and ultimately possessed by the Ottoman Turks. Cyprus remained in Turkish hands until 1878 when it was ceded to Great Britain in return for various guarantees. As a result of Cyprus's diverse historical past and strategic position, it has never been successful at establishing sovereignty nor the characteristics accompanying this status. The constraints of conformity have prevented Cyprus from creating a strong Cypriot consciousness or developing strong state institutions through which a national ideology could be embraced and nurtured.[5]

In terms of politics, Cypriots identified themselves not as Cypriots but as Greek or Turkish Cypriots. The politically salient identities of people are critical. The ethnic identity of the Cypriots was directly relevant to their political identity. Cypriot ethnic identity was preserved by institutions built into the government. The principle of consociationalism functioned to reinforce ethnic identity in Cypriot society. Part of the definition of consociationalism is that representation is parceled out on the basis of group membership. To worsen matters of separate ethnic identity, the 1960 Constitution guaranteed Turkey and Greece the right to ensure that Turkish and Greek Cypriots could maintain their own educational, cultural, and religious institutions, all derived from the homelands. (See appendix 2, table 2.)

TABLE 2: THE ORIGINS AND MAINTENANCE OF POLITICIZED IDENTITIES

NATURE OF POLITICALLY SALIENT IDENTITY	NATURE OF INSTITUTIONAL BASIS TO PRESERVE IDENTITY	
	INFORMAL	FORMAL
NATIONAL		
ETHNIC		CYPRUS

5 Panteli, *Cyprus* 3–36.

Table 2 elaborates on the institutional and ideological weaknesses of Cyprus. Not only did Cyprus lack strong state institutions and ideology, but its leaders had to contend with antinational ideologies and institutions that existed among the people.

B. Development of a Bicommunal Cypriot Society

The tumultuous nature of Cyprus's past contributed not only to its lack of a national consciousness, but also to the development of a bicommunal Cypriot society. The communal character of the Cypriot society was permanently impacted by its colonization by the ancient Hellenic world, Byzantine influence, and Ottoman rule. The ancient Hellenic world left its first significant mark on Cyprus during 14 BC. The Myceneans linked the island to a civilization and legends which introduced Cyprus to what was later known as the Greek world, a characteristic feature that Cyprus has strongly retained throughout history. The Hellenic connection was strengthened by a great influx of Achaean Greeks who vitalized the economy by establishing Cyprus as one of the cultural and commercial centers of the ancient Greek world. The Cypriot King, Evagoras, implemented further expansion through the development of a Greek literacy heritage. This historical phenomenon partly explains the recurring Greek Cypriot claim to an intimate affinity with the Greek civilization.

More important to the shaping of the Cypriot people, however, was the introduction and assimilation of the Christian religion in AD 45–46. "The modern Greek poet, the late Constantinos Palamas, wrote that, though through the years Cyprus was ruled by many 'despots, her heart was ruled by Greece."[6] The island's history, so deeply influenced by the Hellenic Christian religion that it could be seen even in the patterning of politics after the Byzantine politico-religious alliance, was thereafter to be dominated by Christianity.

Ottoman rule left its indelible mark on the island as had the ancient Hellenic world. For 307 years the Cypriots suffered while

---

6 John Koumoulides, *Cyprus and the War of Greek Independence 1821–1829* (London: Zeno Booksellers & Publishers, 1974) xi.

they endured earthquakes, epidemics, plagues, oppression, and misgovernment by the Ottomans. The island was politically restructured to accommodate the millet administrative system and the autocratic nature of Ottoman rule. The economy and general well-being of the islanders were paralyzed by unjust taxes. The oppressive measures and famine which permeated the island produced a depopulation of the Greeks.

Amid this harsh persecution, intimate camaraderie compelled the Greek Cypriot population to collaborate with the Greeks. They fought for independence despite the devastating consequences of such a decision. By the early nineteenth century, Cypriots, Greek and Turkish alike, were suffering from the repercussions of Turkish misrule as were the Greeks on the mainland. The Turks had plundered much of the island's wealth and reduced it to a state of neglect and desolation. As a shortsighted remedy which had burdensome long-sighted consequences, the succession of Cypriot archbishops was driven to borrow money from European consuls, particularly those of Britain and Russia. Because all Greek affairs fell under the cognizance and management of the archbishop, jealousy subsisted between the Turkish dragoman, or the interpreter of the palace, and the archbishop.

After enduring the tyrannical rule of the Ottoman administration for four centuries, a February 24, 1821, letter announced to all Greeks of the mainland, the island's and the Diaspora that the time had come to break free from the oppressive clutches of the Ottoman rulers. Greek Cypriots, whose Hellenistic heritage, ideals, traditions, language and spirit had been preserved through the nurturing efforts of the church and the unceasing hope that their freedom would someday be recovered, copartnered this cause. Kyprianos, the acting Cypriot archbishop at the time, pledged his financial and moral support to the independence struggle, but due to Cyprus's close geographic proximity to Ottoman territories, he could not actively participate. Even though Cypriot involvement was covertly executed, Kuchuk Mehmed, the recently appointed governor of Cyprus, caught wind of Cypriot involvement in the Greek revolution. For the next three months and beyond, "the orgy of slaughter proceeded fast and furious."[7] In addition to the Archbishop, Bishops, high-ranking Greek priests, merchants, and all notably rich and influential individuals, hundreds of Cypriots were slaughtered, beheaded, or hanged, their properties confiscated and their families imprisoned.

The decade following the massacres of 1821 was an extremely difficult one for the Greek Cypriots. Thousands of Cypriots risked their lives as they attempted to escape from the island. By 1829 the population of Cyprus had diminished to under sixty thousand inhabitants, a decrease that directly affected the economy. Commerce was estimated as being "near zero" by 1830. The Ottoman administration made attempts to maintain order on the island primarily through the importation of troops. However, these efforts only exacerbated the poor conditions. Despite the countless obstacles against them, the Greek Cypriots held firm to the dream of liberating Cyprus from Turkish rule and achieving enosis with Greece. After Cyprus had struggled for seven years for the right of independence, the great powers—Great Britain, France, and Russia—decided to assist in bringing peace to the East. The noncooperative attitude of the Turkish administration induced the British and French consuls to remain on the island until an agreement could be reached.

The Greek Cypriot people suffered tremendously for their decision to play a leading role in bringing freedom to the motherland. Many emigrated, including those who fought literally hand-in-hand with the Greek forces, while those who remained behind endured economic depression and extreme oppression. In spite of the heavy price, an independent Greece was re-established with the assistance of the three great powers under the Treaty of London. This revitalized Cypriot hope and confidence that the spiritual link, an unmistakable cultural identity between the peoples of Cyprus and Greece, would one day be physically manifested in union.[8]

When the period of Ottoman rule ended in 1878, the Cypriot Muslims comprised approximately 18 percent of the total population, and Cyprus was distinctly bi- communal. Another important

[7] Koumoulides, *Cyprus and the War of Greek Independence 1821–1829* 58.

[8] Koumoulides, *Cyprus and the War of Greek Independence 1821–1829* 27–78.

consequence of Ottoman rule in Cyprus is reflected in the character of modern Cypriot society. The roots of the present Muslim Cypriot community can be traced to the army of Sultan Selim II, consisting of some 20,000 soldiers who were awarded permanent residence on Cyprus.[9]

1. British Arrival and Bicommunal Intensification on Cyprus

Bicommunalism intensified as the British arrived on Cyprus. The British colonial policy of "divide and rule" extended and reinforced the ethnic, administrative, and political separation inherited from the period of Ottoman rule. Like those forces before her, the British government did not assume the administration of Cyprus with a regard for the island or its inhabitants, but rather because Britain saw Cyprus's geographic position as a strategic point for safeguarding her interests in the near and far east.[10]

The British administration did not engender or foster a unifying native Cypriot consciousness. The Greek and Turkish communities were treated as separate groups for administrative purposes, and the psychological gap between them was instrumental in securing British control. Numerous factors — Church dominance, the millet system, segregated education, antagonistic national loyalties, political diversity, and "the divide and rule" policy of Britain—contributed to both the preservation of the ethnic identities of the Greek and Turkish Cypriot communities and the great rift between them. Communal segregation was further reinforced by mutual uncertainty, fear, suspicion, and animosity.[11]

Great Britain set out to liberate Cyprus from her three-hundred-year history of oppression and misgovernment Under

---

[9] C. W. Orr, *Cyprus Under British Rule* (London: Zeno Publishers, 1972) 44–46; and Kyriakides, *Cyprus* 4–7.

[10] C. W. Orr, *Cyprus Under British Rule* 44–46.

[11] See Panteli, *Cyprus* 76–78; and Joseph, *Cyprus* 29–30.

Turkish rule by establishing an efficient system coupled with the protection and security of the British military. Over the course of the first four decades of British rule, administrative, fiscal, legislative, and social reforms were implemented. Generally speaking, by reducing and simplifying taxation, establishing a just and impartial administration, and by enforcing and maintaining law and order, British rule improved the standard of living for the Cypriot people, and made material progress possible. Results such as these were possible only through the services of a trained bureaucracy and the enforcement of a rigid economy with prudently managed resources. However, as is characteristic of all systems, those qualities which tend to promote positive conditions have defects. The inherent vice in an efficient and conscientious bureaucracy is its reliance on precedent, which tends to inhibit progress and change. Specifically, the main defect in the administration of Cyprus was excessive centralization and extreme conservatism, which is hardly conducive to imaginative or innovative thought.[12]

In 1882, the British administration established a Cypriot constitution that not only failed to provide a base for bicommunal cooperation, but encouraged animosity between the two ethnic communities. Divisiveness was fostered between the Greeks and Turks since the operation of the Legislative Council depended on the Turkish minority. The Greek members became a permanent opposition to the British-Turkish alliance which supported the traditional Ottoman system of social organization based upon the religious millets. Consequently, British administrative practices contributed to the destruction of the possible bases of an integrated Cypriot society. In addition, the British simultaneously provided the leadership for potential ethnic conflicts by preserving and politicizing traditional power structures, most importantly the Orthodox Church and its civil functions. The preservation of traditional power structures

[12] Orr, *Cyprus Under British Rule* 44–177.

enabled the colonial administration to maintain ultimate control by allowing the play of one community against the other.[13]

It would be incorrect, however, to conclude that the overly bureaucratic British government was completely responsible for the division which characterized the island during the first four decades of British administration. The Cypriot people themselves did not exhibit the qualities conducive for integration. The failure of the people to unite for the purpose of expressing an opinion regarding commercial enterprise or the general welfare of the community demonstrated complete dependence on the government. The only display of collective agreement on the island was exhibited by a section of the Greek community concerning the political aspiration of enosis which predated British occupation. This inadequate Cypriot constitution of 1882 remained unaltered when Britain annexed Cyprus in 1914. Despite modifications in 1925 when the island became a crown colony, the new arrangements failed to satisfy the Greek Cypriots because they still did not provide majority rule.[14]

The fact that Greek nationalism among Greek Cypriots and Turkish nationalism among Turkish Cypriots were maintained led to transnational nationalism. This nationalism was binding on Greece and Turkey to act on behalf of their coethnics. Hence, what is usually thought of as international relations and foreign affairs—events in another country—became domestic politics in regards to the Cypriot situation. (See appendix 2, table 3.)

---

[13] See Koumoulides, *Cyprus and the War of Greek Independence 1821–1829* 45–46. Also, for a detailed account about the end of the Ottoman rule and British administrative practices on Cyprus, see Panteli, *Cyprus* 76–78 and 87–112; and George Hill, *A History of Cyprus* vol. IV (Cambridge: At the University Press, 1952).

[14] Orr, *Cyprus Under British Rule* 180.

TABLE 3: TRANSNATIONAL NATIONALISM-CULTURE AS A VARIABLE IN INTERNATIONAL RELATIONS AND DOMESTIC POLITICS

PURPOSE OF TRANSNATIONAL NATIONALISM	TYPE OF TRANSNATIONAL NATIONALISM	
	PAN-TURKISM	PANHELLENISM
LEGITIMATION FOR INTERVENTION	TURKEY	GREECE
LEGITIMATION FOR REUNIFICATION	TURKISH CYPRIOTS	GREEK CYPRIOTS

Table 3 demonstrates the consequences of the cultural maintenance guaranteed under the 1960 Constitution. Turkish and Greek leaders maintained a serious approach regarding their responsibilities to their compatriots. A Panhellenic ideology called enosis and a Pan-Turkish ideology named taksim were accepted by both Greek and Turkish Cypriots, as well as by Greeks and Turks in the home countries. While American ethnic identity does not lead to intervention in the United States by nationality countries, this role of ethnic identity is called for in Cyprus. Cypriot Greeks believe in union with their homeland, as do Cypriot Turks. Greeks and Turks believe they are totally obligated to protect and maintain the culture of their comrades in Cyprus.

2. British Dissatisfaction and the Development of Enosis

As dissatisfaction over British administration activities and intercommunal animosities mounted, so too did the Greek nationalist movement for enosis. The enosis movement first stirred on the island early in the nineteenth century with Cyprus's responses to the Greek War of Independence. In December 1921, a political organization called the National Assembly was established to unite all Greek Cypriots under the Archbishop to promote union with Greece. This political body functioned as the Greek counterpart to the British government's Legislative Council. It countered Britain's educational policy on Cyprus by insuring that Greek Cypriot youths were nurtured with Greco-Byzantine heritage. At the same time, the National Assembly became the source of demands for reform. By the time of the 1931 uprising, Greek Cypriots regarded this political organization as their legitimate constitutional representative.

There were three general causes for the 1931 uprising: economic problems stemming from the depression which was omnipresent in all of Europe during the 1920s; conflict in the Legislative Council over taxation which was ultimately imposed by the Executive Order; and the announcement that the Tribute collected from the Cypriots was to repay the Ottoman loan of 1855. An uprising against the British during which Greek Cypriot protestors rioted and burned the Governor's house revealed that Church leadership could mobilize the entire Greek Cypriot community behind the enosis cause. The constitution, which had undergone modifications in 1925 was abolished. An Advisory Council replaced the Legislative Council and immediately banished Church leadership for its incendiary role in the uprising. Moreover, in 1937 the government passed three laws to confine the activities of the Church. But the more the Church was curbed, the more it promoted the cause of enosis among its people.[15]

To aggravate the tensions which stemmed from enosis, economic discontent sprang from the poverty and underdevelopment prevailing in Cyprus up until World War II. This discontent increased the attractiveness of nationalism. Greek Cypriot nationalism emerged as a byproduct of social and political change, domestic political problems, and external influences. At the end of World War II, political developments in Cyprus entered a new phase, partly as a result of international instability.

[15] See Kyriakides *Cyprus*, 17–25; and Kitromilides, "From Coexistence to Confrontation," *Cyprus Reviewed* 41–42.

The United States emerged from World War II as a superpower without being fully aware of Great Britain's simultaneous decline. Early in 1947 Great Britain found herself unable to continue assisting Greece and Turkey. Great Britain notified the United States that it could no longer supply the 250 million dollars in economic and military support that was needed to maintain the non-Communist status quo. The United States responded with the proclamation of the Truman Doctrine on March 12, 1947. United States military and economic assistance became the primary source of the American presence and influence in Greece and Turkey. In September 1951, NATO foreign ministers approved Greek and Turkish admission to NATO, followed by the signing of separate bilateral agreements regulating United States bases in both countries.

Throughout the early postwar years, the United States found its diplomatic task trouble-free because Greek and Turkish bilateral relations remained on good terms. It was not until 1955 with the emergence of the "Cyprus Question" that United States policy makers began to realize that the serious disputes over Cyprus were jeopardizing both the southeastern flank of NATO and the strategic Greek-Turkish space. The United States, as the leader of the Western Alliance, was delegated the task of carving out policies that would lead to a satisfactory settlement between the three NATO countries of Greece, Turkey, and Britain, without impairing the cohesiveness of the strategic southeastern flank of NATO.[16]

C. The Origins of the Cypriot Dispute

The Cypriot dispute began to erupt in the mid-1950s following a number of undiplomatic rejections by British officials to inquiries and requests by Greeks and Greek Cypriots. The Greek Cypriots, strongly supported by the Papagos government in Athens, struggled for the self-determination of Cyprus. They were confident that the

[16] Couloumbis, *The United States, Greece, and Turkey* 7–20.

British would consent to their enosis demands as a reward for Greek efforts on the side of the Allies during the war. Simultaneously, the post-World War II British stand toward Cyprus was to encourage limited self-government. However, because Greek Cypriots expected more, irreconcilable differences persisted. All British attempts to promote limited self-government were countered by the Church's sole political goal of enosis. The most militant Church elite of the post–World War II enosis movement was Makarios, who refused to consider any British offer short of enosis.[17]

1. Greek and Turkish Cypriot Ethnic and Cultural Polarization

As nationalism grew among the Greek Cypriots and demands for greater political participation rose against British colonial rule, Turkish Cypriots became increasingly conscious of their ethnic identity and rights in regulating the affairs of the island. The political outlook of Turkish Cypriots leaders was in constant opposition to Greek nationalist demands and their drive for union with Greece. During this time, Turkish "irredentism" extended to include the territorial and political union of Cyprus with Turkey. In the worst case, Turkey would concede to taksim. Regardless of the ultimate outcome, the Turkish Cypriot community was expected to integrate with Turkey and be appropriated by Turkey; in other words, "Turkish-Cypriots simply becoming Turks living in a Turkish province."[18]

Prior to the 1950s, Turkish Cypriot society had not progressed as far as the Greek Cypriots in terms of political mobilization and organization. It was not until the anticolonial campaign of EOKA threatened the island's status quo and an intercommunal conflict broke out that Turkish Cypriots began to develop close ties with the Turkish military. On April 1, 1955, the EOKA organization, under the leadership of General George Grivas, commenced its campaign to liberate Cyprus

[17] See Kyriakides, *Cyprus* 26–28; and Panteli, *Cyprus* 237–64.

[18] Ioannides, *In Turkey's Image* 49.

from British control. Grivas had appropriated the nom de guerre "Digenis," the name of a legendary Byzantine hero, and from that time forth became known as George Grivas- Digenis.[19]

EOKA was established to crusade in the struggle for national self-determination which was certain to lead to enosis with Greece, a manifestation of the ideology of modern Greek nationalism. Originally the focal points of Greek nationalism were Megali Idea—the goal of liberating all Greeks still under Ottoman Turkish rule, including the Greeks of Cyprus—and to create Megali Ellas (Great Hellas)—a revived Byzantium. The bifold dreams of Megali Idea and Megali Ellas were forgotten in 1922 following the Greek defeat known as the Mikerasiatike katastrophe. The question of Cyprus did not die, however, but remained a consideration in all of Greece's subsequent decisions, including the diplomatic maneuvering which took place during World War II.

Cyprus proved to be on Turkish minds as well. Pan-Turanianism (Pan-Turkism), greatly influenced by Turkish Islam, was an extreme form of Turkish nationalism which originated in the nineteenth century during the close of the Ottoman Empire. Pan-Turkism was not simply a popular notion, but an official program of the Turkish government, with its origins at the upper echelon of Turkish leadership. Its utopian objective was to unite the Dis Turkler or "outside Turks." In the context of Cyprus, Pan-Turkism entailed the notion of Kibris Turktur (Cyprus is Turkish). The Kibris Turktur ideology surfaced in an organization bearing the same name in August 1954. The organization revealed that its objectives were to introduce to public opinion the idea that Cyprus was Turkish, and to defend the rights and privileges of Turks with regard to Cyprus. Slightly over a year later in September 1955, the Volkan group appeared on Cyprus with the objective of countering the Greek Cypriots. By the fall of 1957, the Volkan group was superseded by TMT,

[19] Ioannides, *In Turkey's Image* 50.

which soon grew into a politico-military force capable of influencing the affairs of the Turkish Cypriot community.[20]

Following Britain's post-war decision to retain Cyprus as a crown colony, the Greek Cypriot crusade for enosis resumed and culminated in the EOKA guerrilla movement of 1955. Unable to restrain the EOKA campaign, Britain solicited assistance from Turkey and together they calculated measures against EOKA. As a result, hostilities between Greek and Turkish Cypriots intensified. Even though EOKA's original policy was one where the Turkish community was not involved in the conflict, the Greeks soon found themselves fighting on two fronts, one against the British and one against the Turkish Cypriots. "[T]he dispute in Cyprus, which started as an anticolonial movement increasingly assumed the character of an ethnic conflict between Greeks and Turks."[21]

Turkish violence against the Greeks was induced by the Turkish government via two secret organizations in Cyprus—the Volkan group initially, and TMT subsequently—and was also fostered by British authorities. The British position on the Cypriot issue, to oppose self-determination and support colonial rule for the island, was adopted by Turkey, NATO, the United States, and the anti-Communist bloc in Europe and the Middle East as well. The British government advanced the following political reasons for its position on Cyprus: first, the necessity of maintaining the island as a British base in the Middle East; and second, to ensure that Turkey was not alienated because it occupied a vital strategic position in NATO.

As hostilities between Greek and Turkish Cypriots intensified, the British solicited assistance from Greece and Turkey. The "Cyprus Question" was transferred from one set of hands to another for the next four years as solutions to reconcile the communities' differences were proposed. Finally, in 1959, the Cypriot Agreements, which stood as the basis of the Constitution

---

20 Ioannides, *In Turkey's Image* 52–125.

21 See Ioannides, *In Turkey's Image* 57. For additional information, see Panteli, *Cyprus* 265–323.

of the Republic of Cyprus, were negotiated between the Greek and Turkish Prime Ministers and then presented to Archbishop Makarios, who was required to sign without any prospect of amendment. Makarios was forced to yield when faced with an ultimatum from the British to the effect that if he did not comply, the British might carry out unilateral partition.[22]

The scenario exemplified in Table 4 is an obvious recipe for disaster. This scenario is when two countries, which have historically been at war, see themselves as holding contrary goals regarding the same third country. This recipe is evident in the Cypriot situation. The face-off over the Cyprus issue in 1959 was resolved only by giving countries a role in the domestic politics of Cyprus. (See appendix 2, table 4.)

TABLE 4:
TRANSNATIONAL NATIONALISM AS A CONSTRAINT ON FOREIGN POLICY CHOICES OPEN TO GREECE AND TURKEY

DOMESTIC PERCEPTIONS OF TURKISH LEADERS' DUTY IN I.R.	DOMESTIC PERCEPTION OF GREEK LEADERS' DUTY IN INTERNATIONAL RELATIONS	
	NO RESPONSIBILITY FOR CYPRUS	RESPONSIBILITY FOR CYPRUS
NO RESPONSIBILITY FOR CYPRUS		
RESPONSIBILITY FOR CYPRUS		CYPRUS

Table 4 shows the consequences of transnational nationalism for policy makers in the countries of origin. Pan-Turkism

---

22 Panteli, *Cyprus* 309–23.

leads Turkish decision makers to view protection of Turkish Cypriots as a duty. Likewise, Panhellenism means that Greek leaders must protect Greek Cypriots. Protection extends not just to border issues, but to maintenance of culture itself.

2. British Advances

Britain made advances toward both Greece and Turkey, which were drawn into the arena for the first time by British diplomat Sir Anthony Eden. A tripartite Conference convened to examine the Cyprus Question which, after bearing no fruit, broke up indecisively on December 7, 1955. The next move by the Eden government was to replace the existing governor of Cyprus with Field Marshal Sir John Harding.

Harding arranged a meeting with Makarios during which he proposed economic aid, amounting to thirty-eight million pounds, in exchange for the acceptance of a limited self-government with the possibility of self-determination at some future date. Under Karamanlis, the Greek government accepted the proposals, but Makarios rejected them. Harding proclaimed a state of emergency and under the powers derived from such a proclamation, Makarios was arrested and deported, leaving Grivas in sole command.

Lord Radcliffe made a second attempt at a political solution by drafting constitutional proposals. His proposals included the conditions that Cyprus remain under British control; that Britain retain use of the island as a military base; and that the British were to monitor external affairs, defense, and internal security. With these conditions in place, the Greek Cypriot majority was allotted more power than it had ever been offered before. Additionally, any partition of the island or form of federation was excluded. The Radcliffe Constitution was rejected by Karamanlis, Makarios—who refused to consider any proposals while he remained in exile—and the Turkish government, which demanded partition.

The "Cyprus Question" was subsequently transferred into the hands of Harold Macmillan, who released Makarios from exile with the provision that he not return to Cyprus. Makarios arrived in Athens on April 17, 1957. In autumn of that year, the United Nations failed to receive the necessary two-thirds majority to receive consideration by the General Assembly. Meanwhile, Sir John Harding resigned as governor of Cyprus and was replaced by Sir Hugh Foot. The new governor proposed a truce which was accepted by Grivas, but posed a problem for Makarios, who negotiated in Athens with the Greek and British governments.

The Athens government began exerting pressure on Makarios to settle for something less than self-determination and enosis. The Athens government suggested a united and independent Cyprus with self-determination as a future possibility. The government of Karamanlis in Greece was willing to accept some form of independence for Cyprus as long as it was honorable and excluded partition. There were two obstacles to such a solution: public opinion in Cyprus itself, and the Turkish demand for partition. The first obstacle was overcome by enhancing the position and prestige of Archbishop Makarios. The demand for Turkish territory could be countered by providing the Turkish minority with guaranteed rights and privileges. By the same token, Greece could be given equal rights without cession of territory or an actual constitutional union.

Pressure from America convinced the British government that the Cyprus issue had to be settled within the context of NATO, where the interests of both Greece and Turkey could be safeguarded. Needless to say, the interests of the Greek Cypriots were neglected. Their interests were used only to effect a tripartite deal between Britain, Greece, and Turkey that was designed to strengthen the Eastern Mediterranean flank of NATO. The 1960 Constitution of the Republic of Cyprus was organized by the Cyprus Zurich Agreement which was negotiated by the Greek and Turkish prime ministers on February 11, 1959. The Zurich Agreement was then incorporated into the London Agreements concluded on February 19 of the same year between these governments and that of Great Britain. On that date the accords were also presented to Archbishop Makarios, who was required to sign without any prospect of amendment.

Finally, Makarios was forced to yield when faced with an ultimatum from the British colonial secretary to the effect that if he did not comply, partition might be unilaterally carried out by Britain. Moreover, it has been argued that the Constitution was imposed by Turkey and accepted by Greece and Cyprus in order to avoid war.[23] Makarios himself offered an explanation for his constitutional endorsement in a public statement made on May 21, 1959. In his announcement, Makarios stated: "'I signed the London Agreements fully conscious of my responsibilities towards the people of Cyprus. Failure of the London Conference on Cyprus because of refusal to sign would have had catastrophic consequences for the failure of Cyprus."[24] Thus, the Republic of Cyprus was born.

The Constitution became a basis of continual friction between the two ethnic communities. From the inception of the republic, the Greek and Turkish communities solidified into two opposing groups, with rigid positions toward the Constitutional framework. The opposition and rigidity posed an obstacle to compromise. The irreconcilable attitudes of the two communities over the implementation of the Constitution created suspicion and distrust. The magnitude of this distress was manifested in the intercommunal fighting of 1963–1967. The threat of war between two NATO allies prompted Great Britain to intervene as a peace-keeper. Even though a crisis was averted in 1963–64 and 1967, physical and psychological separation of the two communities resulted. The 1960 Constitution guaranteed both countries a permanent voice in Cypriot affairs. The goals of Pan-Turkism and Panhellenism were deferred to a later time, but still held salience. (See appendix 2, table 5.)

---

[23] Interview with Lagakos.

[24] See Clerides, vol. 1, 80. For more information regarding these arrangements see Clerides, *Cyprus* vol. 1, 69–96; Panteli, *A History of Cyprus: From the Earliest Times to the Present Day* 309–23; and Vanezis, *Makarios: Faith and Power* 84–104.

TABLE 5:
THE CHICKEN GAME FOR GREEK AND TURKISH DECISION MAKERS, 1959

		GREECE	
		COOPERATE	DEFECT
TURKEY	COOPERATE	CYRPUS'S 1960 CONSTITUTION	PANHELENISM
	DEFECT	PANTURKISM	WAR

Table 5 exhibits the situation Greek and Turkish leaders faced in the 1959 Cypriot dispute. The leaders were playing a "chicken game": In a chicken game, the two rivals start off, for example, by driving their automobiles at each other at full speed. Whoever flinches and veers loses the game. Cooperation means veering and risking loss of the game, whereas defection means driving straight and risking death. If both cooperate, a peaceful coexistence results; if both defect, they are both destroyed. Applying this game to the prospect of war in 1959, Turkish and Greek leaders opted to cooperate. The 1960 Constitution guaranteed both countries a permanent voice in Cypriot affairs. The goal of Pan-Turkism and Panhellenism were set aside for a later time, but still held salience.

D. The 1960 Constitution

The overall political and constitutional settlement that was based on the Zurich and London Agreements was set at two levels: the international, within the context of the three treaties; and the internal, within the context of the 1960 Constitution. Focusing on the international treaties, the Treaty of Establishment in effect safeguarded British strategic interests in Cyprus. It recognized the independence of Cyprus only after British military interests were secured, thus providing for the retention of British influence in the Middle East. The Treaty of Alliance was a defense treaty between Cyprus, Greece, and Turkey that provided for the permanent stationing of Greek and Turkish troops on the island. Lastly, the Treaty of Guarantee was a pact between Cyprus, Greece, Turkey, and Great Britain that ensured the three Guarantor Powers the constitutional right to restore Cyprus's status should any change or disturbance occur, or in the event of a breach of the provisions of the Treaty. Moreover, enosis and taksim were excluded. The conclusion of the treaty, which Turkey later made reference to in its justification for military intervention, directed the guarantors to consult each other regarding measures to be taken to ensure compliance with the provisions. If concerted action proved impossible, each of the three guarantors reserved the right to act with the sole aim of re-establishing the environment created by the present treaty.

1. The Constitutional Provisions

An examination of the 1960 Cypriot Constitution reveals an overwhelming bicommunal character. The major provisions of the 1960 Constitution acknowledged and legitimized bicommunalism, and at the same time established and regulated community interests. The two communities were defined and equal recognition was accorded to them regarding the official languages of the republic, the selection of its flag, the right to celebrate the Greek and Turkish national holidays, and the right to fly the Greek or Turkish flag. Additionally, the Constitution ensured bicommunal participation in all spheres and levels of political and social activity; the Constitution attempted to create a balance of interest by establishing minority community participation in government through fixed numerical ratios. The character of the Constitution, regardless of whether it referred to the national or local level, recognized the Turks and Greeks of Cyprus principally as members of their respective communities with political and constitutional rights. The Turks and Greeks of Cyprus were not regarded as citizens of Cyprus, but as members of one or the other community.

The Constitution provided for two communal chambers, each chosen separately by its own community. The chambers held the exclusive legislative power to impose direct taxation and direct policy within the confines of their communal laws. The chambers were also invested with the power to exercise administrative control in a manner that promoted the security of the republic and the rights and liberties guaranteed by the Constitution regarding religious, educational, cultural, instructional matters, personal status, the composition of courts trying civil disputes, and issues "'[w]here the interests and institutions are of purely communal nature."[25]

By the very nature of the communal chambers and the existence of these provisions, the political allegiance of the two communities became fragmented. The two communities were granted special relationship rights with Greece and Turkey which included, among other things, the right to receive subsidies from Greek and Turkish governments for institutions and purposes of education, culture, athletics, and charity. Because education and culture were viewed strictly as communal concerns and not state responsibilities, no effort was made to integrate these institutions or processes into the realm of state activity. The fact that each communal chamber could receive direct assistance from Greece and Turkey not only strengthened the ties between the two communities and their mother countries, but tended to undermine the authority of the government of Cyprus.

The strong bicommunal character of the Constitution was particularly evident in the area of communal participation in the political system and the distribution of governmental powers. The executive branch was comprised of a Greek president and a Turkish vice president, along with a Council of Ministers composed of seven Greek and three Turkish ministers who

[25] Polyviou, *Cyprus* 17.

jointly ensured executive power. Council decisions were made by absolute majority and were issued immediately by the president and vice president unless either one exercised the right of veto or return. Legislative power was exercised by the House of Representatives which was also compositionally and functionally bicommunal. The bicommunal composition of the House was based on a fixed ratio of 70:30, where thirty-five of its fifty representatives were Greeks and fifteen were Turks. The bicommunal system was strengthened by the electoral method, which provided that Greek and Turkish representatives were elected separately by their respective Greek and Turkish communities. Furthermore, the President of the House had to be Greek, while the Vice President was Turkish.

In addition to a legislative branch, the Cypriot government consisted of an operable judicial branch which institutionalized the segregation of the two communities in the administration of justice. The Supreme Constitutional Court was composed of three judges: a Greek, a Turkish, and a neutral presidential judge. The Court held executive jurisdiction and conclusive authority over the allocation of power in the various organs of the republic and maintained the constitutionality of legislation. The judicial branch also consisted of the High Court which was comprised of two Greek judges, one Turkish judge, and a neutral presidential judge who had two votes. The primary function of the High Court was appellate review of civil and criminal offenses.

In terms of public servants, the 1960 Constitution specified that they be selected according to a ratio of 7:3, as were the security forces of the republic, which were divided into the police and the gendarmerie. A public service commission of ten members was in charge of public service appointments, and its decisions were ushered in by simple majority, but this was qualified to include a minimum number of Greek and Turkish votes depending on whether the decision related to a Greek or a Turk. In other words, a power of veto was given to a section of the Greek or Turkish members to frustrate majority decisions.

The system is an example of the ways in which communal participation in government can vary in form. In some governments communal involvement is represented by numerical equality, in others it is based on a fixed ratio, while in still others the power is shared between two individuals on a loose basis of equality.

Aside from its bicommunal character, the 1960 Constitution was characterized by a second feature, that of an elaborate checks and balance system which ensured that the major affairs of state were subject to the agreement of the representatives of the two communities. Executively speaking, both the president and vice president, either separately or jointly, could delay or veto decisions. The right of final veto could be exercised on decisions of the Council of Ministers concerning foreign affairs, defense, or security and was extended to matters originating from any law or decision of the House of Representatives. Furthermore, numerous decisions or acts within the president and vice president's authority, such as the choice of flag, the issuance of legislation by the Council of Ministers, and the appointment of ministers and high public officials, required joint action by both leaders. In the legislative realm, a separate simple majority of both the Greek and Turkish representatives was required for the modification of electoral arrangements, the adoption of laws relating to the municipalities, and for the enactment of any law imposing duties or taxes. Some less important articles could be amended with separate two-thirds majorities, but a great number of the 1960 Constitutional provisions were declared to be unamendable.

A third feature of the Constitution which deserves attention was the fragmentation of component functions and their apportionment among a number of governmental and communal bodies. In the executive area, there were separate presidential powers, separate vice presidential powers, powers shared by both the president and the vice president, limited executive powers held by the Communal Chambers, executive powers vested in the individual ministers, and general executive power "in all other matters" which was exercised by the Council of Ministers. Even though the Constitution theoretically established a "presidential regime," practically speaking, it was more accurately a vice presidential one. The powers of the Turkish vice president and the obstructive potential of his privileges made his authority comparable to the president. At the same time, since the Council of Ministers was entrusted with general executive power, in actuality this body appeared to be the chief executive organ of the state. This was only a facade, however, because not only did the president and vice president convene Council meetings and ensure executive power, but they also held the power to terminate ministerial appointments. Similar fragmentation and dispersal of responsibilities was found in the three legislative bodies of the House of Representatives and the two communal chambers. Because separate majorities were often the standard, the communal groups were forced to divide, which naturally led to an increase in the number of bodies which could exercise or frustrate legislative authority. More remarkably, the judicial branch suffers from similar confounded provisions.[26]

The Constitutional conflict entered a new stage in 1968 when the two communities, attempting to restore a spirit of cooperation, embarked on intercommunal negotiations. These negotiations continued until 1974 when a greatly improved constitutional settlement had nearly been reached. The new Constitution, which would have established Cypriot sovereignty, proved to be too serious a threat to the governments of Greece and Turkey. Motivated by factors external to the Cyprus question and political expediency, Greece and Turkey pursued the destruction and division of Cyprus by way of an externally inspired coup and invasion. War nearly ignited follow-

[26] For official documents and an analysis of the Zurich and London Agreements, see Clerides, *Cyprus* vol. 1, 385–400 and 114–26; and for an additional analysis of the 1960 Constitution, see Polyviou, *Cyprus* 13–25; and Kyriakides, *Cyprus* 53–71.

ing a Greek-inspired coup and a Turkish occupation. Partition, whereby neither Greece nor Turkey would be rejoined with Cyprus, was the worst outcome. Bilateral defection meant neither side achieved its goals, and the guaranteed influence each side enjoyed under the 1960 arrangements had ended. (See appendix 2, table 6.)

TABLE 6:
THE CHICKEN GAME FOR GREEK AND TURKISH DECISION MAKERS, 1974

		GREECE	
		COOPERATE	DEFECT
TURKEY	COOPERATE	CYRPUS'S 1960 CONSTITUTION	PANHELENISM
	DEFECT	PANTURKISM	PARTITION/ SEPARATION

Table 6 displays the logic of the "chicken game" when it is replayed in the context of 1974. The Greeks and Turks narrowly avoid war and Cyprus is partitioned. Lest we discount the importance of transnational nationalism, we must note that this time defection was the dominant strategy.

Although the 1960 Constitutional provisions of Cyprus, particularly the treaty of guarantee, appeased the mother countries by assuring them their participatory status, it failed to provide a sound framework for the government of the republic because of its serious defects in terms of both political balance and its functional capabilities. The most onerous of its numerous undemocratic, inequitable, and politically controversial elements were the absolute veto given to the president and vice president, the legislative separate majorities, and the heightened Turkish involvement in security and public service. Undeniably, the Constitution gave exaggerated powers to the Turkish community—at that time only 18 percent of the total population—and granted their leadership disproportionate obstructionist potential unrelated to the Turkish Cypriots' need for security. This inequity frustrated the Greek Cypriots, who comprised over 18 percent of the population, because the excessive Turkish rights seriously limited them in the pursuit of their interests. Ironically, even though the Turkish community enjoyed ample political power, it could not be exercised directly or positively and therefore could not provide them with either psychological nor practical assurance of security.

2. Tensions Stemming from the 1960 Constitution

Because of Greek Cypriot resentment and Turkish Cypriot mistrust, and as a result of the inherent complexity and impracticality of many of the constitutional provisions, it was not long before serious disputes arose and began dividing the Greek and Turkish Cypriots. The first issue to create dissension was the attempted implementation of the 70:30 ratio in the public service sector. The Greek Cypriots regarded the allocation of civil service posts to Turkish Cypriots as discriminatory. Appointments and promotions were no longer based on universally accepted criteria such as individual qualifications, efficiency, or the general suitability of candidates, because ethnic and communal factors were given primacy. The Turkish Cypriots disagreed with Greek allegations of discrimination and defended the ratio as necessary for securing adequate Turkish representation in all spheres of governmental activity. Controversy over appointments persisted as the Turkish leadership complained about the lack of adherence to the constitutionally prescribed ratio. In retaliation, Turkish members of the House of Representatives refused to vote for the budget. This refusal naturally had deleterious effects on the economy since the republic was left void of tax laws. Both communities relied on their communal chambers for income tax legislation, which caused a greater rift between the two communities and limited the prospects of constitutional government to a greater degree.

A second source of tension was the proposed creation of a Cypriot army. Turkish officials insisted that Greek and Turkish soldiers be quartered separately because of linguistic and religious differences, while the Council of Ministers argued for an integrated army. By exercising his right of veto, the Turkish vice president created a deadlock when he negated the Council's decision. A resolution to the army deadlock was never found and therefore it remained a dormant source of tension.

The issue that proved the most volatile of all was the separation of the municipalities. The 1960 Constitution provided for the formation of municipalities in the five largest towns for a period of four years, at which time a decision would be made by the president and vice president as to whether or not this separation of municipalities should be continued. Difficulties arose in the implementation of this feat because the Greeks and Turks coexisted rather than living exclusively in "ethnic" areas in any of the towns.

When committees established to reach an agreement on the definition of separate Greek and Turkish regions proved unsuccessful, President Makarios proposed the establishment of a united municipal authority with proportional representation in each town. In order to further safeguard the rights of Turkish citizens, Makarios suggested the staff of the municipal authorities be proportioned in reference to the population. In addition, Makarios proposed that a predetermined percentage of the annual budget of each municipality be dispersed according to the suggestions of the Turkish municipal council members. Furthermore, in each of the five municipalities where the mayor was a Greek, the deputy mayor was to be a Turk, if this balance was appropriate in light of the Turkish population.

Denktash rejected the proposal the following day. Clerides expressed his view that each of the five towns should be administered by mixed councils consisting of representation in proportion to the population. The councils were to enact safeguards to assure Turkish citizens that discriminatory practices would not be implemented against them, and to decide how to allocate the fixed budget. Denktash agreed to consider the compromise. A press announcement stated that "common ground" had been found, although this announcement came shortly after the Turkish side reverted to its initial position and demanded geographical separation of the towns.

By 1963, key governmental operations had come to a virtual halt, in part because of the two communities' mutual suspicion and hostility, and partly because of the complexity of the constitutional arrangements. The state was dysfunctional. On November 30, 1963, three years after the adoption of the Constitution, President Makarios issued several proposals to revise the constitutional provisions which impeded the smooth functioning and development of the state.

The first of Makarios's "Thirteen Points" of 1963 entailed abandonment of both the executive veto and the constitutional provisions regarding separate majorities. Other proposals included: unification of the administration of justice and organization of the municipalities; reduction of the proportion of Turkish Cypriot involvement in public service and armed forces to 20 percent; enhancement of the positions of Turkish vice president and Turkish vice president of the House of Representatives by providing they be deputized for the president of the republic and House respectively in the event of the latter's temporary absence or incapacity; the number of public service commission members be reduced and a simple majority used to determine all decisions; abandonment of the division of security forces into police and gendarmerie so that numerical strength could be determined by law; and finally, abolition of the Greek communal chamber. Archbishop Makarios assured the Turkish Cypriots that his proposals were not intended to deprive them of their rights and interests nor their safeguards, but to ease the friction by correcting the provisions which led to the bicommunal deadlocks. In contrast, the Turkish vice president ascribed the causes of the deadlock to the Greek Cypriots' unwillingness to cooperate with the Turkish community within the structure of the 1960 Constitution. On this basis, the Turkish vice president rejected the thirteen points.[27]

The irreconcilable attitudes of the two communities over the implementation of the 1960 Constitution created suspicion and distrust. The magnitude of this distrust manifested itself in the intercommunal fighting of December 1963. The constitutional conflicts and the inability of the leadership of the two communities to cooperate brought dormant fears and mistrust to the surface. Given the prevailing atmosphere of tension, it did not take long for serious violence to engulf the island. Persistent opposition and the resulting bicommunal constitutional deadlocks provided extremist groups the opportunity to press harder. While EOKA-B members pushed for radical solutions to the deadlock and demanded enosis, TMT demanded taksim.[28]

The outbreak of intercommunal violence sparked the historical animosity between Greece and Turkey. Turkey began military preparations for an invasion of Cyprus. As Turkish troops stationed on the island moved into position to support the Turkish community, so too did the Greek contingency. The more the tension in Cyprus heightened, the closer Greece and Turkey came to direct confrontation. In late January 1964, the United States government suggested to President Makarios that a NATO peacekeeping force be dispatched to the island, yet this proposal was quickly rejected by the Cypriot government. In March 1964, however, the Security Council set up a United Nations force in Cyprus. There were sporadic incidents of violence, and the accumulation of armaments and forces, followed by a further drifting apart of the two communities. Although a conference was called in London in January 1964 in an attempt to reach a settlement, the attempts failed. By the beginning of

---

[27] Dr. Fazil Kuchuk's letters to the secretary-general of the United Nations, in Kyriakides, *Cyprus* 177–80.

[28] Kyriakides, *Cyprus* 111.

1965, the 1960 Constitution was effectively dead and communal separation had become necessary.[29]

Meanwhile, bilateral Greco-Turkish talks without Cypriot participation took place intermittently. Although the government of Cyprus "agreed" to these talks, Archbishop Makarios stated emphatically that as a nonparticipant in the talks, his government would not be obligated by any solution which conflicted with the wishes of the Cypriot people. Greco-Turkish dialogue culminated in a meeting held in Thrace in September 1967 between the prime ministers of Greece and Turkey. During the meeting it was determined that the gap between the positions of the two countries—Greece still striving to achieve enosis and Turkey determined to implement partition—was unbridgeable.

Just prior to the end of Greco-Turkish discussions, a military junta under Colonel Papadopoulos took power in Greece as the result of a coup. United Nations authorities, sensing the urgent need for an alternate procedure to allow a peaceful settlement of the problem, began consultations with the interested parties. These efforts were obstructed by an outbreak of intercommunal violence in the Kophinou-Ayios Theodhoros area, which resulted in a full-scale military confrontation between Greece and Turkey. Intercommunal violence erupted when Cypriot police resumed their patrolling activities in the area of Ayios Theodhoros. Turkish Cypriot "fighters," who were preparing to convert the ethnically mixed village into another Turkish enclave, resented the intrusion. The government of Cyprus complained to UNFICYP about the paramilitary activities in the region and requested assistance in reactivating the ordinary police patrol in the area. UNFICYP leadership shared the anxieties of the Cypriot government and therefore made numerous representations to both the Turkish government and the Turkish Cypriot leadership in order to restore police activity.

---

[29] For the full text of United Nations mediation on Cyprus, or the Galo Plaza Report, see Clerides, *Cyprus* vol. 2, 403–65.

UNFICYP proposed a time-table for the gradual resumption of Cypriot police patrols to commence on November 2, 1965; the proposal was immediately accepted by the Cypriot government, but was submitted under review by the Turkish side. On November 3, the Turkish government agreed to accept the proposed timetable, but only if the National Guard was withdrawn from the Larnaca area. Meanwhile, the Cypriot government expressed concern at the delay in the resumption of police patrol and decided on November 14 to wait no longer. The government sent two police patrols into the village without problems, but on the following day the patrol encountered gun fire by the Turkish Cypriot "fighters." The National Guard immediately opened fire and within a few hours the fighting grew more intense as General Grivas ordered his troops to launch an attack on additional Turkish Cypriot fortifications. Serious hostilities broke out between the National Guard and the Turkish Cypriot "security forces" until a cease-fire was negotiated.

Meanwhile, the Turkish government mobilized an invasion force and warned the United Nations that a full-scale war with Greece was imminent unless the Greek government would consent to withdraw all Greek troops from the island who were numbered in excess of those accorded in the Treaty of Alliance, and dissolve the Cypriot National Guard. Additionally, the Turkish government demanded that General Grivas be recalled to Greece and banned from the island. Although the Greek government hastily recalled General Grivas, it did not withdraw its armed forces. Greek Foreign Minister Panayotis Pipinelis immediately initiated consultation with the Turkish and American governments, while at the same time he persuaded Colonel Papadopoulos of the need to cooperate.

On November 21, 1965, mediation efforts commenced in London among the United States, Britain, and Canada. These efforts ultimately led to five propositions which were subsequently submitted to the governments in Athens and Ankara. These proposals included the following tasks: Turkey should disassemble her invasion force out of respect for the territorial integrity and sovereignty of Cyprus; both Greek and Turkish troops should be reduced to the numbers designated in the Treaty of Alliance; the United Nations should enlarge and fortify its force on the island; compensation for the Turkish Cypriots who had suffered losses during the latest outbreaks; and the future security of the Turkish Cypriot community should be assured. In light of these proposals, it became apparent that third-party mediation efforts were crucial. These efforts were provided by Jose Rolz-Bennett for the United Nations, Cyrus Vance for the United States, and Manlio Brosio on behalf of NATO.

3. Further Proposals to End Conflict

After several days of negotiations, a final agreement was reached on November 30, 1967. The basic elements of the agreement were the following: removal from Cyprus of Greek and Turkish troops in excess of the permitted numbers under the Treaty of Alliance; Turkey would not launch an attack; the Greek Cypriot National Guard would be disbanded and its weaponry surrendered to the United Nations peace force, which would assume responsibility for the stability of Cyprus; and reaffirmation of the independence and integrity of Cyprus. Archbishop Makarios refused to disband the Cypriot National Guard, however, unless complete demilitarization of the island was effected by way of withdrawal of all Greek and Turkish troops, even those authorized under the 1960 Constitution. The Cypriot government eventually agreed to allow the "legal" Greek and Turkish military forces to remain on the island, but it refused to disband the National Guard. Even though the crisis was effectively over with the acceptance of the agreement on the part of Cyprus, Greece, and Turkey, physical and psychological separation of the two Cypriot communities persisted.[30]

---

[30] For an analysis of the constitutional breakdown and the ensuing conflicts see Kyriakides, *Cyprus* 72–162; and Polyviou, *Cyprus* 25–61. And for official documentation regarding these events see generally Clerides, *Cyprus*, vols. 1 and 2.

Despite political violence within the Cypriot communities and mounting conflict between the Greek and Turkish governments and that of Cyprus, intercommunal negotiation continued. By early 1974, a comprehensive settlement regarding the internal constitutional problem had nearly been reached. Because the newly reconstructed and soon-to-be implemented constitution posed problems to both Greece and Turkey as a result of their exclusion, the two countries felt compelled to intervene in order to prevent its effectuation. Thus, Greece staged a coup, and shortly thereafter Turkish military forces invaded the island and partitioned Cyprus.

The political saliency of Greek and Turkish identities for Greek and Turkish Cypriots meant that Makarios and Denktash had to respond to the needs of their followers in order to connect with their homelands. At the same time, they were striving to build a sovereign state where Greek and Turkish Cypriots would place primary importance on their identity as Cypriots. Makarios and Denktash had to reinforce transnational nationalism in order to retain their credibility and further independent nationalism. (See appendix 2, table 7.)

TABLE 7:
THE CHICKEN GAME FOR GREEK AND TURKISH CYPRIOT DECISION MAKERS, 1974

		GREEK CYPRIOTS	
		COOPERATE	DEFECT
TURKEY CYPRIOTS	COOPERATE	CYRPUS'S 1974 CONSTITUTION	PANHELENISM
	DEFECT	PANTURKISM	CYRPUS'S 1960 CONSTITUTION

Table 7 reveals the logic that faced Greek and Turkish Cypriot leaders in 1974. The leaders attempted to overcome the stalemate within the country. They wanted to maintain Greek and Turkish Cypriot communities, yet allow cooperation between them. This was to be achieved by removing Greek and Turkish influence, which had consistently led to interventions and conflict.

Due to the 1967 Crisis and the evacuation of Greek and Turkish troops from the island, a major thrust toward a resolution of outstanding differences, including political and constitutional ones, was consummated. The constitutional conflict entered a new stage in 1968 when the two communities, attempting to restore a spirit of cooperation, embarked on the Intercommunal Negotiations which continued until 1974. An exploratory first meeting between Clerides and Denktash occurred in Beirut on June 11, 1968. From the outset, it was agreed that the discussions would be aimed at exploring options for solving the constitutional problem of an independent, integral and sovereign state. Upon settling Cyprus's constitutional problem, the international position, specifically in regards to the Treaties of Alliance and Guarantee, would be addressed.

At the preliminary meeting, Clerides and Denktash jointly acknowledged that the Zurich settlement contained unfair provisions for both Greek and Turkish Cypriots. The first phase of the talks was dedicated principally to an exchange of views and investigation of the attitudes of the two ethnic communities. The main objective of the Greek Cypriot position was to obtain substantial revisions to the 1960 Constitution along the lines of the thirteen proposals, while simultaneously ensuring protection of the Turkish Cypriots.

Turkish Cypriot willingness to compromise followed these lines: they agreed to reduce the percentage of their participation in the civil service, and reduce the police and legislature to that of their population ratio; they accepted that the president and vice president of the House of Representatives would be elected by all the House members, but that separate electoral rolls would be required for elections to the House; they conditionally agreed to the unification of the courts. In addition, Turkish Cypriots made the following requests: executive participation in accordance with their population ratio; retention of the office of the vice president with concession of the right of the vice presidential veto and other established executive powers; that areas for local administration need not be established on racial grounds, provided that an agreement be reached as to those areas where the Turks would be in the majority; and immunity from modification by ordinary legislation. Furthermore, the powers and functions of local authorities would be in accordance with laws enacted by the House of Representatives.

The Greek Cypriot side, even though in full support of Turkish protection and security, could not agree with the Turkish proposals regarding the structuring and power of local administration, nor were they in favor of retention of the vice presidential office. Upon the completion of the first phase of the talks, the representatives issued a joint statement. The statement revealed that while an agreement had been reached on a number of points, common ground had not been established on others, but the existing gap between the two sides could be narrowed with persistence and patient negotiation. At this stage the attitudes of both Greece and Turkey toward the intercommunal talks were positive and the reserved optimism held by both communities was justified.[31]

However, after the completion of the first phase, both Clerides and Denktash consulted with the Cypriot and Turkish governments respectively, which some maintain resulted in a hardening of attitudes. During the second phase, the two negotiators exchanged concrete proposals regarding the executive, legislative and judicial branches, as well as the police and local government. Clerides emphasized to the Council of Ministers the presidential nature of the regime, while acknowledging the

---

31 For official documents and an analysis of the first phase of the intercommunal talks, see Clerides, *Cyprus* vol. 2, 217–63; and for an additional analysis, see Polyviou, *Cyprus* 62–69.

need for Turkish Cypriot participation in proportion to their population. Clerides' legislative proposals allowed for a House of Representatives consisting of sixty members: forty-eight Greek Cypriots and twelve Turkish Cypriots. The House of Representatives would be characterized by: common electoral rolls; three officers, one president and two vice presidents, one of the vice presidents to be mandatorily a Turkish Cypriot; all officers to be selected by majority vote from among the representatives; and all legislative decisions determined by majority vote. In addition, the House of Representatives was to appropriate funds for the financing of education in both communities in proportion to their respective student populations. Regarding the judiciary, Clerides proposed the establishment of a system of courts that would administer justice juridically and not based on ethnic criteria. The highest court would be a Supreme Court consisting of no more than seven judges. In order to assure Turkish Cypriots of judicial impartiality, special appeal procedures would be established. As to the police, Turkish Cypriots would be represented in proportion to their population.

The detailed proposals submitted by Denktash differed significantly from those of the Greek side. The Turkish proposals provided for a Turkish vice president, although his powers and responsibilities could not be designated at this stage. Regarding the administration of justice, Turkish and Greek Cypriots alike had the right to be tried by a judge of their own language rather than according to jurisdictional criteria. Pertaining to the Supreme Court, the Turkish demanded the proportion of Greek and Turkish members be at least 3:2 respectively. As to legislative functions, the Turkish Cypriot position was to accept a decrease in its participation to 20 percent of the total number of representatives, but no less than fifteen members, in order to ensure Turkish participation at all committees. Additionally, common electoral rolls would not be accepted. As of yet, a general election procedure that would satisfy the Greek Cypriot aim of unification, while preventing Greek voters from forcing unacceptable Turkish candidates on the Turks, had not been discovered by the Turkish side.

The primary issue at the beginning of the second phase of negotiation was unquestionably that of local government. Denktash proposed that communal areas consisting of a group of villages should each elect a representative entrusted with the coordination and exercise of local government activities. Furthermore, he suggested that two central bodies, one Greek and the other Turkish, be invested with communal and local governmental powers and responsibilities, and be empowered to issue regulations. Regarding the police, Denktash proposed the establishment of two separate security forces, one at the governmental level and one at the local administration level.

In response to the Turkish side's strong interest in the matter of local government, Clerides presented new proposals in an effort to reduce the differences between the two communities. He suggested the second tier of local government, the grouping of a number of villages, be based on geographical proximity to one other, rather than racial criterion. The third and final tier of local government was to be the district.

In addition to considering the new proposals on local administration, Denktash contemplated other Cypriot proposals such as: the Turkish Cypriots were to enjoy complete autonomy on matters of education, culture, religion, and personal status; representation in the three branches of government, civil service, and police should be in proportion to the population; and the police force in areas predominately populated by Turks should consist mostly of Turkish police officers belonging to a unified police force. Addressing the latest proposals, Denktash expressed the general view that separation of functions between the three tiers was unrealistic. This response signaled the end of the second phase of negotiations.[32]

---

[32] For official documents and an analysis of the second phase of the intercommunal talks see Clerides, *Cyprus*, vol. 2, 263–309; and for an additional analysis see Polyviou, *Cyprus* 69–74.

The third phase of the talks commenced on August 11, 1969, at which time Denktash gave Clerides two documents. The first contained the Turkish views on the Greek proposals of April 24, 1969, and the second document was a complete set of new Turkish counterproposals on autonomous local government authorities. Serious disagreement persisted over principal issues. Denktash viewed the Greek side's position as simply a re-arrangement of the village administration system by the government and not one which gave basic rights or autonomy to the communities for the administration of their own affairs. Most particularly, the Turkish side did not agree with the idea of mixed grouping because they were sure that such conditions would inevitably result in the loss of identity in areas where the Greek population dominated. The key Turkish counterproposals were as follows: the constitution was to provide for local authority and power and not leave this to the discretion of the lawmakers; retention of currently established Turkish municipalities; implementation of grouping based on communal criteria; constitutional incorporation of two central organs of local administration, one authority for Turkish villages and another for Greek villages; and coordination of the government and local authorities through a board linked to the president and vice president.

As the Turkish proposals were discussed on August 18, 1969, it became clear that the various points of contention were focused on the philosophy and functions of local administration, structuring of local authorities, and the organs of central governmental control. The Greek side interpreted the Turkish counterproposals as creating an unworkable system of government for Cyprus based on three exclusive governments which would not create a unitary state: one for the Turks, one for the Greeks, and a central government consisting of Greeks and Turks. As a result, the Greek side found the Turkish counterproposals as failing to offer a satisfactory solution to the issue of local government. Denktash concluded that the Greek side's objections to his proposals were not due to practical considerations, but stemmed from political ones. Greek Cypriots were unwilling to acknowledge the Turkish community as anything but a minority on the island. As a result of these exchanges over the question of local government, the gap between the two sides widened.

By now, it was apparent that positions were becoming entrenched and attitudes were hardening. All things considered, on November 30, 1970, Clerides exerted a final effort to approach the Turkish point of view by offering Denktash a "package deal." The Greek Cypriot side modified its position significantly on many issues and made important concessions on others. The "deal" accepted all of the following: a Turkish vice president of the House and a House of Representatives composed of sixty Greek and fifteen Turkish members; election of Greek and Turkish members of the legislature on separate electoral rolls; the Supreme Court could appoint a judge whose native language was that of the litigants in cases where both parties shared the same language; and the grouping of villages to form areas of Turkish local government. In exchange for these concessions, the Turkish side would need to abandon its proposal of separate central and local government authorities for Greeks and Turks, agree that matters of local government would be legislated by the House of Representatives, and concede that governmentally appointed district officers could refuse to sign any local government regulation deemed contrary to the laws of the House or outside the realm of local authority.

Before responding to the package deal, Denktash flew to Ankara to consult with the Turkish government and decide upon a response. A reply in the form of independent Turkish Cypriot counterproposals was handed to Clerides on April 27, 1971. The counterproposals were prefaced with a reaffirmation of the terms of the intercommunal talks and a presumptive condition upon which all adjustments were to be made. First, Denktash noted his understanding that the aim of the discussions was "a permanent solution based on independence," not an independence to be manipulated by one side or the other for the furtherance of "national aims and aspirations."[33] Secondly, for the sake of clarity, he reaffirmed that to settle the different viewpoints based on the package deal, there could be no misunderstanding that the remaining parts of the constitution would remain in their present form.

The key points of the Turkish Cypriot counterproposals were as follows: retention of vice presidential duties and powers as delineated in the London and Zurich Agreements, except for the veto; establishment of separate legislative assemblies in charge of communal matters; implementation of separate sound and vision broadcasting services; local police forces based on ethnic organization; and conduct of judicial business, including trials, according to communal criteria. Additionally, the Turkish side demanded the creation of communal local courts to administer local or communal matters, with the duties, powers, and jurisdiction of the courts defined in the constitution. Local government should be coordinated by central authorities, such as the Greek and Turkish communal chambers or the president, vice president, and their communally elected committees. Lastly, autonomous local bodies should not be subordinate to the district officer or any central government authority figure.

Turkish response widened the gap by reopening subjects previously agreed upon and raising new ones. Extremely disappointed by these results, Clerides submitted a new set of proposals with further concessions on June 26, 1971. Clerides was prepared to make the following concessions regarding the police: in areas where the Turkish Cypriot majority approached 100 percent, the police force would consist exclusively of Turkish Cypriots; the head and deputy head of the police could be from different communities with the condition that they be appointed by the president; the numerical strength of the police force was to be regulated by law. Finally, in a major concession, Clerides agreed to accede to local government authorities having civilian inspectors with the power to enforce regulations, orders, and by-laws.

---

33 Polyviou, *Cyprus* 80.

Regarding the judiciary, Clerides agreed to a Supreme Court consisting of six Greek Cypriot and three Turkish Cypriot judges selected by the president and confirmed by the vice president. The Supreme Court would also contain honorary justices who would try cases in which regulations, orders, or by-laws were in question, provided the justices be selected by the Supreme Council of Judicature. Concerning the legislature, differences no longer remained between the two sides. In terms of the executive, the vice president would make recommendations to the president regarding the appointment of positions, and the president was to act on such recommendations. Additionally, the vice president had the right and duty to challenge House decisions before the Supreme Court and promulgate and return all decisions of the Turkish communal chamber.

Clerides's final proposals pertaining to local government can be summarized as follows: the House of Representatives would legislate local government issues while delegating powers to local authorities to make regulations, rules, and by-laws; local authorities would administrate jurisdictional matters; a unit of local government should be formed for each Turkish village; and a number of Turkish villages could be grouped to form an area of local government under a local council. The Greek Cypriot side would not agree, under any circumstances, to the issue of Greek or Turkish central local government authorities.

Denktash's response to Clerides's final proposals was that even though a near settlement had been reached on the difficult issues of the police, judiciary, legislature, and executive, settlement was possible only because of the Turkish side's initial concessions on its existing rights in exchange for a system of local autonomy derived directly from the constitution and not subject to central control. Denktash emphasized there could be no compromise on this issue; therefore, the talks were terminated.[34]

---

34 For official documents and an analysis of the third phase of the intercommunal talks, see Clerides, *Cyprus* vol. 2, 310–45; and for an additional analysis, see Polyviou, *Cyprus* 74–101.

The breakdown of the intercommunal talks in 1971 was beset with danger; therefore, United Nations officials interceded without delay in order to reactivate the talks which commenced on June 8, 1972. Both Turkey and Greece expressed their support for reactivation of the discussions because they thought that the dialogue would provide the most suitable framework for solving the Cypriot problem. Turkey emphasized the Turkish Cypriots' complete distrust of Greek Cypriot intentions. Because Turkish Cypriots adamantly opposed enosis, they firmly maintained the validity of the treaties which forbade both partition and enosis. Turkish Cypriots insisted the future of Cyprus rested on the cooperation of two autonomous communities through a balanced partnership. The Greek government acknowledged the impracticability of achieving enosis and therefore supported an independent, sovereign, and unitary state. The Greek government, as did the Turkish government, feared that the long-term goal of the other side was to create an infrastructure for partition. Accordingly, they believed the treaties associated with the Zurich Agreement should be maintained.

In addition to Clerides and Denktash, the two negotiators of the first stage, the discussions were attended by Tafall, the secretary-general's special representative in Cyprus, as well as Dekleris and Aldicasti, the Greek and Turkish experts. It was decided that the second round of talks should be approached with greater tactical flexibility. An exclusive emphasis on direct exchange between the two chief representatives was set aside for a "two-stage" negotiation technique. A mediator would speak with the two sides separately, prepare alternate formulae in order to narrow outstanding differences, and then conduct face-to-face meetings to agree upon and implement solutions.

Between 1972 and 1974, intensive negotiation and compromise took place in the legislature, executive, judiciary, and particularly local government. Considerable progress was swiftly achieved in most areas pertaining to the organization of central government. The few legislative issues that remained unresolved from the first round of talks were satisfactorily resolved during the early stages of the reactivated dialogue. It was agreed that the two communal chambers would be abolished in favor of a bi- communal House consisting of Greek and Turkish representatives. It was also agreed that the House would consist of seventy-five members, sixty Greek and fifteen Turkish members, to be elected on separate rolls. The president, elected by the House as a whole, should be Greek. One of the two deputy presidents was to be a Turk, the other a Greek. The Turkish side also agreed to the abolition of the separate-majorities provisions, except in the cases of the electoral law, amendments to constitutional clauses, and organic law containing the provisions of local government. Concerning these cases, a specially reinforced majority of the House, which included a specified number of Turkish representatives, would be required.

Reorganization of the judiciary proved to be an even more difficult task. The two issues which appeared from the early exchanges to be the most problematic were composition of the Supreme Court and the criteria to determine jurisdiction. After examining numerous formulae, both sides leaned toward a solution whereby aspects of international adjudication would be combined with the organization of a distinct branch within the Supreme Court. For a period of seven to ten years, a special judicial body operating within the Supreme Court and consisting of two Greek and two Turkish judges would exercise complete jurisdiction over the constitutionality of laws and decisions of the House and its branches. The president of the Supreme Court would preside over this special branch, and in case of a 2:2 disagreement, the president of an International Court would issue an advisory opinion.

Resolving the difficulties associated with the executive branch proved even more trying. According to both sides, the crucial issues pertained to the designated powers of the various executive organs and the executive appearance of the state. Early on in the exchanges, it was decided that the regime would continue to be a presidential one. The Greek president and Turkish vice president would be assisted by a Council of Ministers composed of Greek and Turkish Cypriots proportioned to the population (thus, the Turkish side accepted a decrease in its participation to 20 percent). In addition, it was agreed that the separate executive responsibilities of the vice president would be significantly reduced and both the presidential and vice presidential vetoes would be abolished. Some powers and rights, at one time jointly shared by the president and vice president, were converted into ones held exclusively by the president.

Even though these issues were resolved with relative ease, two particularly troublesome problems persisted: first, the source and derivation of executive power, and secondly, the method for the appointment of ministers. Regarding the former, an agreement was finally reached whereby "[executive power would derive from and be exercised by the executive organs of the state [the president, vice president and the Council of Ministers] according to the specific and detailed provisions of the constitution."[35]

Finally, several months into 1974, a compromise on the appointment issue was reached. The president would endorse the instruments of ministerial appointments and would be constitutionally required to endorse Turkish Cypriot appointments designated by the vice president. Likewise, the vice president would be required to countersign, not as a "joint signature," but to announce his concurrence.

The most acute disagreements throughout the intercommunal dialogue surrounded issues of local government, and specifically whether there should be a Greek and Turkish central authority. The Turkish side was absolutely committed to such an arrangement and firmly believed the functions of the two communal chambers should be broadened to include appropriate local government functions. The Greek side, which had expressed stiff opposition to this position until 1972, was forced to agree both to the recognition of two branches of the House and that local governmental affairs would be its responsibility

[35] Polyviou, *Cyprus* 110.

if it wanted negotiation to continue. Both sides concluded it was imperative that there be uniformity in enactment and regulation of the various powers among the local authorities. This meant that common standards would be set legislatively by the House of Representatives and amendable only by a two-thirds majority of the House (the House would include one-third of the Turkish votes). By March 1974, few issues remained unresolved. Had it not been for the coup of July, many believe that a complete agreement would have been reached by August 1974.[36]

4. Escalation of Violence

Transnational nationalism was politically salient for the leaders of Greece and Turkey, Ioannides and Ecevit faced pressures from Greek and Turkish citizens to reunify Greek and Turkish Cypriots with their homelands. Control of Cyprus was not sought as an international security concern, but as a cultural priorit. Ioannides' Greek intervention in Cypriot politics, justifying Turkish occupation, appeared irrational in terms of international relations, but rational in light of his concern regarding his hold on power in Greece. Because transnational nationalism was taken seriously in Greece and Turkey—where enosis and taksim were actual goals—the 1974 Constitution was seen as a threat in these countries, and the Crisis emerged.

Even though remarkable progress had been made concerning constitutional matters, circumstances within the Greek Cypriot and Turkish Cypriot communities and governments, as well as the relations between the governments of Turkey and Cyprus, were straining the discussions. Terrorist activity within the Greek Cypriot community increased following the crushing defeat of the enosist candidate, Dr. Evdokas, during the presidential election of 1968. A number of terrorist organizations,

[36] For official documents and an analysis of the 1974 constitutional model, see Clerides, *Cyprus*. vol. 2, 346–60 and 368–97; vol. 3, 36–109 and 194–246; and for an additional analysis of the 1974 agreements see Polyviou, *Cyprus* 102–53.

the most vociferous being the National Front, became more vocal and visible as they stepped up their acts of sabotage and violence, including the attempted assassination of Archbishop Makarios on March 8, 1970. Deep divisions in sections of the Greek Cypriot community surfaced, and the explosive nature of this precarious situation was exacerbated by the secret return of General Grivas to the island in early September 1971. Grivas promptly established a new terrorist movement called EOKA-B, designed to implement union with Greece. Even though the Grivas guerrillas were few, they were supported by many Greek officers serving with the Cypriot National Guard (the Greek Cypriot army). The guerrillas were successful at infiltrating the police and Cypriot security forces which, as a result, could no longer be relied upon by the government.[37]

Not surprisingly, Turkish attitudes became increasingly rigid, and the political climate in which the talks were held was inevitably influenced by violence within the Greek Cypriot community. It must also be noted that TMT was not dissolved when Cypriot independence was achieved in 1960; in fact, the influence of Turkish officers in Turkish Cypriot affairs became predominant from the 1960s onward. Aggressiveness was injected into Turkey's policy regarding Cyprus during the early 1960s when the Mucahit (Fighters of Islam) force organized by TMT became the military force (although primarily paramilitary) employed to defend the Turkish Cypriots.[38]

Intimately linked with the movement toward enosis was an eruption of conflict within the Church of Cyprus when three members of the Holy Synod of the Greek Cypriot Church turned against Archbishop Makarios by challenging his ecclesiastical authority. Their motives were unquestionably not ecclesiastical but political, as was manifested by their complaints

---

[37] See *The New York Times*, February 17, 1973; *The New York Times*, April 9, 1973; and *The New York Times*, July 30, 1973. For details regarding the effects of Grivas's organization on the domestics of Cyprus see Clerides, *Cyprus* vol.1 110–64.

[38] See Ioannides, *In Turkey's Image* 130 and 134.

about Makarios's abandonment of enosis for independence. On March 2, 1972, the three bishops asked Archbishop Makarios to resign as president. Because this request went unheeded, they attempted to depose Makarios for allegedly violating canon law in continuing to hold the secular office of president while exercising ecclesiastical authority. Even though the final decision of a synod of Eastern Orthodox churches on this matter was a comprehensive victory for Archbishop Makarios, and one in which the three bishops were unfrocked, it was a reflection of the political schism within the Greek Cypriot community. The conflict could not help but exacerbate the already difficult task of reaching a negotiated internal settlement of the Cypriot dilemma.[39]

Of even greater significance, however, was a marked deterioration in the relations between the Greek junta and the government of Archbishop Makarios. Early in 1972, the Greek government under Colonel Papadopoulos issued an ultimatum to President Makarios demanding: first, that a quantity of arms imported to Cyprus from Czechoslovakia be surrendered to the National Guard, whose officers were under direct orders of the junta; second, that Makarios dismiss any ministers of his cabinet who were considered hostile to the Greek regime; and lastly, that Makarios and his government comply with future policies established by the Athenian junta. Makarios's response was that neither he nor his government would cower to Greek pressure or tolerate Greek interference in the domestic affairs of Cyprus. The culmination of the Papadopoulos policy regarding Cyprus was acceptance of a secret agreement with Turkey. According to the agreement's terms, Greece would accept basic partnership principles in the constitutional reconstruction of Cyprus and the extension of substantial local autonomy for Turkish Cypriots, in exchange for a guarantee from Turkey that it would

---

[39] See *The New York Times*, March 10, 1973; May 19, 1973; July 6, 1973; and July 8, 1973. For official information regarding the request for Makarios' resignation see Clerides, *Cyprus*, vol. 3, 398–418.

not unilaterally invade Cyprus unless it had first consulted the Greek government.

Throughout 1972 and early 1973, the Turkish government was willing to oblige Papadopoulos, but it eventually lost patience. Demanding an immediate solution to the Cypriot problem by either intercommunal talks or a separate agreement between Greece and Turkey, the Greek regime decided the only way to settle the problem was to overthrow Makarios and replace him with someone who would be more receptive to its suggestions. As 1973 drew to a close, transitions in the political leadership of both Turkey and Greece exacerbated the previously existing tensions between the two countries. "In Turkey, [a]t the [October] 1973 elections Bulent Ecevit and his center left party, the RPP, secured a slim plurality with 33.5 percent of the national vote and 185 out of 450 seats in the National Assembly." Because a party needed at least 226 votes in the assembly to secure a vote of confidence, Ecevit was forced to seek coalition partners. Ecevit eventually was forced to form a coalition government with a most unlikely partner, the national salvation party (NSP), whose leader was Necmettin Erbakan.[40]

During the same time, Greece experienced political upheaval. In November 1973, a more extreme junta under Brigadier Ioannides overthrew Colonel Papadopoulos and ushered in the beginning of the last phase of relations among the Greek dictatorship, Turkey, and the Cypriot government.

The importance of the Cypriot situation to both Greece and Turkey escalated with each successive administration; in the late 1973 and early 1974, the situation became the paramount consideration. Ecevit realized there were advantages to be reaped by "creating facts" from an opponent's weakness, and this strategy was his golden opportunity for not only a tremendous diplomatic victory, but even more importantly, a chance to alter the social, geographic, and political position of the Turkish Cypriot minority. As early as December 1973, Turkish

[40] Couloumbis, *The United States, Greece, and Turkey* 156.

officials prepared plans for an attack on Cyprus should the junta stumble. Because he was a minority premier in parliament, the preservation of Ecevit's political position as prime minister was ultimately contingent upon the outcome of the Greco-Turkish issues. Just as Greece and Cyprus were of great importance to Ecevit, Turkey and Cyprus were at the forefront of the reconstructed junta's concerns during its eight months in office.[41]

The Ioannides regime developed a rigid attitude toward Makarios and the mounting Turkish announcements regarding claims in the Aegean, Ioannides, with the aid of officers who had served in Cyprus, covertly organized the Cyprus Bureau at the Greek Pentagon in order to deal effectively with Cyprus. One of the tasks was to prepare EOKA-B to play the secondary role in a coup launched by the Greek contingent and the Cypriot National Guard. Diplomatically, Makarios began "leaking" information on the regime's intentions in an attempt to preempt Greek action through diplomatic pressure. Problems for the military junta were compounded when Archbishop Makarios's publicly blamed of the Greek government for renewed outbreaks of violence on April 7, 1974. Furthermore, shortly thereafter Makarios revoked the amnesty offered to Grivas' followers, outlawed EOKA-B, and insisted on personally selecting the officers of the National Guard, Ioannides, cognizant that his political position was being jeopardized by a host of domestic problems, knew Makarios's threatening actions would secure his demise. An obsession with the retention of power cast light on all of Ioannides' subsequent decisions. Both Ecevit and Ioannides, keenly aware of their precarious positions, strove to make decisions that would win the support of their communities and secure their roles as leaders, Ioannides perceived Makarios as

[41] Theodoracopulos, *The Greek Upheaval* 58. Ecevit gained popularity and secured his position as prime minister in the 1977 general elections for his role in the Cypriot invasion. See Evriviades, 'The Problem of Cyprus," *Current History* 41.

the obstacle to his plans for enosis who needed to be eliminated, rather than realizing the Turks posed the greatest danger.[42]

The events of the weekend of July 6–7, 1974, convinced Ioannides once and for all to go forward with his plan to overthrow the Archbishop. Upon receiving an official letter from Makarios on the evening of the July 6, President Gizikis (the newly selected president of the 1973 Ioannides regime) immediately notified Ioannides of its contents. Makarios not only accused the Athens government of plotting to overthrow him by inciting a revolution, but of assassination attempts as well. Because he stated unconditionally that "[t]he roots of the evil is very deep, reaching as far as Athens," Makarios demanded that the Greek officers of the Cypriot National Guard be recalled to Greece. Makarios maintained that "[t]he Greek government has been following a policy calculated to abolish the Cyprus state." He concluded the letter by expressing, in no uncertain terms, his aversion for the nondemocratic Greek junta.[43]

Outraged by the provocative letter, Ioannides, "[c]ursed the 'treacherous priest,' called him a communist at heart, 'who would sacrifice Cyprus to the Turks in order to keep absolute power for himself.'"[44] Feeling humiliated, Ioannides called for immediate action but was persuaded by Gizikis to postpone a meeting of the chiefs of staff until the following Monday. But on Sunday morning, July 7, Cypriot newspapers published the Archbishop's letter, and even though the censored press in Athens carried no news of the letter, word traveled fast to the Greek mainland. Because Makarios, as evidenced through public statements in addition to his letter, stood as an obstacle to enosis, the Greek regime set its Akritas Plan, to assassinate Makarios, in motion. Even though Turkish ships had been seen embarking troops and equipment in the south coast ports of

---

42 See Evriviades, "The Problem of Cyprus," *Current History* 21; Denktash, *The Cyprus Triangle* 64; and Woodhouse, *The Rise and Fall of the Greek Colonels* 150.

43 Denktash, *The Cyprus Triangle* 123 and 125.

44 Theodoracopulos, *The Greek Upheaval* 27.

Turkey, Ioannides's serene demeanor indicated he was confident they were only holding exercises and displays of their military strength, and there would be no violent Turkish reaction.[45]

Makarios made a serious error of judgment in that he was convinced that Ioannides would not attempt to eliminate him because the Turks would be the beneficiaries.[46] He also underestimated the intentions of Washington by focusing solely the "practical" side of American policy which tolerated him and Cypriot independence. He never anticipated to be overthrown because of the United States influence over Greece, nor did he expect that the United States would allow a Turkish invasion given their track record in 1964 and 1967.[47] Even though Makarios was sure Ioannides would not act so foolishly as to jeopardize the Greek Cypriots on the island, he made contingency plans for any eventuality. Makarios was aware that the Athens-Nicosia relationship was crumbling because of his association with the Communist bloc countries and his recent crackdown on pro-enosis elements.

Although Grivas had died by this time, he was replaced as leader of EOKA-B by Colonel George Karousos, a former officer in the Greek army. However, because Karousos realized the futility of terrorist activity and the serious consequences of a Turkish military intervention should conflicts degenerate into civil war, Brigadier Ioannides forced Karousos to leave the island. It might be argued that Grivas' death left Makarios in sole control of the political future of the Greek Cypriots, thus liberating them to show greater flexibility and make further concessions to the Turks in the intercommunal talks. However, in light of increasing terrorist activity within the Greek Cypriot community and in the relationship between Cyprus and Greece, Makarios and his government were caught

---

45 See Denktash, *The Cyprus Triangle* 180; and Woodhouse, *The Rise and Fall of the Greek Colonels* 156.

46 Woodhouse, *The Rise and Fall of the Greek Colonels* 151.

47 Coufoudakis, "United States Foreign Policy and the Cyprus Question," *Cyprus Reviewed* 129.

in the midst of a painful dilemma. On the one hand, constitutional agreement and political settlement were more urgent than ever before. On the other hand, Makarios and some of his chief supporters realized a final solution with the Turkish side, which would unavoidably entail exclusion of enosis, would be beset with serious dangers. Namely, efforts instigated in Athens to remove Makarios would provide Turkey with the opportunity to invade. Consequently, Makarios chose to play a waiting game with hopes that the Greek junta would fall, American policy would turn in support of the intercommunal talks, or terrorist activity on the island would be eliminated.

In addition, Makarios sensed that Ioannides' regime was floundering because of a dramatic decline in popularity on both the domestic and international fronts.[48] Makarios felt that the benefits to be reaped from dispatching the fateful letter were immeasurable and the possible damages were negligible because "[i]f Ioannides backed down and withdrew the Greek officers from Cyprus, Makarios would have eliminated the most powerful pro-union element from his realm. If Ioannides refused, or tried something foolish, his plan was to call on the superpowers for support, knowing full well that Athens would have trouble finding any great power to back her cause."[49] After sending his letter, Makarios alerted his proletarian guard and the secret police to be prepared for any eventuality. Makarios was so certain of his own security, he departed for his annual summer holiday in his chalet in the Troodos Mountains. The oddest thing about this highly publicized conspiracy was that both Ioannides and Makarios were calm and displayed the utmost confidence. But the peaceful attitude of both Makarios and Ioannides was due to fatal errors of judgment: Makarios miscalculated what Ioannides was liable to do, and Ioannides misjudged the Turks.[50]

---

48 The Ioannides regime fell from power shortly after the unsuccessful coup.
49 Theodoracopulos, *The Greek Upheaval* 29.
50 Woodhouse, *The Rise and Fall of the Greek Colonels* 153.

In July 1974, the National Guard staged a coup against Makarios's government under the direction of Greek army officers. President Makarios escaped assassination and sought refuge in London. Nikos Sampson, an EOKA-B gunman with a record of violence against Turkish Cypriots and dedicated to enosis, replaced Makarios.[51] Turkish officials viewed Sampson, the new president of Cyprus, as a threat to the Turkish Cypriot community. Greece denied any involvement in the coup by referring to it as an "internal affair" of Cyprus, but offered to withdraw her officers from the island. Realizing cooperation with the new Sampson government or the unstable and uncooperative Greek regime was unattainable, the Prime Minister of Turkey, Bulent Ecevit, flew to England and informed British officials that the Turkish government had exhausted every effort short of war before invading Cyprus. Upon arrival, Ecevit informed British officials:

We have appealed to the government of Great Britain for joint action. We haven't made a similar appeal to the third guarantor of power, the Greek government, because we regard, as so many people in the world do, the Greek government as the instigator of the intervention against the independent state of Cyprus. We hope that we will achieve results in these talks with our friends and allies, the British, which will contribute to the establishment of peace.[52]

Unable to reach a peaceful settlement, Turkey invaded Cyprus on July 20, 1974, using the July 15, 1974, coup as an alibi for invading and assuming the role of guarantor of the

---

[51] See Parker T. Hart, *The Two Nato Allies at the Threshold of War* (Durham: Duke University Press, 1990) 130–31. For an account of the effect Ioannides' regime had on the Cypriot dispute, see *Woodhouse, The Rise and Fall of the Greek Colonels* 142–60; and Theodoracopulos, *The Greek Upheaval* 26–55. Also, for an analysis of the repercussions of Grivas's death see Clerides, *Cyprus* vol. 3, 286–335.

[52] Evriviades, "The Problem of Cyprus," *Current History* 39. The following statement made by Prime Minister Ecevit was recorded on *The History of Modern Greece*, by George P. Kontakos, Greek Video Records and Tapes Inc., 1988.

island's independence. Just as the Greek government implemented their Akritas Plan during the coup and failed assassination attempt, so too did the Turkish government execute their Attila Plan. "Attila is quite a common first name in Turkey . . . The code name 'Attila' was given at one stage to the Turkish army's move on Cyprus." Through the success of the Attila Plan, Turkey partitioned the island and established itself as the protector of their Turkish Cypriot counterparts.[53]

Deeply deploring the violence and bloodshed, and gravely concerned about its serious threat to international peace, the Security Council called upon the three guarantors to immediately enter negotiations in Geneva to restore peace among the rivals and constitutional government in Cyprus. Unfortunately, the Geneva conference was doomed to fail from the start. Not only had it been preceded by war, but no prior preparations aimed at narrowing rival differences had been attempted. Foremost in importance, however, was the fact that the Turks were already enjoying superiority on the island and were not receptive to any agreement unless it reflected the political and strategic advantage which they held as a consequence of their invasion.[54]

After the breakdown of the Geneva conference, the Turks launched their second and final attack on Cyprus, during which time the Mucahit force effected the de facto partition of Cyprus, thus "redeeming" the Turkish Cypriots. The Islamization process was initiated as soon as the Turkish army began to occupy Northern Cyprus. One of the first manifestations of the process was the army's conversion of the Church of Panagia Glykiotissa

---

[53] Christopher Hitchens, *Hostage to History: Cyprus from the Ottomans to Kissinger* (New York: The Noonday Press, 1989) 119.

[54] The American administration had just undergone the unsettling effects of the Watergate Scandal and was either unable or unwilling to act decisively, and the British foreign secretary was not strong enough to affect events. See Polyviou, *Cyprus* 185. For a detailed analysis regarding the two phases of the Turkish invasion and the Geneva Conference see Polyviou, *Cyprus* 154–202; and Clerides, *Cyprus*, vol. 4, 17–85.

(Church of the Virgin Mary, Healer of Pain) in Kyrenia into a mosque so that invading troops could pray upon landing at a nearby beach. The conversion of the Church of Panagia Glykiotissa symbolized a Turkish victory over the *gavurlar*, or the Christian Greek "unbelievers," and signified the commencement of the Islamization process which followed throughout the newly occupied territory.[55]

Turkification became intertwined with the Islamization process as the Greek names of localities—villages, towns, cities, and districts—were replaced by Turkish names. The cultural transformation of occupied Cyprus was accompanied by the Unilateral Declaration of Independence which established the "Turkish Republic of Northern Cyprus" (TRNC) in 1983. To the Turks, this "state" was formulated because the Turkish Cypriots desired to exercise their "inalienable right to self-determination." According to Turkey, the "official" name of the occupied area or "state" is Kuzey Kibris Turk Cumhuriyeti (Turkish Republic of Northern Cyprus).[56]

The Turkification of the region necessarily included the eradication of all evidence of the history and culture of the Greek Cypriots who had previously inhabited the area. Greek monuments and symbols were replaced with those symbolizing the Turkish culture, and villages were transformed into Muslim communities with the transfer of settlers from Turkey to the empty Greek towns. Turkification occurred in the economic realm as well, since the model of development and the economic policy of TRNC fell under the jurisdiction of the Turkish government. The total economic dependence of the TRNC on Turkey, Turkey's cultural absorption of the region, and the political consolidation of Turkish Cypriots and Turkish colonizers acted to transform Northern Cyprus into a de facto

---

55 Since 1974, more than 59 Christian Orthodox Churches in occupied Cyprus have been converted into mosques, a greater number than anywhere in the Islamic world in recent history. See Ioannides, *In Turkey's Image* 178–79.

56 Ioannides, *In Turkey's Image* 84.

province of Turkey. From the Turkish view point, this process irreversible, while to the Greeks it is incomprehensible.[57]

IV. UNDERSTANDING THE CONFLICT

Years of conflict between Greece and Turkey, each striving to strengthen its position in the Mediterranean and to extend its nationalistic ideology transnationally to Cyprus, culminated in the 1974 Cypriot Crisis. Cyprus has always held strategic regional importance, particularly for Turkey. From Turkey's perspective, Cyprus sits in an ideal position for controlling its Mediterranean ports; therefore, if Cyprus were to pass into Greece's hands, Turkey would be left vulnerable, particularly in the event of war. While Greece has no strategic interest in Cyprus, it shares with Turkey an interest in and a responsibility for the community of its coethnics on the island. The Cypriot problem is fundamentally one of communal frustrations of two distinct populations, intensified by the island's geographic proximity to Turkey and Greece, and by ethnic pride and national obligation for Greece and Turkey. As such, Cyprus became trapped between the historic rivalry of the two motherlands rather than by mere ethnic diversity.[58]

In an attempt to fulfill their similar yet antagonistic goals, each rival promoted its cause and implemented plans for the union of Cyprus with its respective homeland by way of its own cultural institutions. Tension mounted as these ethnic groups opted to pursue union. It has been argued that the Greek regime's chief preoccupation was how to preserve itself in power when it sensed obstacles to its control of events, which were believed to emanate from Cyprus as a place which had a predominantly Greek population.[59] Finally, an unstable Greek regime staged a coup in 1974 to retain its position of power, even though Greece was incapable of countering an imminent Turkish attack. Turkey invaded

---

57 Ioannides, *In Turkey's Image* 165, 177, 179, 184, 186, and 188.

58 Harry J. Psomiades, 'The United States and the Mediterranean Triangle: Greece, Turkey, and Cyprus," *Cyprus Reviewed* 203–05.

59 Interview with Marios Evriviades, Press and Information Officer, Nicosia, June 23, 1992.

Cyprus using the coup as its pretext and ultimately implemented its goal of taksim, while forcing Greece to abandon enosis.

Why did the United Kingdom, the United States, and the Soviet Union fail to intervene on behalf of Cyprus? Because the new arrangements were unacceptable to Britain and the United States, these nations opted to abandon their responsibilities as mediators. The 1974 constitutional proposals might have introduced a Soviet presence in the Mediterranean, strategically located near the Suez Canal. Hence, American and British policy makers had no incentive to protect Cyprus's ability to enact the 1974 document. (See appendix 2, table 8.)

TABLE 8:
COLD WAR IMPLICATIONS FOR AMERICAN AND BRITISH DECISION MAKERS

PRESENCE OF SOVIET ALLIANCE TO GREECE AND/OR TURKEY	ABSENCE OF SOVIET THREAT	
	YES	NO
YES		
NO	CYPRUS'S 1960 CONSTITUTION	CYPRUS'S 1974 CONSTITUTION

Table 8 outlines the situation facing American and British decision makers, whose foremost concern was the Cold War. It is clear that many world powers anticipated the events in Cyprus, yet did nothing to prevent the destruction of the united Cyprus. Ironically, Cyprus was spared the kind of intervention that might have maintained its independence because it was not a Cold War issue.

Because Greece and Turkey were both NATO allies, Cyprus was stable as long as it was controlled by them. A sovereign Cyprus could have been a threat to Western interests because it could have chosen to ally with the Soviet Union. The 1974 constitutional arrangements negotiated between the two Cypriot communities were a threat for two reasons: first, because an independent Cyprus could ally with Russia; and second, because Makarios had made overtures and there was some evidence that he might choose the Soviet Union as the single guarantor power designated under the 1974 constitutional proposals.

Throughout Cyprus's history, she has played a valuable role not only to Turkey and Greece, but for the Western powers as well. The island served as a central point in Britain's military position from the time of its acquisition in 1878 until well after World War II. Even after Cyprus gained its independence, Britain retained two key base areas: one at Dhekelia and another at Akrotiri. By incorporating the interests of the British, Greeks, and Turks into the structure of the Constitution, namely the Treaty of Guarantee, the Guarantor powers were provided with a perfect means of destroying the emerging republic.

The eruption of intercommunal violence in 1963 marked a pattern of internationalization of Cypriot ethnic disputes. Greece, Turkey, and Britain were the first external powers to intervene, provided for by the Treaty of Guarantee. The former two intervened in order to protect their respective communities, while the latter strove to restore peace and protect its interests on the island. As hostilities mounted, Britain found herself incapable of restoring peace and reconciling the opposing ethnic factions, which set the stage for superpower participation. The ethnic conflict became entangled in Cold War rivalry as the United States stepped in to replace Britain and the Soviet Union intervened to counteract Western interference. Although Britain had a legal right and moral obligation to intervene in the 1974 Cypriot Crisis, she refrained from doing so because of the policy consideration that a divided Cyprus was more beneficial to Britain.[60]

As with Britain, the United States and the Soviet Union have been drawn into the affairs of Cyprus, principally because of the island's potential effect on their strategic concerns in Greece and

[60] John Zarocostas, "Cyprus," Mohammed Ayoob ed., *Conflict and Intervention in the Third World* (London: Croom Helm) 108 and 126.

Turkey. Cyprus is strategically important because of its location at the crossroads of three continents and the chief routes that link the West to the East. Because of its close proximity with the region, Cyprus can also serve as a base for extensive land, sea, and air operations in the Middle East.

In addition to its strategic location, the foreign policy implications that the Cypriot ethnic conflict could have on the parties involved were major concerns for the two superpowers. Repeated outbreaks and threats of the ethnic conflict escalating into a Greco-Turkish war made the island a symbol of Western disunity and a challenge to Western security rather than a locale of defense. Greco-Turkish friction and the risk of an armed intra-alliance war had a destabilizing effect on NATO in that it undermined the operational utility of NATO's southeastern flank, an obvious threat to the United States' position but a definite advantage to the Soviet Union.

As the United States stepped in on behalf of Great Britain to safeguard the interests of the West, its objectives became the prevention of an escalated crisis, preclusion of both United Nations and Soviet Union involvement, and a permanent peaceful solution of the Cypriot dilemma within a Western setting protecting Western strategic interests. Its proposed solution, the Acheson Plan, safeguarded United States interests in the region, provided Greece with its long-desired enosis with Cyprus, and offered adequate guarantees for Turkish political rights and strategic concerns. The Acheson Plan fulfilled the requests of all parties concerned, except one: the Republic of Cyprus would have to sacrifice its independent status. Naturally, Makarios could not embrace such a provision. Greece's rejection of partition, however, was an obstacle to the American objectives in Cyprus which could be readily satisfied through Cypriot dismemberment.[61]

The Soviet Union, on the other hand, saw the conflict as an opportunity for an extension of its influence. Therefore, Soviet intervention took the form of diplomatic and military support for the Cypriot government, which countered American goals and tactics.

---

[61] Douglas Brinkley, *Dean Acheson: The Cold War Years 1953–71* (New Haven: Yale University Press, 1992) 215.

Since superpower involvement transformed the conflict into a Cold War dispute, another dimension was added to the issue to further complicate existing local and regional ethnic controversies. The result was the merging and amplification of ethnic and ideological antagonism, which aggravated resolution attempts.

The two superpowers were again challenged to intervene in the short but intense 1967 Cypriot Crisis. The United States hastily intervened to prevent a catastrophic war and disruption within NATO. Although American negotiators found the "Castro of the Mediterranean," as Makarios was known in Washington, unreceptive and nonconciliatory to Western proposals, they successfully resolved the crisis by exercising pressure on the Greek military junta and satisfying most of the Turkish demands.[62] By this time, it was clear that the United States was unable to impose a settlement on Cyprus. Consequently, the two Cypriot communities began negotiations for an internal solution. Greco-Turkish efforts received the conditional blessings of the United States as long as their actions did not create a threat of Soviet involvement in Cyprus. Consequently, while peace emerged from the Crisis, the basic ethno-political aspects of the conflict were overshadowed and remained unresolved as a result of the strategic and ideological goals of the Cold War rivals.[63]

The Cold War strategic principles which had directed United States and Soviet policies toward Cyprus during the crisis of the 1960s again came into play in 1974. The primary United States goal remained the NATO-ization of Cyprus, while the Soviet objective was maintenance of a nonaligned Cyprus with a pro-Soviet government. In the middle of these two conflicting policies stood Makarios, who pursued a policy aimed at establishing Greek Cypriot dominance within an independent, unitary, and nonaligned Cyprus.

The delicate balance of power on Cyprus was upset when the Greek junta staged a bloody coup against Archbishop Makarios. The Soviet Union lost its leverage on the island when Makarios fled the

---

62 Joseph, *Cyprus* 134.

63 Coufoudakis, "United States Foreign Policy and the Cyprus Question," *Cyprus Reviewed* 123 and 125.

country. Turkish troops wasted no time in descending upon Cyprus under the pretext of securing the safety of their Turkish community. Throughout the intense sessions of the Security Council which convened from July 16 to August 15, 1974, the Soviet delegate repeatedly blamed the Greek junta, the United States, and "certain NATO circles" for attempting to liquidate the Cypriot state in order to convert the island into a military base.[64] Not one word was directed toward Turkey regarding its invasive role. The sharp contrast in Soviet attitude toward Turkey between 1964 and 1974 was attributed to an impressive improvement in Soviet-Turkish political and economic relations, largely the product of deteriorating United States–Turkish relations which began in 1964 as a result of the Cypriot situation. Because the ultimate Soviet Union goal was severance of Turkey from NATO, the delegate said and did nothing to offend Turkey when its army advanced on Cyprus.

The United States attitude was also conducive to Turkish invasion of Cyprus. Although Washington expressed concern over the possibility of a destructive Greco-Turkish war, it did nothing to avert the coup or the invasion because its objective, to limit Makarios's political action capability, was already obtained as Turkish troops now occupied 40 percent of the island. Because United States influence on Turkey was limited at this time, and it was believed that any forceful military intervention would foster Soviet-Turkish relations, the United States maintained a policy of tolerance toward Turkey. Both Washington and Moscow interpreted Turkey's behavior as a tactic to preserve or extend influence over that strategic country. Consequently, superpower rivalry over Turkey created attitudes and conditions very different from those of 1963–64 and 1967 that encouraged Turkey to invade Cyprus and determine the outcome of the 1974 conflict.

While an independent, united Cyprus did not threaten the strategic position of the superpowers, the geographic interdependence of Greece and Turkey has been recognized as a critical geopolitical factor from ancient times to the present. The Cold War superpow-

---

[64] Joseph, *Cyprus* 146.

ers realized the defense of Greece and the Greek islands would be affected greatly by the defense of Turkey and vice versa. If either Greece or Turkey was to opt for a nonaligned policy, or worse yet, alignment with the Communist camps, the security of the other would be severely compromised. Greece without Turkey, or Turkey without Greece, could lead only to irreparable damage to NATO's southeastern flank, if not total destruction. In addition, because the United States quest for a stable international order was under severe attack by the 1973 Arab-Israeli War, the prospects of a reopened Suez Canal, factors such as strong Soviet involvement in the Eastern Mediterranean, and the need to protect oil shipping routes and guarantee energy supplies increased Cyprus's strategic value. American security interests in this critical region and concerns with "unreliable third world regimes" intensified after 1973. Thus, a divided Cyprus and a severely restricted Makarios regime ameliorated United States interests.[65]

V. CONCLUSION: HOPES FOR A UNITED CYPRIOT STATE

In sum, the problem of Cyprus is fundamentally one of the communal frustrations of two distinct populations, intensified by the island's geographic proximity to Turkey and Greece, and by ethnic pride and national obligations to Greece and Turkey. Cyprus became trapped between the historic rivalry of the two homelands rather than by mere ethnic diversity. Furthermore, years of conflict between Greece and Turkey, each country striving to transnationally extend its nationalistic ideology to Cyprus, culminated in the 1974 Crisis and the developments thereafter. Each rival promoted its cause and

[65] See Psomiades, "The United States and the Mediterranean Triangle," *Cyprus Reviewed* 200–03; and Coufoudakis, "The United States Foreign Policy and the Cyprus Question," *Cyprus Reviewed* 130–31. For an analysis for international involvement in the Cypriot Crisis, see *The New York Times*. July 18 and 20, 1974; and Laurence Stern, *The Wrong Horse; The Politics of Intervention and the Failure of American Diplomacy* (New York: The New York Times Books, 1977).

implemented its plans for the union of Cyprus through its own cultural institutions. Great Britain, United States, and Soviet Union, who were drawn into the affairs of Cyprus principally because of the island's potential effect on their strategic concerns in Greece and Turkey, did not prevent the crisis situation. Thus, the interactive effects of these factors culminated in the Cypriot developments.

Although the island was partitioned, neither Greece nor Turkey was successful at fulfilling their nationalistic aspirations. The Cyprus question remains unresolved to this day. Even two decades later, a solution to the Cypriot dilemma has not yet been found. The arduous search for a viable and durable political and constitutional settlement has only struck obstacles. Efforts to compromise on differences and thus break the deadlock have been met without success. Are the Cypriot people forever condemned to live in segregated regions of the island, fortified by armed barriers?

Some feel that there is still time to raze these barriers and build a common society. In order to draw closer to a more united state and a more cohesive society, particular attention must be given to two factors. First, the constitution must be reconstructed so that community interdependence and future interaction, without the loss of essential security, are maximized. Federal arrangements should be flexible and workable, and should contain all possible guarantees and safeguards of individual and communal rights. Secondly, nothing less than a social revolution is needed, particularly in attitudes and habits. The Cypriot people must be reeducated to develop a public conscience and a sense of public responsibility. In so doing, the two communities can accept each other as partners and cohabitants rather than as grudging and unwelcome neighbors. Generally, a transformation in attitude and habit can occur only through a laborious process of effort and failure, mistake and correction, frustration and reattempt. The Cypriot people, through some fault of their own and through the operation of forces beyond their control, have at one time or another met with all the above.[66]

---

[66] Polyviou, *Cyprus* 234–37.

Do the Cypriots now possess the good sense and maturity, derived from tragedy and now required for the survival of Cyprus, to reverse the legacy of the past? The central irony of the Cyprus case is that Cypriot nationalism was sacrificed on the altars of enosis and taksim. Nationalism is a zero-sum concept. The ethnic identities of Greek and Turkish Cypriots thwarted their identities as Cypriots. It is evident that nationalism is a powerful force, possessing the ability to aid in overturning a country, yet it is also limited—one cannot create it overnight. Nationalism is a cultural link between the state and the individual. Group-based citizenship is inherently less stable than individual citizenship. Consociationalism is an unstable form of government because it promotes group citizenship. Cyprus was the weakest kind of consociationalism government because foreign countries were given power in its decision- making. But what could the 1960 Constitution writers do but acknowledge the realities of the time? A document does not erase cultural institutions any more than it erects them. Sadly, however, as Cyprus lies bare on the pages of history, there is no question that her fate does not rest in her own hands. She has been tossed and turned by Greece and Turkey because of their cultural ties with the island's inhabitants over the course of her existence.

Still today, Cyprus lies vulnerable to the mother countries, who each remain loyal "unyieldingly, inflexibly, uncompromisingly" to the oaths of the respective forefathers. For Greece, the cry is for "enosis and only enosis," while "partition or death" is hailed by the Turks. Cyprus will never be relinquished from the hands of the enemy without a sacrifice of life and blood. Therefore, the dispute between Greece and Turkey over Cyprus to this day wages on.

CHAPTER 5

UNDERSTANDING POLITICAL IDENTITY AND IDENTITY CONFLICT: AN OVERVIEW OF NATIONALISM IN THE CASES OF NORTHERN IRELAND, PALESTINE, LEBANON, AND BOSNIA-HERZEGOVINA

> ONCE UPON A TIME all the world spoke a single language . . . . 'Let us build ourselves a city and a tower with its top in the heavens, and make a name for ourselves; or we shall be dispersed all over the earth.' Then the LORD came down to see the city and tower which mortal men had built, and he said, 'Here they are, one people with a single language, and now they have started to do this; henceforward nothing they have a mind to do will be beyond their reach. Come, let us go down there and confuse their speech, so that they will not understand what they say to one another.' So the LORD dispersed them from there all over the earth, and they left off building the city. That is why it is called Babel, because the LORD there made a babble of the language of all the world; from that place the LORD scattered men all over the face of the earth.
>
> —Genesis 11:1–10

I. INTRODUCTION: LANGUAGE AND POLITICAL IDENTITY

Society has suffered from the curse of "a babble of the language" from the earliest of times. There have been relentless efforts to counter the disruptive plague of multilingualism and return to a common means of communication, but such efforts have been unsuccessful.[1] This curse, exemplified on the island of Cyprus, has frustrated the establishment of a unifying political identity. Has citizenry been defined according to identity in Northern Ireland, Palestine, Lebanon, and Bosnia-Herzegovina, or do they, like Cyprus, suffer from the malady of disunity? Would the use of an indigenous official language assist in the establishment and preservation of a united identity in these cases? It has been argued that a state is composed of its citizens who are defined by self-understanding or identity to a greater degree, and self-interest to a lesser degree. Because a state's legitimacy is contingent upon its success in serving its bounded citizenry, an indigenous official language for multilingual states must be selected and practiced.

Despite the ease with which the state has come to be identified as the product of its citizenship, a fundamental definition of the nature of citizenship has not received similar universal acceptance. In spite of its contested identity, citizenship is considered a powerful instrument and an object of social closure from both an internal and external perspective. States claim to be of and for their citizens, and a state's legitimacy is contingent upon its success in advancing the interests of its bounded citizenry. Judgments as to what is in the best interest of the state or the citizenry are influenced by cultural idioms—ways of thinking and speaking about nationhood. Cultural idioms are not simply impartial agents for the expression of preexisting interests, but the fabrication of interests and expressions for effectuating self-understanding. Therefore, "[t]he politics of citizen-

[1] *The New English BIBLE WITH APOCRYPHA* (Oxford: University Press, 1970) 11.

ship . . . is a politics of identity, not a politics of interest."[2] As a "politics of identity," citizenship concentrates on the individuals that compose it in order to achieve a level of understanding, as opposed to the effectuation of self-interest. The "interests" are not asserted from a material perspective, but are "ideal." The central question underlying the politics of citizenship is not "who gets what?" but "who is what?"[3]

Upon defining its citizenry, a state must choose and implement an official language with which to govern and unite its citizens. The problem of selecting an indigenous official language for multilingual states is one of coordination, and the mechanisms for reaching a solution are difficult to find. The most prevalent solution is based on simple market conditions of language coordination across space and time without state-enforced legislation, but this solution is problematic because it lacks efficiency. At the same time, it has been found that state-induced coordination of a national language is difficult to achieve.

The "3±1" ("three-plus-or-minus-one") formula is a linguistic strategy that permits the institutionalization of an indigenous national language without yielding to language rationalization. The model proposes that a national language, one of neutrality, would be used for purposes of education, business, and political administration, while the chief vernacular would be employed for official interstate communication and popular culture such as film, music, and television. In addition, each district would promote its own district language for instruction in primary education and administration. As dialects of a district, they could still be spoken on the personal level. Although the 3±1 language outcome is not a definitive solution to a state's curse of multilingualism, it is an example of how coordination problems can be overcome.[4]

---

2 Rogers Brubaker, *Citizenship and Nationhood in France and Germany* (Cambridge: Harvard University Press, 1992) 182.

3 Brubaker, *Citizenship and Nationhood* 182.

4 David D. Laitin, "The Tower of Babel as a Coordination Game: Political Linguistics in Ghana," *American Political Science Review* vol. 88, no. 3 (September 1994) 622–23 and 630–32.

A state, in and of itself, is the product of its citizens and exists solely to serve its citizens. In fact, a state's very subsistence is contingent upon its ability to represent and promote the interests of its citizenry, which are influenced by the cultural vernacular. Language is the means by which traditionally held interests are expressed, but it has the additional capacity to fabricate interests. Because citizenship is delineated by self-understanding and identity, as disclosed through communication, an indigenous official language for multilingual states is crucial. The coordination problems of such an enterprise may be solved by implementing the 3±1 formula as a linguistic strategy. But irrespective of the linguistic strategy a state selects to implement, the institutionalization of a unifying language is critical for state survival. Cyprus, unable to institutionalize a common language and therefore propagate a political identity, was ripped in two. Whether the fusion of these two conditions—citizenship defined by identity and the constitutionalization of a unifying language—are sufficient to create stability will be determined upon applying them to the cases of Northern Ireland, Palestine, Lebanon, and Bosnia-Herzegovina.

II. AN EXAMINATION OF NATIONALISM AND LACK OF NATIONAL IDENTITY IN THE CASES OF NORTHERN IRELAND, PALESTINE, LEBANON, AND BOSNIA-HERZEGOVINA

Civilizations have been at odds with one another from the beginning of time, and despite hundreds of years of study, scholars have yet to determine the causes and solutions of disputes and wars. Whether a dispute is among people from the oldest of civilizations, as is the case in Palestine, or a dispute originates during the more modern period, as with Northern Ireland, consistent strands can be seen running through each struggle.

One such similarity between the regions of Northern Ireland, Palestine, Lebanon, and Bosnia-Herzegovina is that they were all subjects of colonial rule for some period of time. Throughout the duration of their subjugated status, not one of these regions successfully established a national identity, but instead they broke free from the shackles of colonialism by clinging to their cultural roots. As a consequence, the identities of these peoples became rigidly entrenched. Such identities between ethnically related communities became unbreakable. Those that found themselves cohabitating in a heterogeneous environment would, with the encouragement of and possibly even initiation from the homeland, struggle for dominance. Others, certain they held rights to their ancestral soil, returned to recover their territory. Whichever was the case, conflicts erupted and instability resulted. Let us now take a close look at the contrasts and commonalities of each case.

A. Nationalism and Lack of National Identity in the Case of Northern Ireland

Ireland, in many respects, was the forerunner of anticolonialism in the British Empire. Dissatisfied with its politically, socially, and economically subordinate status, particularly after the passage of the 1800 Act of Union, Irish, campaigns which sought to replace the existing government with an indigenous one, began to surface. Of the multitude that emerged, Sinn Fein (Ourselves Alone) quickly took center stage as it advanced its cause through the mobilization of popular action. Even though it encountered resistance from the British-directed Ulster volunteers, Sinn Fein, in conjunction with its militant arm the IRA, won independence from Ireland but sacrificed Ulster in the process. Despite its long-awaited freedom, the island continues to be plagued with unrest to this very day as the struggle for Ulster persists. (See appendix 3, table 1.)

Appendix 3

TABLE 1: TRANSNATIONAL NATIONALISM-CULTURE AS A VARIABLE IN INTERNATIONAL RELATIONS AND DOMESTIC POLITICS-IN THE CASE OF NORTHERN IRELAND

PURPOSE OF TRANSNATIONAL NATIONALISM	TYPE OF TRANSNATIONAL NATIONALISM	
	IRISH NATIONALISM	BRITISH LOYALISM
LEGITIMATION FOR INTERVENTION	IRELAND	BRITAIN
LEGITIMATION FOR REUNIFICATION	SINN FEIN I.R.A.	ULSTER PROTESTANTS

Table 1 displays the outcome in Northern Ireland of the cultural maintenance guaranteed under the Act of Union. Irish and British leaders maintained a serious approach regarding their responsibilities to their compatriots. Both ethnic groups in Northern Ireland believed in union with their homelands. The Catholics and Protestants in Northern Ireland, as well as Catholics and Protestants in Ireland and Britain, accepted an Irish nationalistic ideology to pursue union, and a British loyalist ideology to sever the region. Irish Catholics and British Protestants held themselves responsible for protecting and maintaining the culture of their comrades in Northern Ireland.

Ireland has often been considered England's first colony, a byproduct of the great power status she developed in the early modern period. Because England itself was politically unstable in the early Tudor period, Henry VII and Henry VIII hoped to control Ireland as easily and inexpensively as possible. The Irish and their land were to be kept more or less intact and converted to a colonial possession—constitutionally and jurisdictionally at first, and gradually to a cultural colony as well. Both the great Irish landlords and the lesser lords would attend parliament and participate in the administration of the crown's judicial machinery. The plan was never implemented, however. In the 1540s a program of "surrender and regrant" was launched to induce Irish lords to pay homage to the English king, accept an English title, and substitute English land and inheritance laws for their native traditions in return for the regranting of surrendered lands to the nobles. A problem arose when the "loyal English" in Ireland strenuously opposed the cooptation of Catholic elites in this manner.

By the middle of the sixteenth century, in the wake of Henry VIII's severance with Rome and the Anglicanization of the Tudor state, a new type of English settler began to exercise significant influence in the administration of the "Irish lordship." The Protestant fervor of these new settlers, and the ease with which they could effect change to existing land titles, threatened the Catholic aristocracy. The influence and significance of the new Protestant interest in Ireland was reflected in the harshness with which Elizabeth I's officials crushed rebellions in the 1580s and 1590s, the punishment inflicted upon the dissenters, and the unprecedented large plantation policies undertaken during this period.

Crowned as king after the death of Elizabeth I in 1603, James I initiated a policy of reconciliation with the Catholics of Ireland by granting full pardons to the leaders of the Irish rebellions and postponing the implementation of various plantation projects. With the spread of the Reformation at this time, religion added to the existing barriers of geography and culture that divided the two countries. Therefore, the Tudor monarchy soon became committed to a policy of full military conquest. A royal commission for the plantation of

Ulster was established in 1608 to implement the seizure of much of the lands of the great Catholic families. James I hoped to implement the settlement of Ulster in a manner which would generate royal revenue, protect native rights, and benefit the majority enough to outweigh the displeasure of the smaller number of Catholic elites. Such may have been the theory behind the Stuart plantation of Ulster, but in practice, early-seventeenth-century settlement efforts led to extensive expropriations of native land, aggressive segregationist policies toward Catholics, and intense hostility toward English rule.

The plantation under James I neither solved the "Irish problem" by reducing the country to loyal obedience, nor substantially contribute to the king's treasury. When Charles I ascended to the throne in 1625, his government found the state of affairs in Ireland unsatisfactory. Charles I, therefore, offered twenty-six concessions to protect the rights and lands of Catholics in Ireland in return for financial and military assistance in the struggle against Catholic Spain and Catholic France. Objections condemning the royal proposal of toleration for Irish Catholicism brought the proposal to a halt. In 1629 England signed a peace treaty with France, and a year and a half later England signed a treaty with Spain. For the remaining ten years of Stuart rule of Ireland that preceded the outbreak of the civil war, a government that dealt with the Catholics tolerantly prevailed.

During the civil war in Britain, the Gaelic Irish were accompanied by the Catholic elites and rose against the new English settlers, only to be subjugated. In order to establish permanent control, Britain implemented the Cromwellian plantation solution. This entailed retributive laws mandating death for half of all Irish Catholic males, sweeping confiscations of Catholic land, forced emigration, and transplantation of Catholics to Ireland's barren Western province. The effects of the Cromwellian conquest and land settlement were drastic and long-term. The Catholic leadership was annihilated and the Protestant community was firmly established.

The Protestant community held its ascendant position nearly unhindered for the next two hundred years by implementing a rigorous system of "penal laws" and voting restrictions against Catholics. Because of the weakness of the Catholic majority of Ireland in the eighteenth century, politics were dominated by British exploitation and Irish Protestant opposition to British economic policies. Issues like central government efforts to consolidate its rule, settler efforts to suppress natives, or native struggles for autonomy never made it to the agenda.[5]

During the previous century and a half of Catholic struggle to disassemble the system of religious repression, Irish nationalism was born. Even though Ireland's troubled relationship with England was initially political in nature, the social and economic effects of British policy actually provided the mainspring for its successful appeal of nationalism. By the close of the eighteenth century, the political, economic, and social trend of events led Ireland sharply downhill. However, real problems began when William Pitt set the Irish policy of the British government on yet another course with the passage of the Act of Union in 1800. Ireland's population began to grow until the repeated failure of the potato crop, its staple food source. By the mid-1800s the British government was forced to alter Irish policy because of Ireland's economic collapse. It did so by legislating the transfer of bankrupt estates to a new class of "capitalist" landowners who were harsher than the previous owners.[6]

Although Ireland was too economically depressed in 1848 to effectively respond to the wave of revolutionary fervor which was sweeping Europe, a new nationalist movement, the Fenian Brotherhood or "IRB," began to revive the concept of the Irish Republic that was inherent in the very existence of the Irish people. From 1858 to 1916, the doctrinaires of the IRB promoted this ideology and finally achieved their ideal in the proclamation of a republic during Easter week of 1916.

Parallel to the theoretical renunciation of the Act of Union was the development of practical campaigns which sought to dispose of the existing government and provide a representative substitute. Sinn

---

5 Ian Lustick, *State-Building Failure in British Ireland & French Algeria*_(Berkeley: The Regents of the University of California, 1985) 17–38.

6 E. Rumpf and A. C. Hepburn, *Nationalism and Socialism in Twentieth-Century Ireland* (New York: Barnes & Noble Books, 1977) 1–3.

Fein was organized by Arthur Griffith in 1905 as one such campaign. The campaign not only assumed the illegality of "British rule" since the Act of Union was illegal, but also promoted the development of indigenous government organs to provide the order that was imposed at that time by an alien and illegitimate power. Clearly, much of the history of Irish discontent and resistance is rooted in notions and stratagems which defied the Act of Union.

The Act of Union was an act of miscalculation, born of dread of French invasion, revolution, social levelling, and fears of what a frightened peasantry or angry ruling class might attempt in terror. The act appeared to be an appeasing solution. To the British government it promised to resolve the question of national defense and to furnish a solution to the Irish question. Incorporation, or at least containment within a single kingdom, appeared to be more practicable than outright subjection. To the Protestant "nation" in Ireland, the act promised an end to the bloodshed. Moreover, the Protestants were sure that concessions to Catholics were inevitable in light of the current movement toward civil equality. Therefore, the safest environment within which political participation could be granted would be one with enforceable restraints. To the Irish Catholics, the act promised a prime objective—political and civil emancipation.

The provisions of the Act of Union similarly involved miscalculation. The British believed that by providing the Irish with 100 seats in an assembly of 650, she would be rendered impotent while simultaneously assenting to Irish authority. With the development of a British party system, however, even a small organized independent group could exercise influence disproportionate to its numbers. Parliament proved an effective medium for announcing that the majority of its decisions ran counter to Irish assent. It is questionable whether the financial provision of the act, which charged Ireland with two-seventeenths of the national expenditure, represented a reasonable obligation. But the expense of containing Irish discontent stemming from their economic ruin due to the establishment of a free trade area was certainly unforeseen.

While the miscalculations in the act were serious, abandonment and breach of the implied understandings which produced its passage was even more invidious. The decay of the Union's underlying promises constitutes the majority of nineteenth-century Irish history. For the "Protestant nation," the first provision of the contract governed the continued control of local government and the public service, higher education and the professions, land ownership, and the instruments of order. The second provision governed the preservation of the privileges, both honorary and material, of the established church. Even though the third provision initially seemed self-evident, it was only when the others crumbled that direct British authority on the island became a matter of life and death to the Protestant nation. Over the years, the political Union grew in significance, until in the final forty years between 1880–1920, the critical conflict centered on this final provisions.[7]

The hundred years from 1815 to 1914 was a period of slow disintegration of the Unionist position, as a new type of public servant and public service began to emerge. Administration was gradually divorced from politics and the concept of the neutral state began to take root in the Irish system. The growth of this concept was assisted, especially after 1830, by changes in the structure and spirit of English politics. Anglican power weakened little by little as the Test and Corporation Acts were repealed in 1828, the lower-middle-class electorate was enlarged in 1832, the local government took on a greater secular character by the Poor Law Amendment Act of 1834, and by the Municipal Reform Act of 1835. Advances in civil equality accompanied these changes and hastened the pace of "economical reform" while, at the same time, led to infraction of the act's provisions.

The weakest sector of the Protestant front was that which was directly dependent upon religious discrimination; therefore, it was only to be expected that the first losses would be suffered in this realm. The earliest and greatest loss was the Catholic Emancipation Act of 1829, followed by the Irish Poor Law of 1838 and the Irish Municipal Reform Act of 1840. Apart from these Catholic advances,

[7] Oliver MacDonagh, *Ireland: The Union and Its Aftermath* (London: George Allen & Unwin Ltd., 1977) 13–29.

Protestant influence gradually receded as its prominence waned. Political alterations both fed and were fed by the shift in concepts. The national elementary education system of 1831 was theoretically supradenominational, and secular power ruthlessly reordered the ecclesiastical economy; thus, the way was being prepared for disestablishment. The Church of Ireland lost forever its formal preeminence and status as the Crown representative. Once the religious warranty disappeared in 1869, the social and economic provisions were sabotaged by the Irish Land Act of 1870. Even though the act failed to weaken the actual power of the proprietors, it symbolized a defeat for the traditional concept of land ownership as being both absolute and free from tenant obligations.

At the same time, it was decided that British agriculture would not be protected from foreign competition during the failed harvest of 1877–79. The conservative government ignored not only the British, but also the Irish farmers who provided the power for the civil disobedience of 1879–82 and the uniting of the Irish party into a single effective weapon. The government also undermined the morale of the Irish landowners who experienced ruin following the 1885–86 failure which compelled them to finally accept the Land Act of 1881 that introduced a degree of coownership in the landlord-tenant relationship.

The last decades of the nineteenth century marked the beginning of the end of economic privilege and the near monopoly of landed wealth which had been forever guaranteed by the Act of Union. Along with the disintegration of the Union's provisions came the creation of a powerful Home Rule Party in 1880, which finally destroyed any prospects of reconciliation among the Irish protagonists from this time forth. Catholic Ireland's entrance to parliament became contingent upon rejection of the Union and active involvement in the persistent struggle for its overthrow.[8]

The first truly dangerous assault upon the Union itself was Charles Parnell's Liberal Alliance Strategy, that also constituted the basis of the anti-Parnellite Party from 1891 to 1900. Certain

[8] MacDonagh, *Ireland* 33–52.

Nationalists, chief among them the anti-Parnellite John Dillon, continued to claim that Home Rule could be achieved only through a liberal government and opposition to all Unionist reforms regardless of their short-term advantages.

While the formal political objectives and party organization of Parnellism covered nationalist Ireland for twenty-five years, movements either beneath or outside the umbrella of Parnellism began to emerge and expressed other often antagonistic aims. The most significant of all the new movements was Sinn Fein because it offered a complete political strategy. Sinn Fein stood for the removal of all Irish members from Westminster and their reconstitution in Ireland as a native parliament, as well as the new Irish body's assumption of executive powers so that the native "state" might secure international recognition. Sinn Fein's goal was to mobilize popular action in the native system in order to sanction the new structure and to fool British power. Even though Sinn Fein differed radically from revolutionary republicanism in that it neither sought a republic nor was violent, militaristic activity returned to Ireland with the formation of the British-led Ulster volunteers. This provided an opening for once again turning Irish nationalism toward more violent courses. For the first time in over forty years, the Irish advocates of violence had a genuine chance to capture, or at least significantly influence, the mass movement of Irish nationalism.[9]

For a quarter of a century economic and principally agrarian grievances provided the force behind the parliamentary movement for independence and the nationalists; this was the Irish nation's loss. Even though the opponents of conciliation had become uncomfortable with the trend toward agreement since the Local Government Act of 1898, it was the successful Land Conference of 1902 that caused them serious concern. Landlord and tenant representatives proposed a plan for establishing proprietorship on the basis of state loans to cover the difference between the selling and offering price which the Unionist government accepted. Open resistance developed within the Nationalist Party and ultimately created a standing

---

9 MacDonagh, *Ireland* 53–71.

deadlock despite British efforts to reopen the negotiations. The last of these conciliatory efforts, the Irish Convention of 1917–18, also proved ineffective. At the convention, the Nationalists (Sinn Fein) stood for genuine and immediate autonomy in internal matters and for the withdrawal of ail Irish members from Westminster while the Ulster intransigents refused to move from the existing Union. Meanwhile, the Southern Unionist representatives simultaneously tried to pursue both positions.

Although dualism might have been possible in 1908, by 1918 the main body of Irish sentiment had settled on principles of self-determination, separation, and abhorrence of the British connection. Thus, the notion of conciliation faded. At the close of 1917 a junction of the two forces, Sinn Fein and the extremists for revolutionary republicanism, created a single national front under de Valera with two effective arms, military and political. By boycotting the Irish Convention of 1917, the national front advanced in the public image after securing two-thirds of the Irish seats in the 1918 general election. By 1919 Irish volunteers had begun sporadic guerrilla attacks upon Crown forces without Sinn Fein's approval. The principal goal of the attacks was to win international recognition for the new state at the Peace Conference of Versailles. When recognition was withheld and the 1920 Government of Ireland Act became law, it was understood that a new course was necessary since full independence and sovereignty were undeniably unattainable.

By mid-1921, Sinn Fein recognized that the Irish Republican Army (IRA) had no prospect of military success, but chose to hold out until a negotiating position was safeguarded. A truce was called on July 11, 1921, and peace negotiations were set for October 11, 1921, in London. The treaty negotiations involved four main areas of conflict: fiscal and economic autonomy, executive and military autonomy, constitutional autonomy, and lastly, Ulster. On the first two issues the Irish delegates were symbolically, if not materially, successful. On the third issue, the Irish delegates secured an oath that established the primary "allegiance" to the new Irish State, and secondarily "fidelity" to the British government. The last major issue, Ulster, proved to be the least malleable and the most confusing.

Mishandling of the issue on the part of the Irish resulted in a partition with a Boundary Commission Clause that neglected to insure neutral international adjudication and instructions for the transference of territory.[10]

In Ireland, independence was achieved through a single party, which soon after broke into two parts. Attempts to recreate party unity failed because a third force emerged, the republican wing of the army, and because non–Sinn Fein candidates for election were surprisingly successful. The final blow to the prospect of unity came within ten days of the 1922 election when the republican forces incited armed conflict in Dublin and the civil war erupted. Meanwhile, de Valera began the involved process of disentangling himself from violent forces and reconstituting himself as a parliamentarian while he strove to reestablish himself as president. By the end of 1924 de Valera was managing a successful retreat from his former unsupported position. De Valera broke from the IRA in November 1925 when the IRA altered its position to one in support of restoration of Irish unity by force of arms. After 1932, the IRA began sinking in popular estimation as its image changed from one of a powerful body of armed idealists to a divided body whose only common ideal appeared to be an unattainable political dream and an ineradicable belief in violence. In June 1936, the IRA was proscribed as an illegal body; its officials were imprisoned and its public assemblies concluded altogether. Despite its unrecognized status, the early 1950s witnessed a marked revival in IRA activities.[11]

Over the course of the last forty years, the IRA has consistently made advances in the achievement of its "ethos" as "one Ireland and an all-Ireland arrangement."[12] Its latest victory was celebrated this year when the United States lifted its ban on official contacts with Sinn Fein and permitted the organization to hold its first fundraiser in the Woodside section of Queens, New York. Prior to this con-

---

[10] MacDonagh, *Ireland* 72–101; and Rumpf and Hepburn, *Nationalism and Socialism* 28–68 and 164–218.

[11] MacDonagh, *Ireland* 102–21; and Rumpf and Hupburn, *Nationalism and Socialism* 28–68 and 164–218.

[12] *The New York Times*, February 23, 1995.

cession, IRA supporters in the United States had made their contributions through Noraid, an organization which tunneled cash to the IRA. Furthermore, in recent months the prime ministers from Britain and Ireland submitted proposals upon which negotiations regarding the future of Northern Ireland may rest.[13]

What is at the heart of this protracted argument? Is the surrender of a strategic defense center the concern for Great Britain? It does not appear so, because even the most extreme republicans in Ireland have been prepared to accommodate Britain on this issue. Does Britain fear that the Irish, being incapable of governing themselves, may become an unstable neighbor? Again, this fear is groundless because if anything, Ireland's fault has been to reproduce itself too faithfully as a model of England. Could Great Britain's concern for free trade within the British Isles and fiscal control of the region be the core of the problem? Once again, there would appear to be no foundation for such anxiety because, although the Irish would in theory have the right to pursue an independent economic course, they would suffer first and foremost in the event of such a decision. Although these and other issues have bearing on the circumstances, the cultural elements the two communities of Ulster share with their respective homelands provide them with an identity that will not permit them to forsake their cultural roots for a new national identity.

B. Nationalism and Lack of National Identity in the Case of Palestine

The land of Palestine gave birth to what is now one of the most ancient of all civilizations. Over the course of history, a unique culture developed and the Palestinian people cultivated a highly developed national consciousness. One of the greatest ironies of history is that as Palestinian society was dismantled and dispersed during the mid-twentieth century, the historic fact of Palestine's prior existence as an entity and the Palestinians as a people was questioned

13 *The New York Times*, February 23, 1995; and *The New York Times*, March 13, 1995.

and represented as an apparition of improbable authenticity. In order to displace the moral issue of transforming another entity's homeland into Eretz Yisrael and to establish an aura of legal justification around Zionist attitudes and goals, the dehumanizing image of the Palestinians emerged and was propagated. Since the dismemberment of Palestine, the Palestinian people have sought to establish an authority capable of voicing the inherent national rights of their people. The Palestine Liberation Organization (PLO) accepted the challenge of mobilizing Palestinians to liberate Palestine despite the nearly insurmountable obstacles it faced.[14] (See appendix 3, table 2.)

TABLE 2:
TRANSNATIONAL NATIONALISM-CULTURE AS A VARIABLE IN INTERNATIONAL RELATIONS AND DOMESTIC POLITICS—IN THE CASE OF PALESTINE

PURPOSE OF TRANSNATIONAL NATIONALISM	TYPE OF TRANSNATIONAL NATIONALISM	
	PALESTINIAN HOME	ISRAELI CONTROL
LEGITIMATION FOR INTERVENTION	ARAB WORLD	ISRAEL
LEGITIMATION FOR REUNIFICATION	P.L.O./ HAMAS	WEST BANK SETTLERS

Table 2 illustrates the effects of cultural saliency in Palestine. By denouncing Palestinian claims to the land as well as the very existence

14 Edward_W. Said, Ibrahim Abu-Lughod,_et al., "A Profile_of the Palestinian People," in Edward_W. Said and Christopher Hitchens eds., *Blaming the Victims: Spurious Scholarship and the Palestinian Question* (London: Verso, 1989) 235–57.

of the Palestinians as a people, Zionists reclaimed Ertz Yisrael under the Balfour Declaration. Despite international recognition of Israel, the Palestinian people have collectively preserved a national will, and with the support of the Arab world have been granted access to their ancestral homeland. Israeli Zionists, supported by their Jewish counterparts outside Israel, struggle even today to maintain their dominant position, while the Arab world corroborates with the Palestinian community and they strive to coexist peacefully.

Designated as present-day Israel, the land encompasses a significant portion of what was once regarded as Palestine. Three thousand years ago the Jews labeled the territory Eretz Israel, "Land of Israel," and themselves, "Bnei Israel," the people or tribe of Israel. At approximately the same time the Philistines, a people of Greek origin, settled in the coastal plains of the area and referred to the land as Filastin or Palestine. The distinctiveness of Israel lies in the monotheistic belief that Yahweh is the one God of the universe, while most other cultures of that day were polytheistic and the people believed in multiple gods.

Jewish political and military unity emerged under Saul, the first king of Israel, in response to a Philistine challenge. Upon defeating the Philistines, the Jewish army established Jerusalem as a religious sanctuary. Despite a less-than-stable empire, Jewish independence endured until the region, known briefly as Judea, was incorporated into the Roman Empire as an autonomous unit by 63 BC. Shortly thereafter, due to numerous rebellions incited by the Jewish population, Palestine/Judea lost its autonomous status and became a Roman colony known as Syria Palestina. With the birth of Jesus and spread of Christianity came the newly acquired importance of Palestine, Jesus's birthplace.[15]

The balance of power that had existed in the region for over two millennia was shattered in AD 632–633. with the Arab invasion and their new religion of Islam. Those who profess faith in Allah

[15] Charles D. Smith, *Palestine and the Arab-Israeli Conflict* 2nd edition (New York: St. Martin's Press, 1992) 1–5.

as the only God are called Muslims, described as "those who submit."[16] Because the Muslims consider Islam the perfect culmination of the Jewish and Christian traditions, both of which fail to adhere to the commands of Allah but nevertheless are in the lineage of Islam, Muslims claim to be superior to Jews and Christians. Under the Islamic tenets, non-Muslims were permitted to practice their religious beliefs, but were commanded to maintain a humble status through mandatory compliance with discriminatory practices such as clothing and additional tax stipulations.

For a time, Palestine fell under the domain of those who controlled Egypt, the Sunni Muslims followed by the Shii Fatimid dynasty, until the crusades took Jerusalem in 1099 and reestablished Christian control. Within less than a century Palestine was recaptured by the Mumluks, a Muslim military elite, and then conquered by the Ottoman Turks in 1516–1517. Palestine resumed its Muslim character over the course of the nearly four-hundred-year period of Ottoman rule, even though Ottoman Jews advanced and prospered, in part because of their economic contributions and contact with foreigners who were granted trading privileges with the empire. Treaties that ultimately weakened Ottoman sovereignty accompanied European commercial expansion during the eighteenth and nineteenth centuries, the major actors being Great Britain, France, and Russia.[17]

The progressive decline of Ottoman power in the nineteenth century weakened the stability of Muslim society, particularly Muslim-Christian relations that underwent change as a result of European interference and Ottoman response to such intrusion. In an effort to internally strengthen Ottoman power and counter external threats, the tanzimat, or reordering of society, was implemented. Tanzimat commenced with granting equal rights to all Ottoman subjects, Christians and Jews included, as initially proclaimed in the Hatti Sharif and subsequently in the Hatti Humayun. The reformation of land laws to regularize the structure of land ownership and

[16] Smith, *Palestine* 7.

[17] Smith, *Palestine* 5–15.

its use was one method of reducing separatist tendencies and thus stabilizing the empire. Additionally, foreigners were granted the right to own land in exchange for an agreement to pay land taxes, which facilitated extensive outside investment. Some of the first people to find Palestinian land attractive were notables of the land, followed by Christian, Lebanese, and European merchants, representing a major transformation of Palestine landholding patterns during the late 1860s.[18]

Paralleling the revisionary efforts of the Ottoman Empire during the latter half of the nineteenth century were strides toward legal and social equality in Europe. Despite these advances, latent hostility toward Jews periodically surfaced. While Jewish equality with non-Jews was declared in Western Europe at this time, portions of Eastern Europe, particularly Russia and Poland, experienced heightened anti-Semitic prejudice. In the midst of prejudicial mistreatment, the wish to establish an independent Jewish existence in Palestine began to grow and lay the foundation of the modern Zionist movement. As the number of Russian Jewry expanded significantly with the partition of Poland, new laws which restricted Jewish residence to only designated areas formed the Pale of Settlement. Although these laws were not always strictly enforced, they reflected an official attitude of suspicion and hostility that led to a tax on Jewish communities, the catalyst for some Jews to seek refuge in Palestine.

Those that envisaged a Jewish state in Palestine founded on the principles of Jewish labor and agriculture became known as BILU. Although BILU met with meager success, it left a lasting impression on later Zionists, including Theodor Herzl whose efforts produced the World Zionist Organization in 1897. To assist in the fulfillment of its goal of "[t]he creation of a home for the Jewish people in Palestine to be secured by public law," the organization created its own Bank in 1899. In 1901 the Jewish National Fund was established for the express purpose of land purchase and development in

[18] Odeh, *Lebanon* 173-86; Smith, *Palestine* 248-51; and Cleveland, *A History of the Modern Middle East* 348.

Palestine for Jewish settlement.[19] A substantial wave of immigrants came to Palestine between 1904 and 1914, increasing the number of resident Jews to approximately 85,000. Among these immigrants was David Ben-Gurion, who later became Israel's first prime minister. By 1914 and the outbreak of World War I, Arab Palestinian suspicion and disapproval of Zionist goals flourished, and Zionist officials in Palestine were cognizant of Arab fears.[20]

Prior to the war, European stability was contingent upon the maintenance of Ottoman territory, and yet future harmony relied on the equitable parceling of Turkish-controlled land in accordance with nineteenth century diplomatic traditions. To advance its strategic interests, however, Britain defied diplomatic criteria, which radically transformed the future of the Middle East, including Palestine. For the first two years of the war, Palestine was of little strategic interest to Britain except that it stood as a potential buffer zone between French-held territory in Syria and Lebanon, and British-controlled Egypt. Palestine and Zionism became increasingly more attractive by the beginning of 1917 when Russia appeared as though it might withdraw from the war, permitting the Germans to concentrate all of their forces against France and Britain.

In an effort to retain Russia's war efforts and gain additional American assistance via the encouragement of their respective Jewish populations, the British aligned themselves with Zionism. Obtaining Jewish support for its interests was not only a means of furthering Britain's immediate wartime needs, but of guarding the Suez Canal, which ensured Britain's long-range imperial goals. These factors, in addition to a concern for the fate of European Jewry, led to the Balfour Declaration of November 2, 1917, which promised a national home for the Jews in Palestine. At the close of the war, the League of Nations decided and confirmed that the French would hold mandatory rights in Syria and Lebanon, as would the British in Palestine and Iraq. Britain was additionally bound by the obligation to establish conditions in Palestine to assist the immigrating Jewish

---

19 Smith, *Palestine* 30.

20 Smith, *Palestine* 27–36.

population in its path toward ultimate dominance as stipulated in the Balfour Declaration.[21]

The Palestine land that the British set foot upon in December 1917 was significantly different from what had existed in 1914. Immediate steps were taken to provide food and medical supplies to the needy and to restore social and economic stability to the region. In the midst of these efforts, British officials confronted Arab hostility toward Zionism that was motivated by the Balfour Declaration and the presumptuous attitudes of the Jews in Palestine who believed the establishment of a Jewish state was imminent.

Shortly after the Zionist commission was formed in 1918 for the purpose of representing Zionist interests, it requested that the Hebrew language be granted equal status with Arabic and that Jewish representation in government equal that of Arab representation. Compliance on the part of British officials fanned the flames of animosity. The sparks did not begin to fly, however, until a new wave of over 10,000 Jewish immigrants, predominately young and enthusiastic socialists, arrived during 1919 and 1920, followed by another large group in 1921. In order to quell the disturbances, the British government issued a White Paper stating that Britain did "[n]ot contemplate that Palestine as a whole should be converted into a Jewish National Home, but that such a home should be founded in Palestine."[22] Appeased by the British declaration and a sharp decrease in Jewish immigration during the mid-1920s, Arab leaders turned inward to broaden their influence against one another.

Even though both communities in Palestine served the British with divided loyalties, their primary allegiance was to the retention or attainment of their respective nationalist existences, which rested on the issue of land. For the Palestinian Arab community, especially its 90 percent Muslim component, land was the heart of its subsistence because it was an agrarian society. For the Jews in Palestine, land possession was essential to the establishment of the future Jewish state. Due to changes in land laws and the escalation of indebtedness,

---

[21] Smith, *Palestine* 38–65.

[22] Smith, *Palestine* 73.

which was endemic but worsened after the war because of Palestine's destruction, many Arab peasants were forced to transfer their land titles in order to avoid conscription and tax assessments. Zionist organizations like the Jewish National Fund and the American Zion Commonwealth purchased large land areas, thus fueling Zionist optimism. In response, riots erupted in 1936 as fears mounted that because of Jewish immigration and land purchases, the Arab population would be deprived of its livelihood and subjected to Jewish economic domination.

Equally important to the increase in overt Arab resistance was the emergence of several secret societies that advocated more open defiance to British authority. In 1937, Britain's Peel Commission introduced resolution proposals to partition Palestine into separate independent Arab and Jewish states, but the Arabs immediately rejected the proposals. The ensuing tensions led to a more violent stage of the Arab revolt which lasted from September 1937 to January 1939.

British attempts to resolve the crisis in Palestine throughout the 1936–1939 period of the Arab revolt occurred against a backdrop of increasing tensions in Europe and the Mediterranean, which had tremendous impact on Britain's Palestine policy. The British chose to reinstate a slightly amended white paper that placed restrictions on Jewish immigration and land transfers. As was the case with the Balfour Declaration of 1917, the White Paper of 1939 was an act of expediency motivated by strategic concerns related to war efforts. Because Palestine was a crucial link in Britain's system of imperial air defense and communications, a reversal in Palestine's policy served Britain's immediate war-time and possibly long-range imperial designs in Palestine, despite the fact that it outraged Zionists and dissatisfied the Arabs.[23]

The impact of World War II on Palestine and the future of Zionism was far- reaching. In 1941 Adolf Hitler began exterminating people, principally European Jews, designated as "inferior" by the cult and its ideology of Aryan supremacy. To the Jews in Palestine

23 Smith, *Palestine* 68–108.

and elsewhere, particularly the United States, Palestine was the most appropriate location for housing war refugees because of the steps which had already been taken there to establish a Jewish state. To that regard, a cabinet committee on Palestine was established in 1943 that recommended the partition of the region; however, partition was never officially approved. In 1946 the British proposed provincial autonomy in Palestine with Arab and Jewish areas specifically demarcated, and Negev and Jerusalem under British trusteeship. This plan, too, met with opposition. By the end of the war, Zionism and the fate of the remaining European Jewry had become intertwined with United States interests, creating dissension within Britain over post-war policies.

Already confronted with Zionist terrorism in Palestine aimed at driving them out, the burden became too great for the British, who handed the matter over to the United Nations in 1947. The United Nations Special Committee on Palestine (UNSCOP) was formed and charged with the task of investigating conditions that resulted in the call for partition. To the jubilation of the Jews, on May 14, 1948, the state of Israel was proclaimed to exist within the borders awarded it by the UNSCOP partition plan.

Anticipating such an outcome, Arab Palestinians prepared and launched various plans for mobilization. Even though there had been major structural changes in Arab Palestine between 1939 and 1945, they were no match for the highly trained, organized, and committed Jewish forces. By the end of 1948, not only had Israeli forces taken over much of West Galilee, which was designated as Arab land according to the partition plan, but they had incorporated into Israel the Negev and the eastern shore of the Gulf of Agaba as well.[24]

The era that followed the signing of the armistice agreements between Israel and the Arab states was neither one of war nor peace, but rather one of belligerence. The cardinal issue prohibiting official Arab or international recognition of the status quo was the question of the Palestinian Arab refugees. Each side insisted that the other take a

---

[24] Odeh, *Lebanon* 173-86; Smith, *Palestine* 248-51; and Cleveland, *A History of the Modern Middle East 348.*

preliminary step before a peace talk would be considered, but neither side would fulfill the prerequisite. Arbitrarily drawn armistice lines encouraged border clashes and hostile incidents, particularly along the Jordanian line as Israeli retaliation forces organized Palestinian infiltration and attacks. Although relations along Egypt's border were relatively mild until 1955, Egypt's refusal to permit the passage of Israeli ships through the Suez Canal prompted Israel to embark on a campaign to seek additional weapons. Hostilities were aggravated as Western powers entered security pacts with Arab countries to ensure opposition to Soviet overtures in the Middle East. Although neither rival's ambitions suited Western strategic interests, Egypt's decision to nationalize the Suez Canal set in motion a series of events that led to a coordinated Israeli-French-British attack on Egypt.[25]

The decade between 1957 and 1967 was characterized predominately by inter- Arab rivalries that pivoted on the personality and influence of Egypt's Gamal Abd al- Nasser. Nasser sought to preserve his status as leader of the Arab world as rivals began challenging his vast political influence. From 1964 onward, Nasser's principal antagonists were Syrian rulers who sought to establish themselves as the true representatives of the Arab nationalist cause by exploiting Palestinian grievances against Israel. This new Arab commitment to liberate Palestine became the objective of the PLO, which held its inaugural conference in May 1964. When Nasser outmaneuvered the PLO's initial demands for militant action at the Cairo Summit of July 1964, a smaller Palestinian organization, al-Fatah, began preparations to undertake operations into Israel.

Unlike most of the factions that identified with the current trend, Palestinian liberation could only occur with Arab unity. The leaders of Fatah advocated the argument that militancy and militant action were the predecessors to politics, and by mid-1965 Arab-lsraeli hostilities, dormant for a season, intensified once again because of Fatah's militant activities. As 1966 drew to a close, the Arab political world remained as fragmented as it previously had been. In an attempt to restrain Syria and reassert his prominence, Nasser employed anti-Is-

---

[25] Smith, *Palestine* 111-47 and 151-74.

raeli tactics that were acknowledged by American and Israeli leaders. The United States appeared willing to permit Nasser to peacefully restore the dilemma through a face-saving compromise, but the Israelis were not as amenable. Israel was determined to define new territorial boundaries, while the Arab governments strove to restore the pre-1967 borders. Consequently, the Israelis seized the opportunity to obliterate the Egyptian forces amassed in the Sinai. As for Fatah, it emerged as an independent force in Arab politics.[26]

Diplomatic proceedings were seriously hampered by governmental and organizational factionalism between 1967 and 1975. The Arab heads of state and the Israelis held dissenting views regarding peace terms, and the PLO opposed all efforts to achieve peace because it feared that its political objectives would be disregarded. Despite the resistance Fatah encountered as the movement became increasingly fragmented by the end of 1969, its militant activity increased on both the Jordanian and Lebanese borders of Israel. At the same time, because Israel decided to try to destroy Nasser, vast numbers of Soviet personnel infiltrated Egypt, neutralizing the environment along the Suez Canal. The United States pressed for a cease-fire which was achieved in August 1970. The cease-fire was an obstacle to their Palestinian agenda. They made an unsuccessful attempt to destroy the cease-fire by overthrowing Jordan's King Hussein, forcing the PLO to withdraw from Jordan and relocate in Lebanon.

Regional developments were beneficial for Israel in the short run. Upon Nasser's death in September 1970, Anwar al-Sadat assumed the office of president. Sadat attempted to involve the United States with the hope of regaining territory in return for some form of peace. However, an American response never materialized. With the outbreak of the 1973 War, the United States reversed its position by forcing talks between Egypt and Israel. These negotiations and later discussions with Syria yielded the 1974–75 agreements to disengage Egyptian forces both in the Golan Heights and the Sinai.

Political events ushered in new phases of power in the United States and Israel in early 1977. Jimmy Carter was elected president

---

[26] Smith, *Palestine* 177–200.

of the United States in January, and Menachem Begin became Israel's prime minister in June. At the same time, the PLO sought participatory status in a Geneva conference and thus involvement in international diplomacy. Within the same time frame, outbreaks of unrest besieged Egypt, the result of economic instability. Sadat hoped that by addressing and resolving the Palestinian question, he might stabilize his country, his own political position, and his relations with the United States.

Administrative officials, including Carter's advisors, also acknowledged the need to resolve the Palestinian problem and therefore agreed to convene. During the period of diplomacy that culminated in Camp David, major developments took place on the West Bank and in Lebanon. On the West Bank, settlement projects in violation of commitments to the Carter administration multiplied, while struggles among Palestinian groups were on the rise in Lebanon. As the fate of these two regions became increasingly intertwined, particularly in regard to Israel's vital interests, Begin's willingness to concede to an agreement with Sadat heightened, culminating in the Camp David Accords. In turn, these agreements provoked the PLO and induced Israel to once again invade Lebanon in order to secure a stable border.[27]

With the withdrawal of American forces and Israeli troops from Lebanon in 1984, the hostile situation in the region seemed little changed. Despite the intensification of diplomatic bargaining among various Israeli-Arab leaders over the course of the following years, an agreement could not be reached because of a mutual denial of the agreement's inhumane political terms. During these years, a war ended and a resolution began in the Middle East that yielded new tensions in the region and tested the new relationships formed at the end of the Cold War and the introduction of the post–Cold War period. The revolution was the Palestinian Intifada that broke out in Gaza in December 1987 and incited an uprising against Israeli domination in the occupied territories. The uprising breathed new life into the PLO and encouraged it to declare an independent state

---

[27] Smith, *Palestine* 204–73.

of Palestine and recognize the existence of Israel in the later months of 1988. As a result, the United States acknowledged the change in PLO direction and agreed to a dialogue with the organization through its newly established embassy in Tunis.

In June 1990, United States President George Bush suspended the United States-PLO talks following an abortive Palestinian raid on Israel. The interruption of the dialogue followed a period of heightened violence in the occupied regions and the United States veto of a Security Council resolution requesting an investigation of the treatment of Palestinians under Israeli subjugation. With these developments came increasing desperation for the PLO because of unsuccessful America-initiated negotiations with Israel regarding the territories and because of the consequences of Soviet glasnost, Moscow's decision to permit massive Soviet Jewish emigration. The territories were proclaimed as necessary for the accommodation of the thousands of new Jewish immigrants.

The war that ended on July 20, 1988, was between Iraq and Iran, with the former victorious despite few tangible gains. The Iraqi ruler, Saddam Hussein, found himself debt-ridden to those who had financed his war, particularly the oil-reach countries of the Persian Gulf; consequently, he was unable to rebuild his military and economy. Hussein also found his regional ambitions curtailed by his isolation within the Arab world.

With the onset of the post–Cold War era, Syria, Iraq's archrival in Arab affairs, sought access to the peace process by aligning itself with Egypt upon announcing its willingness to settle differences with Israel. Saudi Arabia and Jordan followed Syria's course of action shortly thereafter. Major decisions faced Palestinian and Israeli leaders, but Arafat was on record as supporting American peace efforts. It was not until September 13, 1993, that a breakthrough occurred in the century-old conflict between Arabs and Jews in Palestine with the signing of the Oslo Accord. Behind a thick veil of secrecy, unofficial talks in Oslo, Norway, between representatives of the PLO and the

Israeli position established the conceptual framework of the Israel/PLO accord.[28]

The Israel/PLO accord was comprised of two parts. The first was a mutual recognition of Jewish and Palestinian nationalism. Israel, represented by Prime Minister Rabin, not only acknowledged the Palestinians as a people with political rights, but also formally accepted the PLO as its representative. Likewise, Chairman Arafat confirmed the PLO's commitment to recognize Israel's legitimacy. The second part of the accord, the Declaration of Principles (DOP), set the framework for negotiation on Palestinian self-government in the occupied regions, commencing with Gaza and Jericho in the West Bank. Even though many considered the signing of the DOP and the implementation of the Gaza-Jericho phase to mark a new era in the history of the Middle East, Peres, the Foreign Minister of Israel asserted: "We have to overcome a great deal of difficulties, and we are trying to do our best. We are building a new history."[29]

Unfortunately, the difficulties the two communities are currently experiencing do not involve merely the logistics of internal implementation, but also external interference from patronized groups striving to impose their conflicting agendas. In Gaza on April 3, 1995, thousands of supporters of the militant Islamic group Hamas marched in a memorial procession for fellow Palestinians killed in a bomb blast that blew out a Hamas hideout. Although the marchers blamed Israel and the Palestinian authority for the explosion, the PLO police called the incident a Hamas accident. Israeli officials denied having any involvement in the explosion and commented they were aware of Arafat's attempts to reach an agreement with Hamas leaders to thwart Israeli attacks. In response to previous assaults, Israeli troops opted to retaliate through shootings to demonstrate they are cracking down on Arabs opposed to the Oslo Agreements.[30]

---

[28] Smith, *Palestine* 288–94 and 307–14.

[29] *The New York Times*, January 4, 1995; and Avi Shlaim, "The Oslo Accord," *Journal of Palestinian Studies* vol. XXIII, no. 3 (Spring 1994) 24–25 and 30.

[30] *The New York Times*, April 3 and 4, 1995.

Incidents of this nature not only exacerbate the already formidable task the leaders face, but jeopardize optimism as the leaders attempt to assert control. In the words of Arafat: '"Let no one think that they can scare us with their stronger weapons, for we have a mightier weapon—the weapon of faith, the weapon of martyrdom, the weapon of jihad [holy war or struggle]."[31] Unquestionably, an Israeli-Palestinian struggle wages on. The question remains: will the struggle be magnetic or repellant in nature, barring a harmonious coexistence or creating a zero-sum game?

Even though Zionist and Israeli leaders considered Palestinian national claims to be illegitimate over the last several decades for both ideological and practical purposes, the Palestinian people have collectively preserved a national will and formulated a sense of their future with the intent to establish an independent Palestinian state on their historical national soil. Rather than perpetuating the anomalies of displacement, dispossession, and exile, the Palestinian vision is predicated upon a democratic community. The Palestinians are aware that the road to peaceful coexistence, even under the best of circumstances, is an arduous undertaking. Obstacles regarding the selection of operational methods are inevitable and must be sidestepped through skillful and insightful maneuvering. Additionally, hope dwindles when insults to undermine stability are repeatedly hurled from culturally connected powers outside the region's sphere of influence, like the West Bank settlers and PLO/Hamas.

Therefore, although the Palestinian people are finally recognized once again as a people who share the attributes of nationhood—a common history, language, and set of cultural traditions derived from natal territory and cultural patrimony—serious issues remain unresolved. What are the prospects that two culturally diverse communities, each claiming the same land as the birthplace of their forefathers, can peacefully coexist?

---

[31] *The New York Times*, January 4, 1995.

C. Nationalism and Lack of National Identity in the Case of Lebanon

In the late 1960s, when the Palestinians assumed the task of liberating their homeland, there was naturally a rise in the prominence of Palestinian resistance groups. Even though the leaders of the Arab states expressed support for the Palestinian cause, they were hesitant to offer sanctuary to the guerrilla organizations because of the risks they posed. Yet, without a secure base from which to direct operations in Israel, the commando organizations would have no legitimacy. Therefore, Palestinian demands became a consideration in the domestic politics of all the Arab states, but particularly in the affairs of Lebanon, for it was selected as the organizational base. The 1970s marked the beginning of Lebanon's long civil war, which was waged primarily over issues internal to the country, but was also fought to determine the status the prominent new political force would hold within the country.

Palestinian organizations retained their autonomy in the aftermath of the civil war and continued to mount raids on Israel while building support among the residents of the West Bank. In response to these developments, the Begin government launched an attack on Lebanon in hopes of eliminating the PLO both as a military force there and as a political force in the occupied territories. The invasion successfully disposed of the PLO's military function, but it failed to terminate Palestinian political influence. Palestinian identity had become too deeply ingrained to be eradicated by brute force. Having achieved its principal goal of establishing a Palestinian consciousness, the resistance organizations proceeded to awaken the international community to the realization that the Arab-Israeli conflict was at its heart an issue between the state of Israel and the Palestinian people. Until the two adversaries could agree to negotiate their differences, there would be no advancement toward peace.[32] (See appendix 3, table 3.)

[32] William L. Cleveland, *A History of the Modern Middle East* (Boulder: Westview Press, 1994) 324–25 and 351–52.

TABLE 3:
TRANSNATIONAL NATIONALISM-CULTURE AS A VARIABLE IN INTERNATIONAL RELATIONS AND DOMESTIC POLITICS—IN THE CASE OF LEBANON

PURPOSE OF TRANSNATIONAL NATIONALISM	TYPE OF TRANSNATIONAL NATIONALISM	
	PAN-ARABISM	PAN-JUDAISM
LEGITIMATION FOR INTERVENTION	SYRIA	ISRAEL
LEGITIMATION FOR REUNIFICATION	P.L.O.	ZIONISTS

Table 3 shows the offspring of preserved cultural identities. Syrian and Israeli decision makers retained a rigid stand regarding their liability to the counterparts. Syria and the whole of the Arab world endorse PLO's claims to Palestine, while Zionist consciousness is shared by Israel. Both Syrians and Israelis feel obligated to defend and preserve the culture of their respective brothers.

The history of Lebanon has been an integral part of the historical development of Syria. In the ninth century when the Maronites, the displaced Christians from Syria to the north of Lebanon, a society evolved through an intricate interaction between the Maronites and the Druze, a religious offshoot of Islam living in the South. These communities integrated to establish a secular feudal order that matured and prospered within the emirate of Mount Lebanon. The feudal means of production, accompanied by their attendant political and social institutions, encouraged further integration of the two communities. The need for more agricultural land and production to increase landlord revenues not only promoted integration, but helped to create new independent and competitive social forces on the political scene. This development explains why landlords assigned to the Maronite Order of Monks a significant role in production and thus influence among the peasantry

As an organized social force that shared in the animosity toward the feudal system with the peasants, the clergy made a powerful force which the ruling emir capitalized on in order to consolidate his position against the feudal lords. As the Church sought to become a dominant or exclusive force in the emirate, it united with the emir and relied upon religion to alienate Druze and Maronite peasants from each other. For the most part, despite its influence on the peasants, the Church failed to convert the class conflict into a religious one because it had to betray peasant interests as it bid for its emirate.

Lebanon was affected not only by its domestic revisions, but also by external forces. From the time of the 1831 Egyptian conquest, Western impact upon society in Syria and Lebanon was formidable and extensive. This impact is credited for helping to create new class formations. Social, political, and economic developments marked the disintegration of feudalism as a political institution. The newly established classes grew to share power with the landlord class which retained its superlative position until independence. As the commercial class (Comprador bourgeoisie) increased its economic status, the feudal mode of production decreased because land as a source of wealth had lost its exclusive position.[33]

Measures such as disarmament, conscription, and a regular system of exaction that were undertaken by the Egyptian government to promote public security were not uniformly applied. Eager to win European good will, Christians enjoyed differential treatment and were exempt from many of the impositions levied on Muslims and Druze. The disparity between the religious groups had a lasting impact on Lebanese society.

By the end of the Egyptian affair, the growth of public security, reforms in the fiscal system, rationalization of land tenure, increase

---

[33] J. Odeh, *Lebanon: Dynamics of Conflict* (London: Zed Books Ltd., 1985) 228–38.

in foreign trade, movement of capital, and the broadening of village society, produced a change in the relative socioeconomic and political statuses of the various religious groups. The delicate balance that had held the society together was disrupted and civil crisis was imminent.

When the traditional Lebanese privilege of autonomy under hereditary rule became seriously challenged, the political history of Lebanon turned a corner. Growing Western superiority prompted the Ottomans to advance a new ideology of reform that was articulated in the edicts of 1839 and 1856. Departing from the traditional system, the Ottomans sought to introduce new institutions that would extend autocracy and centralization, thereby undermining all vestiges of local autonomy while promising religious equality. Altogether, the edicts of 1839 and 1856 generated disappointingly few reforms.[34]

French colonialism fostered the integration of Lebanon into the world capitalist system as it strengthened the growth of the comprador by dividing Syria, thus rendering it economically weak and dependent on foreign trade and commercial services. The socioeconomic alterations observed during this period did not evenly benefit all levels of the population. As previously discussed, the burgeoning urban middle class—mostly Christian merchants and agents for European traders—continued to prosper. The remainder of the society, primarily craftsmen, artisans, peasants and small traders, were adversely affected by the increasing dependence of the Lebanese economy on European production and trade. Even more damaging than the socioeconomic disparities, however, were the widening religious cleavages and confessional hostility. The two edicts, which advocated the principle of equality between Christians and Muslims, actually achieved just the opposite: a complete rift between the two chief groups which ultimately instigated the massacres of 1861. Lebanon was clearly in urgent need of swift and comprehensive measures to pacify, rehabilitate, and rebuild the fabric of its dismembered society.

---

[34] Samir Khalaf, *Lebanon's Predicament* (New York: Columbia University Press, 1987) 48–64.

Unquestionably, more than a mere restoration of order and tranquility was needed; political reorganization became imminent.[35]

The issue of independence created conflict within the dominant class because some fractions aligned with the French while others opted for independence. The victory of the forces was attributable to specific class alignments which established in 1943 the first regime, El-Khoury's. Among those that supported the fight for independence were the peasantry, workers, and petty bourgeoisie because they were already divided along confessional lines. At the dawn of independence both the landlord class and the comprador faction conformed to the Lebanese social formation. Despite the power held by the landlord class, the Lebanese state displayed a power bloc in which high finance was hegemonic. The Lebanese state additionally displayed another important feature characteristic of its historic development, that of confessionalism, which enabled it to resolve intra-power bloc conflict and disputes among factions of the dominant classes in the social formation. The Lebanese confessionalist state attended to the "common interests" of the dominant classes and offered polity cohesion.

Confessionalism as an institution helped to prevent conflict within the Lebanese power bloc where the comprador bourgeoisie, consisting mostly of Maronites, were hegemonic. The comprador, however, increasingly strove to improve its political and economic positions at the expense of the other power bloc components. During the period between 1943 to 1975, several hazardous situations emerged that threatened the life of the confessional arrangement. These incidents evidenced that the political system was incapable of accommodating the diverse interests of the dominant class, let alone those of the population at large. Consequently, in 1958 and again in 1975 the intra-power bloc hostility produced two civil wars.[36]

The confessional system allowed the dominant class in the social formation to establish policies contrary to the country's social and economic well-being, thus exacerbating Lebanon's economic ills. Imperialist interests and those of the comprador paralleled one another,

---

35 Khalaf, *Lebanon's Predicament* 66–70.

36 Odeh, *Lebanon* 38–49.

but were diametrically opposed to those of the Lebanese majority. The first major conflict between these two ideologies, "Lebanonism" for the comprador bourgeoisie and "Arab Nationalism" for the majority of the Lebanese, climaxed in the 1958 civil war.[37] Certain power bloc components in support of Arab nationalism attempted to topple the Chamoun regime and enhance their position.

The demise of the Chamoun regime in 1958 was a great affliction to the comprador bourgeoisie and to imperialism in the region. Even though some modern reforms accompanied the ascendancy of Chehab, confessionalism remained intact as did the preexisting economic structures. Upon stepping down from office in 1964, most of the reforms Chehab had planned had not been implemented, as was the case with his successor, President Helou. By the end of the Helou regime in 1970, Lebanon was experiencing serious economic problems.

Just as there were major ideological contradictions within Lebanese society eulogized in "Lebanonism" versus "Arab Nationalism," so too were there opposing political agendas. The Lebanonistic defenders of confessionalism became known as "Maronites" and established the Lebanese Kataeb Party (Phalangists) or LKP, the Party of Free Nationalists (PFN), and the National Bloc (NB).[38] The period after 1967 marked a heightened political consciousness among the masses that was partly due to deteriorating economic conditions within Lebanon, aggressive Israeli attacks that terrorized the South, and the dynamics of the Palestinian question. The masses, no longer content with their voiceless political position, established the Lebanese National Movement (LNM) in 1969 which included "working class" parties as the Communist Party (CP), the Arab Socialist Action Party (ASAP), and the Organization of Communist Action (OCA).[39]

The LNM was a loose coalition of the anticonfessionalistic progressive parties whose members came from all the religious sects (Muslims, Christians and Druze). They strove to institute reforms

---

[37] Odeh, *Lebanon* 122.

[38] Odeh, *Lebanon* 94.

[39] Odeh, *Lebanon* 124.

by utilizing the political process and they were highly successful in mobilizing the masses. Opportunist motivations prompted class alliances between the LNM and Muslim sector of the bourgeoisie and other bourgeoisie factions who opposed right-wing methods. The LNM was content with the fact that its strategic ally, the Palestinian Resistance, was militarily strong and politically capable of instituting reforms in the system. Military dependence proved to be unwise because without a strong military apparatus, the LNM found itself in compromising situations in its relation to the Resistance and more importantly to Syria and the right wing.[40]

Despite the tremendous advances the LMN had achieved on the "political" level, the Maronite right wing was in tight control of the state machinery, particularly the presidency and the military. The right wing provoked hostility with the intention of crushing the LNM and the Resistance through the use of the state's most formidable organ—the army. They had previously employed the military against the Resistance and unarmed demonstrations of students and workers even before the 1975 incident at Sidon which, along with the bus massacres of April 13, 1975, ignited the Lebanese Civil War. These incidents indicated that the right wing was intent on confiscating the other organs of the state from LNM influence. Even though the LNM, LKP, PFN and other pro-system forces were represented in the same cabinet for a time, given the irreconcilable differences between the LNM and right wing, it was most assuredly a temporary arrangement.

The right wing experienced a set back with the resignation of the military government on May 26, 1975, testimony to the fact that the LNM and its allies were strong enough to challenge the president's prerogative. Regrettably, however, the LNM did not pursue its demand for a cabinet which would have heavily represented it. The LNM chose not to pursue the demand because it did not want to undermine the Syrian initiative, which was responsible for the formation of the cabinet, and because it preferred a peaceful settlement through reformism and the parliamentary process.

---

40 Odeh, *Lebanon* 88–126

The formation of the Karami cabinet on July 1, 1975, and the National Dialogue Committee on September 24, 1975, evidenced that the right wing was determined to secure power through any available means. In fact, the right wing had already made preparations for offensive action that would partition Lebanon. The LNM addressed this breach of faith by appealing to diplomatic and political force, but to no avail. The LNM was incapable of staging a preemptive offensive campaign to link West Bank with Karantina, Nab'ah and Tal al-Zatar.

When contradictions within Lebanese polity surfaced, the LNM was forced to assume more "radical" methods in its fight against the right wing. Furthermore, external complications in relation to Syria propelled LNM to differentiate itself from the pro-Syrian forces. This was not the only contribution to its revolutionary development; its solitary Mountain Offensive in March 1976 was also an important move.[41]

The LNM Mountain Offensive was launched because specific events had left the LNM with no other alternative. The Syrians strove to consecrate confessionalism through the same agreement that yielded the Constitutional Document. At the same time the LKP besieged LNM mountain areas, a move which revealed that the Maronite right wing had no intentions of reaching an agreement with the LNM. Moreover, LKP attacks crippled the extremely weak "coup" by Brigadier Ahdab that tried to reunite the armed forces and coerce Suleiman Frangieh to resign.[42]

Despite the Mountain Offensive's victories, the LNM was forced to settle for a cease-fire because of pressures it encountered from Syria and the Resistance. Fearing that the mounting Syrian role could hamper its options, the LNM requested Arab and foreign diplomatic intervention to oppose Syria. As it turned out, however, Syria's role in Lebanon was supported by French diplomatic efforts which hampered the initial United States diplomatic effort.

---

[41] Odeh, *Lebanon* 131–54.

[42] Odeh, *Lebanon* 170.

Elias Sarkis' presidential election illustrated Syria's dominant influence in Lebanon. The right wing, which aligned itself with Syria's diplomatic and military advances against the LNM, quickly adjusted to Syria's new position by uniting efforts to weaken the Mountain Offensive and militarily defeat the LNM. It became obvious that the Mountain Offensive was politically finished when, on the eve of Sarkis' election, its military intervention was completely ineffective. The LNM was still militarily strong, but its strength was soon to be undermined.[43]

The Syrian invasion contained the development of a revolution in Lebanon. All of the LNM gains made during the Mountain Offensive were lost with the Syrian invasion of Lebanon on June 1, 1976. Internally, the National Front and the Maronite right wing endorsed the invasion, but once the Syrians were in power they also gained support from the Muslim majority of the bourgeoisie. In addition, many groups within the LNM chose to cooperate with Syria in order to bring stability to Lebanon. It should be noted, however, that these choices were compulsory to some degree because Israel and the right wing had established a new military front in the south of Lebanon. This cooperation was not one among peers, but one between a victorious occupation army and a restrained LNM.

The Syrian invasion provided the right wing with the opportunity to attack Palestinian and LNM areas, particularly Tal al-Zatar and mountain positions. The Syrians also attempted to drive a wedge between the Resistance and the LNM via the Palestinian-Syrian Agreements of July 26, 1976. The Agreement was never implemented, however, because Syria refused to coerce the right wing to retreat from Tal al-Zatar or divert its buffer troops from the path of the combined forces' relief columns.

Despite Syria's frequent acts of betrayal, LNM was unwilling to sever its ties. The anti-imperialist and traditional nationalist role Syria had previously played, and particularly Syria's role in the October 1973 war, obscured the nature of the Assad regime from most of the political parties comprising the LNM. The Arab Baath Socialist Party

[43] Odeh, *Lebanon* 158–70.

(ABSP) was the only force that persistently cautioned the LNM of Syria's deceitful nature. But because the two wings of Baath—ABSP and the pro-Syrian Baath Party Organization (BPO)—harbored tremendous animosity toward each other, the LNM was reluctant to heed the warnings. The LNM also found it difficult to sever its ties with Syria because Syria supplied the majority of its arms. Because the LNM was dependent on Syrian arms and because it was militarily weak, it could only experience success within the parameters of Syrian design. Syria capitalized on LNM's dependence to maximize and actualize its own interests within Lebanon and to control the LNM's success. Thus, LNM's objectives were greatly hindered.

LNM's failure to perceive the true nature of the state and to sufficiently prepare for armed conflict were perhaps its greatest shortcomings. The LNM was in control of 80 percent of the Lebanon region before the Syrian invasion. An organized, armed, and disciplined political machine with clear direction could have appropriated state power at that point. Instead, the LNM chose to implement a political solution to the conflict that coopted its gains and left intact the mechanisms for its final defeat. It was this bourgeois radicalism and reformism that impeded revolutionary development and the Lebanese right wing's ascendancy to power, whose dominance was secured with the Israeli invasion of Lebanon after June 6, 1982.[44]

At the conclusion of the war and following an Arab summit in Riyadh in October, a deterrent force remained in Lebanon to try to restore peace. The PLO withdrew its forces from central Lebanon and returned to the South where its presence contributed to the problems that ultimately caused the Israeli invasion of Southern Lebanon in March 1978. Meanwhile, the Israelis began establishing relations with the Lebanese, especially the Maronites under the dissident Lebanese army officer Saad Haddad, in order to form a security belt along Israel's northern border. As Haddad began expanding the range of his territory, tensions increased with the PLO which was coexisting in the area. Both Syria and Israel strove to define their areas of interest, hence, the Syrians tried to restrict the PLO's

[44] Odeh, *Lebanon* 173-86.

activities to reduce the potential for a massive Israeli intervention. In July 1977, Syria, the PLO (represented by Arafat), and President Sarkis agreed to withdraw PLO forces from the border areas adjacent to Israel and substitute them with Lebanese army units. Haddad and Begin rejected the idea because they opposed restoration of any central authority that could restrain their freedom of action against the PLO.

These activities occurred during a time of heightened American diplomacy that aimed at establishing an environment suitable for a Geneva conference. The PLO heightened terrorist activity in attempts to sabotage any progress toward a meeting that might foster recognition of non-Palestinian control over the West Bank. The interrelationship of these factors ultimately led to the Israeli invasion of South Lebanon in March 1978.

Once the attack on Lebanon was underway, Israeli officials sought Sadat's approval, something he gave to prevent the derailing of the peace talks. However, due to discrepancies in the objectives of Sadat and Begin over the West Bank issue, the peace negotiations had to be revised. Accordingly, the revisions ensured Israel control of the West Bank, increased Israel-PLO hostilities, heightened Arab resistance to repressive Israeli measures on the West Bank, and propelled the Begin government to invade Lebanon.[45]

When Israeli troops moved into Lebanon in June 1982, they launched what ultimately became Israel's longest and most controversial war. Israeli defense forces set out not only to achieve "peace for Galilee" and destruction of the PLO bases in Southern Lebanon, but also the destruction of the PLO infrastructure in West Beirut and to ensure the election of Bashir Gemayel as Lebanon's next president.[46] The deliberate misleading of Israeli and world opinion regarding the scope of the military operations and the extensive toll they took on civilian lives prompted international mediation efforts. The Israeli

[45] Smith, *Palestine* 248–51.

[46] Smith, *Palestine* 248-51; and Cleveland, *A History of the Modern Middle East* 348.

invasion turned into an occupation of Lebanon that persisted until 1985 when United States and Israeli troops evacuated the area.[47]

Despite their appearance, relations between Israel and Lebanon remain seriously strained even today, ten years after the war's conclusion. Israel recently established a naval blockade along a stretch of Lebanon's Mediterranean coastline in relation for what it calls Lebanese government harassment of its own citizens in Israeli's security zone. Israel asserts that Lebanese soldiers incite friction in the neutral area in order to create a pretext for the abandonment of the zone. All of this developed against a backdrop of consistent conflict between Israeli forces and Lebanese guerrillas that could very well erupt again into an intense exchange of shellfire.[48]

The Lebanese Civil War of 1975–76 was a result of internal contradictions, but possibly even more so the product of regional politics through the Palestinian link. Lebanese and regional politics from that time forth, including the 1982 Israeli invasion of Lebanon, are comprehensible only if the historical contradictions that arose in the region are addressed. Such contradictions include: the impingement of a zionist, exclusivist entity, the economic and political contradictions that accompanied development and underdevelopment, and the interests of imperialists. As important as these factors are, it is cultural identity that binds the Arab world, and at the same time runs counter to zionist consciousness, which ultimately stirs up conflict as each community struggles to recover the territory it claims as belonging to its forefathers.

[47] Odeh, *Lebanon* 173–86; Smith, *Palestine* 248-51; and Cleveland, *A History of the Modern Middle East* 348.

[48] Smith, *Palestine* 248–51; and Cleveland, *A History of the Modern Middle East* 348.

D. Nationalism and Lack of National Identity in the Case of Bosnia-Herzegovina

International recognition of Bosnia and Herzegovina in 1992 provided legal status for an entity that was politically and socially fictitious prior to that time. Legal recognition masks the fact that Bosnia and Herzegovina do not constitute a functioning state with effective central authority. Croatia and Serbia, two of the three national groups which constitute the government, are committed to ensuring that it remains powerless, a favorable environment within which to initiate their agendas -- the partition of Bosnia and Herzegovina.

Although the sources of conflict since 1991 are considered to have developed over centuries of hatred, the proximate cause was division along ethno-national lines as manifested in the 1990 elections. As the citizens formed three distinct camps, Serbian and Croatian leaders proposed plans for division of the republic. Military segregation has been mostly accomplished, but the 1992 Vance-Owen Plan suggested a division of provinces with a propensity for homogeneity, thus undermining any future chance Bosnia and Herzegovina might have of functioning as a single state. Once the powerful political message that the people of Yugoslavia could not coexist within one state was accepted, partition of Bosnia and Herzegovina was as inevitable as the partition of Yugoslavia. For if Yugoslavia could not survive as a common state of Serbs, Croats and peoples, how could Bosnia and Herzegovina survive?[49] (See appendix 3, table 4.)

[49] Robert M. Hayden, "Conflict in the Former Yugoslavia: The Partition of Bosnia and Herzegovina, 1990–1993," *Radio Free Euro/Radio Liberty Research Report* vol. 2, no. 22 (28 May 1993) 1–2, 4, 9, and 11–13.

TABLE 4:
TRANSNATIONAL NATIONALISM-CULTURE AS A VARIABLE IN INTERNATIONAL RELATIONS AND DOMESTIC POLITICS—IN THE CASE OF BOSNIA-HERZEGOVINA

PURPOSE OF TRANSNATIONAL NATIONALISM	TYPE OF TRANSNATIONAL NATIONALISM	
	SERBIAN IDENTITY	BOSNIAN/CROATIAN IDENTITY
LEGITIMATION FOR INTERVENTION	SERBIA	BOSNIA/CROATIA
LEGITIMATION FOR REUNIFICATION	SERBIAN GUERILLAS	BOSNIA/CROATIAN DEFENDERS

Table 4 indicates the derivatives of sustained cultural consciousness under the ineffective central authority of the Bosnia-Herzegovina region. Serbian, Croatian, and Bosnian politicians continue to stand for the preservation of Bosnia's multinational and multireligious character in order to provide their respective governments with the control of their comrades within the region. Each of the three distinct ethnicities comprising the area endorses the partition plans of its motherland because the cultural ties hold fast and persist.

Racial history is the curse of the Balkans. Nowhere within the entire region can a racially homogeneous province be found, let alone a racially homogeneous state. A microcosm of the Balkans is found in Bosnia, which emerged from a complex history of early Slav Bosnia infiltrated by Croats and Serbs in approximately AD 620 and which became an independent state in AD 1180. Even though a majority of the Bosnian territory appears to have been occupied by Croats, or at least by Slavs under Croat rule, and while the Bosnians more closely resembled the Croats in their religious and political history, applying Croatian identity to the Bosnians of this period would be an anachronism. The only conclusion that can be drawn about Bosnian ethnic identity is that they were Slavs who resided in Bosnia.[50]

The history of Bosnia in the high Middle Ages was filled with contrasts. During this time frame, Bosnia expanded to include the principality of Hum (Herzegovina) and a large part of the Dalmatian coast, enabling it to become the most powerful state in the Western Balkans. Not only did Bosnia benefit from territorial enlargement during this time, but it gained prosperity through exploitation of its mineral wealth. Despite these monetary and expansionistic advantages, Bosnia found itself divided, either officially or de facto, as a result of frequent power struggles among local noble families. Eventually, divisiveness in conjunction with Ottoman Turk advancements undermined the stability of medieval Bosnian politics.[51]

In 1463, the Ottoman army swiftly conquered Bosnia while Herzegovina managed to hold out against the Ottomans for nearly two more decades. Until it stagnated and declined, a process which began in the mid-sixteenth century, the Ottoman Empire was a formidable and highly active military enterprise that drew people from Christian Europe (janissary army) into the machinery of the Ottoman state via devsirme (the system of boy-tribute). During the two centuries of operation at least 200,000 children from the Balkans passed through the system.

Even though the members of the janissary corp were mandatorily converted to Islam, conversion was not a state policy, as was control of the country through amassing money, men, and feudal incomes to supply the needs of the empire. Control was maintained through the dispensation of Ottoman law by a local kadi or judge, several of whom presided within a single sancak, or military-administration district. Each sancak was a subdivision of an eyalet or prov-

---

[50] Noel Malcolm, *Bosnia: A Short History* (New York: New York University Press, 1994) 1–12.

[51] Malcolm, *Bosnia* 13 and 24.

ince, the largest constituent of the empire. In 1580, the eyalet of Bosnia was established to include the whole of modern Bosnia and Herzegovina in addition to some neighboring sections of Slavonia, Croatia, Dalmatia, and Serbia. For the duration of the Ottoman period, Bosnia enjoyed this special status as a distinct entity.[52]

Even though the Muslims occupied positions of authority, and being a Muslim was advantageous for anyone in the Ottoman state, Bosnia could hardly be considered an Islamic state. However, the Islamicization of a large percentage of the population under the Ottomans is a significant feature of modern Bosnian history documented in the records of the "defters" or tax registers. The process by which Bosnia gained a majority population of Muslims took the better part of 150 years. In light of the evidence accumulated thus far, it is clear that the interplay of numerous factors contributed to the Islamicization of Bosnia. During the period preceding the Turkish conquest, Bosnian religion was an amalgamation of Christian and Islamic practices because the Bosnian church had become largely defunct. In addition to Bosnia's fractured ecclesiastical history, several economic and social factors motivated Bosnians to convert. Finally, as a result of the wars that dominated the seventeenth and eighteenth centuries, large numbers of Islamicized Slavs from outside Bosnia's borders entered the region, expanding further the Islamic population.[53]

Although the Ottoman Empire prospered by war, warfare and the social changes it produced also contributed to its demise. The feudal cavalry, effectively employed during the establishment of the empire, was defunct by the seventeenth century. The feudal cavalry was replaced by a regular salaried army equipped with modern firearms and artillery. The financial burden of maintaining such a defense system, in addition to an increase in governmental corruption and a deterioration of law and order, hastened the empire's demise. Because the Turks engaged in one war after another, Bosnia was left financially drained and militarily exhausted. Even Turkey's short periods

[52] Malcolm, *Bosnia* 43–46 and 50.

[53] Malcolm, *Bosnia* 49, 51–52, 54, 56–57, 60 and 64–69.

of recovery were marred with inflation, currency devaluation, and epidemics. Amid the unrest, the desire of local representatives to resist central rule was particularly acute in Bosnia. The town officials who led the resistance held the rank of ajan. Through the exercise of this office, and with the support of members of the local landowning class, the officials kept their city in a state of almost permanent resistance to central authority from the 1760s to the 1830s.[54]

The fifteenth century military-feudal system, under which estate holders could be Christians or Muslims and their workers were peasants of either faith, gradually eroded. In its place there arose a nineteenth century local landowning aristocracy, consisting entirely of Muslims, and the great majority of the nonlandowning peasants were Christians. Although conditions of life deteriorated for Christian peasants as a whole, a small minority enjoyed prosperity in the major towns in which the Christian merchant class developed as well as the protection of consular officials from France, Austria and Prussia. The new landowning aristocracy and the rise of Serbia as an armed and quasi-autonomous Christian state intensified the suspicions and fears of the sultans. The most important political problem facing the empire, however, was the growth of autonomy in the hands of local Muslim lords.[55]

Recognizing the critical nature of implementing legal and administrative reforms in order to modernize the system and gain greater control over the local authority, the sultans initiated numerous revisions. The rebellious ajans of Bosnia, among other local lords, resisted central reforms by way of clashes. During this same final period of Ottoman Bosnia, peasant revolts against landowners were on the rise. By mid-1876, this large but local crisis expanded to international proportions when Serbia and Montenegro declared war on the Ottoman Empire and asserted Serbia would annex Bosnia and the latter would take possession of Herzegovina. These plans were interrupted when Russia declared war on the Ottomans in 1877. Since covert negotiations between Joseph II of Austria and Catherine

[54] Malcolm, *Bosnia* 82–83, 86 and 89–92.

[55] Malcolm, *Bosnia* 93–97 and 106.

the Great of Russia regarding a takeover and division between them of the Balkan lands had taken place nearly a century before, upon defeating the Turks a settlement was reached at San Stefano. The great powers of Europe met at the Congress of Berlin in July 1878 to redraw the map in order to counterbalance Russia's dominance in the Balkans and block its access to the Mediterranean. It was decided that Austria-Hungary would occupy and govern Bosnia and Herzegovina. Bosnian troops prepared to resist the arrival of the Austrians, but the Austrian army was far too powerful.[56]

Political problems inherent in a dual monarchy soon surfaced: should Bosnia be ruled by Austria, Hungary, or both? This dilemma was solved when it was decided that Bosnia would become a crown land. Austro-Hungarian administrators set out to develop the Bosnian economy by revising agricultural policy, among other things, and to address the delicate issue of the three main religious communities. The growth of Muslim activism was a particular problem to Benjamin Kallay, the man in charge of Bosnia at the time. His Bosnian policy was aimed entirely at "[i]nsulating the country from the nationalist political movements in Serbia and Croatia, and developing the idea of Bosnian nationhood as a separate and unifying factor."[57] Kallay hoped to extend the term "Bosnian" to all people, regardless of their religious faith.

Kallay believed that in order to establish Bosnian nationhood, Bosnia must first be accepted by the Muslims, because unlike the Catholics and the Orthodox, they had no sponsor-nation outside Bosnia's borders to which to turn. Unfortunately, the modern idea of nationhood began to spread from Croatia and Serbia to the Catholics and Orthodox of Bosnia through the very cultural institutions that Austro-Hungarian policy had helped to propagate. It soon became obvious that Kallay's Bosnian project was doomed to failure. As animosity grew between Croats and Serbs and was kindled by their respective homelands, two secret societies formed to campaign for pan-Serb unification: Narodna Odbrana (National Defense)

[56] Malcolm, *Bosnia* 87, 119, 122 and 133–35.

[57] Malcolm, *Bosnia* 147.

and Ujedjenje ili Smrt (Unification or Death). Serbian resistance mounted and by 1913 relations between Austria-Hungary and Serbia were extremely tense, culminating in the assassination of Archduke Franz Ferdinand, heir to the Habsburg throne, and his wife, Duchess of Hohenberg, during an official visit to Sarajevo.[58]

Within the local Balkan context there were valid reasons for hostility, but not sufficient reasons for war. Without the German drive for war, the assassinations at Sarajevo probably would not have caused even a serious Balkan war, and certainly not one of global magnitude. Most Bosnians, including the Muslim community, supported Austro-Hungarian troops because they did not want to risk the chance of being swallowed up in Serbia's post-war expansion. By mid-1918, Austro-Hungarian war efforts faltered, however, and the leading Bosnian politicians who proposed the formation of a Yugoslav state as an alternative abandoned the preservation of Habsburg rule. A National Council for Bosnia was established and on October 29, 1918, a new sovereign state of Slovenes, Croats, and Serbs was formally declared.

Even though most Bosnian Muslims favored the creation of a Yugoslav state, they were also aware that they needed a powerful political organization to protect their interests; thus, the "Yugoslav Muslim Organization" was founded in 1919.[59] Arguments subsequently arose among the communities over the fundamental principles of the new state. The new Muslim organization under Mehmed Spaho supported Bosnian autonomy within the Yugoslav state as did the Croats. In contrast, Serbs fought for centralism. While Muslims acquired political significance through their majority in the Constituent Assembly, the secularizing influences of the twentieth century eroded their religious foundation. At the same time, the Catholics and Orthodox in Bosnia began to identify themselves as Croats and Serbs, which proved problematic as political tensions between Serbian centralists and Croatian regionalists grew more severe during the 1920s. Attempts to create a unitary political system by, among other things,

---

[58] Malcolm, *Bosnia* 136–37, 141–42, 144, 147–50 and 154.

[59] Malcolm, *Bosnia* 163.

announcing the state would be called "Yugoslavia," were underway when Hitler threatened Yugoslavian dismantlement as he advanced into Czechoslovakia and then Yugoslavia. After withstanding Hitler's forces for eleven days, Yugoslavia capitulated to the German High Command.[60]

The history of World War II in Yugoslavia is actually a series of separate battles fought on different stages by different actors. First, there was the initial war that Germany and Italy commanded against Yugoslavia itself. There was also the ongoing Axis war effort against the allies which involved Yugoslavia for purposes of communication and its supply of raw materials and labor. In addition, there was a war of the Axis-occupying forces against Yugoslav resistance movements. Lastly, there were at least two civil wars. Croatian radicals directed the first against the Serb population of Croatia and Bosnia; the second war was between the two leading Serbian resistance organizations, the Cetniks and the Communist Partisans. While it is impossible to disentangle all of these strands for purposes of determining individual death counts, it is clear that at least one million people died, and a majority of that number was probably Yugoslavs killed by Yugoslavs.

On April 10, 1941, the Germans announced a new "[Independent state of Croatia," (NDH), that incorporated the whole of Bosnia and Herzegovina.[61] The territory was divided into two zones: one zone was militarily occupied by Germany and the other by Italy. The first anti-Semitic law was issued eight days later. The genocidal policy of the NDH provoked thousands of Bosnian Serbs to enlist in one of two resistance movements operating on Bosnian soil. The policy of Cetnik, the first movement, was to build an organization and prepare for an uprising while maintaining a low profile until the allies could dominate the Germans. The other organization, the Communist Partisans, planned a resistance operation under the leadership of Tito not to drive the Germans out of Bosnia, but to initiate a social revolution to establish a post-war Communist state. Meanwhile, most Bosnian Croats

60 Malcolm, *Bosnia* 157, 159, 161–64, 166, 168–69, 171, and 173.

61 Malcolm, *Bosnia* 174.

initially aligned themselves with the Croats of Croatia in welcoming the establishment of the NDH, but joined the Partisans after 1943–44. During the same period, the Muslim position vacillated depending upon the discriminatory practices of the different groups at the time. Finally, at the war's conclusion, the Muslims cast their lot with the Partisans, who, on April 28, 1945, appointed a "People's Government" for Bosnia.[62]

While Tito is often credited for the peace and reconciliation Yugoslavia enjoyed after World War II, the price of Communist power was very heavy indeed. Tito's policies closely modeled those of Stalin, particularly in his campaign against religion. Many churches, both Catholic and Orthodox as well as Mosques, were destroyed and cultural and educational societies were abolished in order to foster the Yugoslav Communist Party belief that all religious, ethnic, and national identities would be buried alongside the institutions.

Official policy began to change in the 1960s, however, when Muslims were allowed to call themselves "Muslims" in an ethnic sense, and the Preamble to the 1963 Bosnian constitution referred equally to "Serbs, Croats and Muslims allied in the past by a common life," implying they were to be regarded as equal nations.[63] This stride toward Muslim recognition as a nation was not an Islamic religious movement, but one led by Communists and other secularized Muslims who desired the Muslim identity to develop along nonreligious lines. In the late 1960s, Muslim nationhood was established and accompanied by constitutional revisions that extended the pursuit of individual republic policy development. The immediate cause for such development in Sarajevo was, of course, the scheduling of the 1984 Winter Olympics.

The trend toward the decentralization of Yugoslavia, which unavoidably entailed at least a minimal concession of the principle of separate national political identities, began creating more problems than it was solving because the appetite for such identities had not been satiated. Not only was discontent internally fanned by the weak

---

62 Malcolm, *Bosnia* 174–77, 184–88 and 191.

63 Malcolm, *Bosnia* 198.

and malfunctioning Yugoslav economy and the political corruption and stagnation that polluted the whole system, but it was externally promoted by national feelings of resentment in Croatia and Serbia. Conditions were ripe for the revival of nationalism. Croats campaigned for greater liberalization of the Yugoslav political system, while Serbs reignited their old historic goal and national idea -- "[t]he unification of the Serbian people into a single state."[64] The Serbian Orthodox Church also saw its opportunity to revive religious identity through the political and literary culture of Yugoslavia.

The political malaise afflicting Bosnia and the whole of Yugoslavia by the middle of the 1980s bred a sense of disillusionment which the new leader of the Serbian Communists, Slobodan Milosevic, seized upon and put to good use. In March 1989, Milosevic convinced the Serbian Assembly to pass constitutional amendments to strip Kosovo and Vojvodina of their political autonomy, thus instigating demonstrations which the Serbian security forces crushed. The environment was perfect for a catastrophe. More specifically, the environment entailed: an ambitious politician in Belgrade; a collapse of the economic system and discontent that aroused a yearning for decisive leadership; and a renewal of Serbian nationalism which successfully restored Kosovo and Vojvodina to Serbian control. As the Serbs gathered into a single political unit under the leadership of Milosevic, it was clear that Serbian forces would either dominate or divide Yugoslavia.[65]

Milosevic assumed an unchallengeable position in Serbia by a combination of Communist methods and nationalist rhetoric that assured him a victory in the upcoming elections. He planned to gain control of Yugoslavia through the existing Communist Party structures, until his plan was undermined with the early 1990 collapse of Communist power in Eastern Europe. If Yugoslavia could not be taken as a single entity, Milosevic would extract from it a new entity, an extended Serbian territory. Meanwhile, Slovene and Croatian politicians pled for a peaceful Yugoslavian transformation from a federal

---

64 Malcolm, *Bosnia* 205.

65 Malcolm, *Bosnia* 193–95, 198, 200, 202–03, 205–06, 211–12.

state, where central laws and institutions are primary, to a confederate state, where republics hold the real authority. Milosevic was opposed to any such transformation.

In Bosnia, as elsewhere, the Communist Party disintegrated and a host of national parties were organized, including the primary Bosnian Muslim Party, the "Party of Democratic Action" (SDA), under Alija Izetbegovic. Wedged between Serbian and Croatian nationalism, the Bosnian Muslims began strengthening their own Muslim nationalism by emphasizing its religious component and taking a stand for the preservation of Bosnia's multinational and multireligious character. When the votes were tallied in the December 1990 elections, Izetbegovic's party, along with the other Muslim party, had gained 99 out of the 240 assembly seats, thus assuming control.

Even though Izetbegovic formed a government of national unity that was structured out of a formal coalition between all three communities, the political atmosphere in Yugoslavia was tense as the struggle intensified between the Serbs on the one hand, and Slovenia and Croatia on the other. As Izetbegovic tried to perform a balancing act, Serbian demands for secession of certain territories heightened threatening Croatia and Bosnia. Despite Izetbegovic's efforts, full-scale war broke out in Yugoslavia providing federal and Serbian irregular forces with the opportunity to confiscate territory. A peace treaty, negotiated by United Nations representative Cyrus Vance, defined the land seized by the irregulars as "UN-protected" zones. For nearly four months, discussions regarding the future of the region took place among a multitude of different leaders, some proposing partition, while others like the European Community suggested cantonal confederation. Although the European Community Plan was initially accepted by all three sides as a basis for further negotiation, the Croats subsequently rejected it because they would have controlled only 12 percent of the land, while 59 percent of the Croatian population of Bosnia and Herzegovina would have remained outside the designated Croatian provinces. The Muslim population also rejected the plan because they perceived as absurd its division on a national basis.[66] Even though all plans would have been disruptive to an element of the Bosnian population, the majority voted for a democratic and independent Bosnia of equal citizens. Therefore, on April 6, 1992, the European community recognized Bosnia as an independent state.[67]

Instead of halting the fighting, recognition of Bosnia triggered an outbreak of further conflict because the Serbs, who proclaimed their independence from the independent Bosnia and Herzegovina, began to establish a military force. On the day of international recognition, Serb paramilitary forces advanced upon Sarajevo and were met by 50,000 to 100,000 Bosnians of all national groups, who proclaimed: "'Let all the Serb chauvinists go to Serbia and let the Croat chauvistists go to Croatia. We want to remain here together. We want to keep Bosnia as one.'"[68] Despite the reprimands hurled at the Serbian forces in Sarajevo, the entire region continued onward, as it does to the present day, embroiled in conflicts directed from soil external to its boundaries.

In August 1992, international diplomatic activity concerning the region changed considerably with the London Conference where a new mediator, Lord Owen, was appointed to work with Cyrus Vance, the personal representative of the Secretary- General of the United Nations. Owen and Vance proposed a solution that calculated the geographical midpoint of the demands of the Serbs, Croats and Muslims. The Vance-Owen Plan sought to divide the republic into ten independent regions, with three regions assigned to each of the three nationalities and Sarajevo to have a special neutral status. Despite Croat and Muslim endorsement, Bosnian Serbs declared the plan unsatisfactory because it required them to relinquish too many of their Serbian-sponsored conquests. Clearly, history reveals that

66 Hayden, "Conflict in the Former Yugoslavia," *Radio Free Euro/Radio Liberty Research Report 7*.

67 Malcolm, *Bosnia* 213-15, 217–19, 222–23, 225, 230 and 233.

68 Malcolm, *Bosnia* 235.

what has consistently endangered Bosnia has not been solely internal tensions, but the ambitions of larger powers and neighboring states.[69]

Prospects of resolving this crisis are bleak, despite the fact that Jimmy Carter has stepped in as a mediator for to broker the four-month cease-fire procured for that purpose. On January 1, 1995, a cease-fire commenced when United Nations officials guided peace talks regarding a proposal which offered 51 percent of Bosnia to a Muslim-Croat federation and 49 percent to the Serbs. The truce was violated within one day of its enactment, and there have been far more serious breaches since that time. It appears that both sides hoped for a reprieve from fighting during the winter months when the weather hindered advancements, but neither side was truly committed to complying with the truce or abandoning its nationalistic claims to the land. Most citizens align with the dubious forecast of the European Ambassador in Zagreb regarding a Bosnian settlement: "'My guess is that when spring comes, we'll see a new hunting season begin . . . .'" Sure enough, at the first sight of sprouting buds, the motors of helicopters and tanks that had lay idle through the winter were fired up. The Bosnian-Serb army ignited the flames of violence as it killed Bosnia's foreign minister when it shot down his helicopter and captured members of the United Nations peacekeeping force.[70]

What does the future hold for this war-torn region? Is a harmonious association out of reach for this ethnically incompatible population? Whether any proposal for the division of Bosnia and Herzegovina is implemented, it is evident that the situation in and around the former Yugoslavia remains troubled and is likely to stay

---

[69] See Malcolm, *Bosnia* 234–35, 238 and 247; Patrick Moore, "Conflict in Former Yugoslavia: Endgame in Bosnia and Herzegovina?" *Radio Free Europe Liberty Research Report* vol. 2, no. 13 (August 1993) 18; and Hayden, "Conflict in the Former Yugoslavia," *Radio Free Euro/Radio Liberty Research Report* 9.

[70] *The New York Times*, January 3.1995: *The New York Times*, January 21 and March 21, 1995; and *The New York Times*, May 29, 1995. For further readings, see Mark Prison, ed., *The Muslims of Bosnia-Herzegovina: Their Historic Development from the Middle Ages to the Dissolution of Yugoslavia*_(Cambridge: Harvard University Press, 1994); and Bogdan Denitch, *Ethnic Nationalism: The Tragic Death of Yugoslavia* (Minneapolis: University of Minnesota Press, 1994).

that way during the foreseeable future. Because the region is compositionally heterogeneous, but more importantly because the three principal communities that comprise Bosnia and Herzegovina have inherited the nationalistic ideologies indigenous to their identities, conflict is inevitable. If the three communities, whether out of choice or for survival, choose to make sacrifices in order to create an environment conducive to harmonious coexistence, interference from the threatened homelands will most certainly sabotage their efforts. Therefore, it is highly unlikely this region will ever be a common country of all Yugoslavs, but it can strive to unite as an association of states that shares interests and the capacity to resolve conflict through peaceful negotiation and reconciliation.

III. OVERALL CONCLUSIONS

What does the future hold for these war-ravaged regions? Even though it is impossible to predict the future with certainty, the odds of an enduring settlement seem to be far outnumbered by the chance of continuing strife. History has repeatedly revealed that because culture fuses together individuals through the functioning of its institutions, it is nearly impossible to sever the union in order to establish a new national identity that will transcend all others. Without a unifying identity, it is likely that stability will exist only in the form of an illusion.

Since conflict continues to torment Northern Ireland, Palestine, Lebanon, and Bosnia-Herzegovina, it appears doubtful that their futures hold much else in store. Each of the four countries remains in its present state of upheaval because not one of them has successfully determined and effectuated the criteria for citizenry or of selecting a common language. Negotiation efforts have been consistently sabotaged by the cultural institutions established within each country and under the direction of their respective homeland because negotiation is a threat to the mother country's ability to exert influence and control.

If these four countries and others including Cyprus that suffer from the same malady can discover and implement a means of eradicating external influence, an environment conducive to the arbitration of these matters is likely to ensue. It remains doubtful, however, that the homelands will forfeit their positions of stewardship without a serious fight because of their responsibility to their people. Thus, in all probability, the reign of instability will persist unless the issues of political identity and the "Babel" of the tongue are addressed and resolved.

CHAPTER 6

CONCLUSION: ABSTRACT THEORIES, CONCRETE REALITIES

A little further
to see almond trees blooming
marble shining in the sun,
the sea rippling with waves
a little further let's go up a little higher[1]
—George Seferes

As in days past, the blossoms of the almond tree will return. Reflections on ancient civilizations— "marble shining in the sun"—remind us of the resiliency of humankind. Each of the theorists included in this research employed past cases to provide insight into present conflicts. Although they take divergent interpretive courses, their research gives us the opportunity to view our present in terms of the past so that we may be enlightened about our future. It is my hope that my research will likewise help to elucidate changing world dynamics and provide a framework through which to examine the new world order.

The eclectic and interactive style of my work is derived first and foremost from my motivation for this study, which did not begin with social science but with my longstanding and intense interest in Cyprus. My research therefore resembles the work of a historian more than that of a social scientist. Social scientists usually begin with a theory and then search for cases to test that particular theory. I, on the other hand, began with a case and searched for theories to explain

[1] George Seferes was cited by Dr. Marianne McDonald at her graduation address to Deree College in Athens on June 17, 1988.

it. Because of this approach, my research suffers from the problem of having more variables than cases, a problem noted in Lijphart's work on the comparative method.[2] However, now that I have formulated a theory, I have begun to test it rigorously with regard to other cases.

My theory of transnational nationalism is not without debts to political science literature. In fact, I discovered transnational nationalism after puzzling over the international relations and comparative approaches and the lack of debate between them. The international relations approach aids in the necessary examination of the Cyprus case in an international context, while taking into consideration the role of influence of Cyprus's neighbors. International relations theories are particularly enlightening where individual powers at the regional level are consistent with multipolarity, and where a balance of power at this level is the ultimate goal. International relations theories, however, are most effective when they are focused on the second level and applied to local regions, rather than on the aggregate levels of hegemony, multipolarity, or bipolarity.

The dependency version of international relations theory appears relevant since Cyprus is only relatively autonomous and is highly influenced by its two dominant neighbors, and these factors conform to the dependency model. However, the relevancy of this approach falters because dependency theorists have stressed purely economic cases, and the Cypriot case does not support this theoretical bias.

The Cypriot case represents military and political action premised upon ethnic dependency rather than on economic motivations. As I have shown, Greek and Turkish activities on Cyprus reflected the need to protect and reinforce culture on the island. This need was incorporated into the divergent political movements of enosis and taksim.

These movements and their cultural content move us beyond the international relations approach to a comparative framework. Comparativists emphasize the need to examine the domestic policies of a country. Unfortunately, however, much of the comparative tra-

2 Arend Lijphart, "The Comparable-Cases Strategy in Comparative Research," *Comparative Political Studies* vol. 8, no. 2 (1975) 158–77.

dition stresses the constitutional structure, elite skill in compromise, and the homogeneous aspects of a state. In stressing these elements, comparative theories ignore the question of whether a national identity exists to preserve the state. The reasons for the failure of 1960 Cypriot Constitution to create a sovereign Cypriot state with a strong national identity can be traced to the intervention of other states. The primary insight comparative theories may provide would be to explain why Greece and Turkey's domestic politics forced their leaders to act as they did in Cyprus.

Comparative theorists fail to take into account international relations, and international relations theorists likewise miss comparative political insights. International relations theorists need to seriously consider domestic politics and comparativists need to pay due attention to events beyond the non-hermetically-sealed boundaries of their case countries. Finally, both international relations and comparative theorists must not ignore culture, which can operate both within and between countries. Both intrastate and inter-state contexts must be examined in order to understand real cases.

The theoretical implications of social science literature provide an understanding of, but not full explanation to, the 1974 Cypriot Crisis. Despite their limitations, international relations and comparative theories help to interpret the causes that triggered the Cypriot Crisis. However, it was not until I attempted to apply both culturally oriented comparative perspectives and game-theoretic international relations models to Cyprus that I discovered the mechanism of transnational nationalism. By combining each theory's applicable insights, I formulated my own hypothesis, one founded on interaction effects and a special consideration to culture. A plural society whose component cultures are tied to other states may serve as the ideal case for understanding the limits and possibilities of nationalism. Specifically, the politics of countries outside the government may prove more influential than politics within the government if cultural bonds between the people and external governments exist and are resistant to political impediments. The most effective agents of transnational nationalism are the cultural institutions which bind together people from different states and preserve their dream of unification.

My analysis of the Cypriot Crisis would be of little value, however, if its relevance were limited exclusively to Cyprus. Upon discovering transnational nationalism, I realized that cultural politics also disrupt the harmony within other countries when foreign and domestic forces strive to achieve transnational nationalism. An in-depth study of the determinants of prolonged conflicts within Northern Ireland, Lebanon, and Israel reveals that in each case, a connection exists between cultural institutions in a dependent country and the domestic politics of a dominant country. Each of these cases demonstrates that internal division intensifies as ethnic groups strive to preserve their national identity by uniting with their cultural counterparts in other nation-states.

Consideration of my alternative theoretical approach is important, not only for its relevance to existing cases like Northern Ireland, Lebanon, and Israel, but to the set of new states that are currently experiencing conflict, such as Bosnia-Herzegovina. Because our world is no longer dominated by two superpowers but is moving from bipolarity to a new world order with a multipolar structure, the conventional wisdom which focuses on hegemonic conditions and the Cold War world order is becoming obsolete. Regional issues will be of greater concern because under this new world order, interaction among small countries will be far more important as nations strive to establish alliances to maximize their individual security. This new structure will likely encourage stronger nations with ethnic ties to smaller countries to establish cultural institutions in an effort to gain greater control and thus strengthen their positions.

As countries attempt to reunite with other countries (particularly neighbors that share a common culture), their intervention inevitably provokes conflict. Conflict is principally a regional manifestation because a majority of wars are fought between neighbors. Conflict is not usually generated because of a disparity of power, but power disparities may be part of the means and the objective of conflict. The existence of an oppressed population in a neighboring state with cultural ties may supply the incentive or opportunity for intervention on the part of a concerned state. The vanity of nationalism, the drive to spread an ideology, the safeguarding of kinsmen in a neighboring land, the hunger for greater territory or commerce, the retaliation for a defeat, the aspiration for superior national strength or autonomy, the desire to impress or solidify alliances -- all are aims that cause conflicts among rival nations.[3]

Beyond the Nation-State

As the dynamics of our restless current world structure adjust and settle in to a new order, the nature of the nation-state and its role in foreign affairs will unquestionably require realignment as well. Will the nation-state respond to internal political pressures and external economic forces in the new world order? International decision makers of the future will have to take into account comparative politics and culture when making foreign policy decisions, as Henry Kissinger discovered to his chagrin.[4]

The world that Kissinger attempted to deal with was at least one in which he had the luxury of focusing on only two cultures

---

3 T. B. Millar, "Conflict and Intervention," *Conflict and Intervention in the Third World* 1 and 5.

4 In terms of the culture of the country involved, the reference is to differing Soviet understandings of detente: "[T]he problem was a more fundamental one. The Russians defined détente (or 'peaceful coexistence,' as they often preferred to call it) differently than did the Americans. To them, detente did not require that they cease support for 'progressive' and 'liberation' movements in the Third World." In terms of the culture of his country, Kissinger's policy was also a failure: "'The acid test of a policy,' . . . 'Is its ability to obtain domestic support. This has two aspects: the problem of legitimizing a policy within the government apparatus . . .; and that of harmonizing it with the national experience.' Ironically, Kissinger's detente policy was to encounter, and fail to pass, the same acid test." Kissinger did not adequately deal with either American or Soviet culture and concomitant understandings of detente. If someone as sage as Kissinger failed with only two cultures to manage, imagine the pressure that future policy-makers will face in a multipolar and infinitely more complex world. See Gordon A. Craig and Alexander L. George, *Force and Statecraft: Diplomatic Problems of Our Time* (New York: Oxford University Press, 1983) 102, 137 and 138.

-- the American and the Soviet. But today's policy makers face multiple possibilities: they live in a multipolar world with a great deal more cultural diversity than diplomats previously had to understand. But if we assume the presence of diplomats, we also assume that the nation-state is reasonably intact as the unit of analysis in international relations. This thesis calls into question the nation-state's international sovereignty and its domestic autonomy. The importance of local culture casts doubt on the integrity of the nation-state as the only player in world politics. (See appendix 4, figure 1.)

Appendix 4

Figure 1

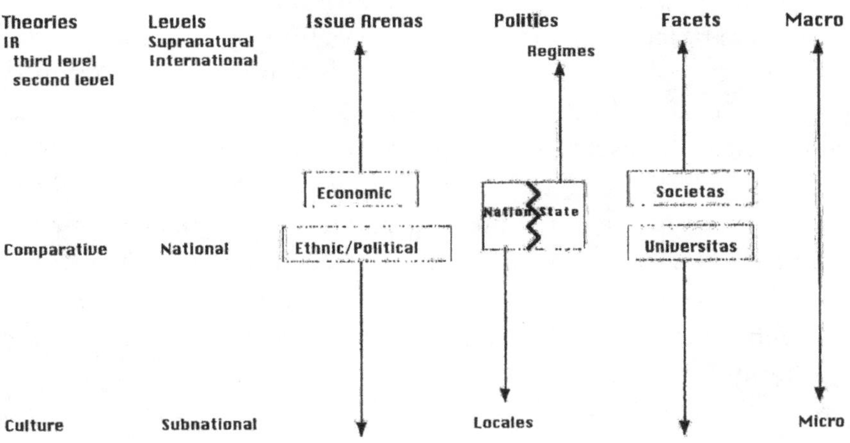

In order to see beyond the nation-state, it remains helpful to examine the way that the nation-state functions as an institution. Michael Oakeshott contends that the legal association known as the state is better understood in terms of its two contesting faces: the societas and the universitas. The societas is an association formed by agreement and based on a set of agreed-upon principles, while the universitas is a corporation united in the pursuit of a substantive goal.

The universitas character of the state is most clearly visible in war. A state at war is an association whose substantive purpose is the goal of survival or expansion. A common cause is only one way in which to indentify a state, however. States are also associations of individuals pursuing their own goals within the terms prescribed by an accepted code of conduct. The societas, or civil association, is not an association with a substantive purpose, but rather a nomocracy directed by laws indifferent to any purpose. These two functions are contradictory yet simultaneous, thus there is an inherent tension within the nation-state which threatens to merge it into a single entity. The contradiction between the state-as-universitas and state-as-societas currently threatens to tear apart the Western nation-states.[5]

The universitas functions of the modern Western nation-state have been directed toward fighting the Cold War. But American efforts to impose liberalization and democratization on one Third World government after another have miserably failed. Sadly enough, the United States' attempts to assist governments confronted with violent internal opposition were not only unsuccessful at insuring that the voice of the people was allowed to direct politics, but actually assisted the usurpation of power by new revolutionary regimes under which the average individual enjoyed fewer freedoms and less personal security than the previous autocracy. In case after case the United States has been led by its own misunderstanding of traditional autocracies where authority is transmitted through personal relations; therefore, the fabric of authority quickly unravels when the authority of the leaders at the top is undermined or extinguished. Ironically enough, the Cold War was won by the United States and the Western nation-states in spite of their efforts to serve as the arsenal of democracy. The societas function of preserving a liberal economic world order did more to win the Cold War than any army in the jungle.[6]

---

5 Michael Oakeshott, *On Human Conduct* (Oxford: Clarendon Press, 1975) 187, 199, 200–01, 272–74, 320–21 and 323.

6 Jean J. Kirkpatrick, *Dictatorships and Double Standards: Rationalism and Reason in Politics* (New York: An American Enterprise Institute Simon and Schuster Publication, 1982) 26, 32–33 and 49.

The societas-like economic functions are now being delegated to economic regimes above the level of the nation-state. In particular, the European Community is a transnational economic regime that is working to break down the boundaries which divide a regional economy. Other examples of regional economic regimes include North America under NAFTA, and Japan and Asia under the proposed renovation of the old Greater East Asia Co-Prosperity Sphere. At an even more aggregated level, the World Trade Organization created by the passage of GATT in 1994 placed trade in the hands of an international institution rather than those of nation-states. International and supra-national economic regimes render the nation-state increasingly irrelevant in economic terms.[7]

As interdependent relationships are established, international political communities will enhance the prospects of eliminating war within their boundaries. Integration, or a sense of community, develops among a population that is extensive enough to assure reasonable expectations of resolutions to social problems by way of peaceful change rather than physical force. The integration or merging of people or governmental units into a single unit may manifest itself in one of two forms: "amalgamated" when independent entities are formally merged under a common unitary or federal government, or "pluralistic" where the communities retain the legal autonomy of separate governments.

The results of this integrative process among any particular group of countries are dependent upon the interplay of the integrative approach, or the effects of background conditions, with the very act of crossing the integration threshold which is affected by moving political events. Timing is everything. Progress toward amalgamation must precede the imposition of burdens that accompany any merger, and rigid party divisions which reinforce boundaries should be on the decline. Leaders should exercise their compromising skills and

[7] Ernst Haas, "The Turbulent Fields and the Theory of Regional Integration," *International Organization* vol. 30, no. 2 (Spring 1976) 173–212.

should not weigh early failures too heavily because failures often contribute to the eventual success of the regional integration process.[8]

Although regional integration theorists anticipated that increasing contact would erase nationalism and ethnicity, cultural analysts would disagree. In reality, ethnicity has not withered away but has grown stronger as the nation-state structure has weakened. If we examine law, the system our culture perceives as the essence of the modern universalist and nationalist development, we find culture still matters. Cultural Anthropologists would not be surprised by this fact. The father of "thick description" argues that "law is local knowledge" in his following commentary:

"Law I have been saying, somewhat against the pretensions encoded in woolsack rhetoric, is local knowledge; local not just as to place, time, class, and variety of issue, but as to accent—vernacular characterizations of what happens connected to vernacular imaginings of what can. It is this complex of characterizations and imaginings, stories about events cast in imagery about principles, that I have been calling a legal sensibility."[9]

If law, the very center of what we perceive as cosmopolitan, is actually parochial, then culture calls our common sense into question.

Culture itself involves local knowledge, and matters like ethnicity, that are often impervious to change by external forces. The case of Macedonia which is currently unfolding before our eyes perfectly illustrates the importance of ethnicity. One of the nation-states produced by the breakdown of the former Yugoslavia has taken the name Macedonia. This name has been claimed by a province of Greece which is adjacent to the former Yugoslavia. The Greeks and Slavs are willing to fight to the death over the issue of which group has the right to claim Alexander the Great as their forefather. If ethnicity did not matter, then why would people be willing to shed blood over a name?

8 Karl W. Deutsch, Sidney A. Burrel, et al., *Politcal Community and the North Atlantic Area: International Organization in the Light of Historical Experience* (New York: Greenwood Press, 1957) 5–6, 32, 38, 71, 76, 90 and 93–95.

9 Clifford Geertz, *Local Knowledge: Further Essays in Interpretive Anthropology* (New York: Basic Books, 1983) 215.

The result of this increasing salience of ethnicity and international economic organization means that the nation-state's two functions—universitas and societas—are devolving upon other institutions. The universitas character may be in the process of being salvaged at the level of subnational and transnational ethnic groups. The societas, on the other hand, is being promoted to the international and supranational levels via institutions like the European Commonwealth and the World Trade Organization. What is left for the nation-state if both its societas and universitas character are removed?

The devolution of economic societas functions has so far been peaceable, but a myriad of conflicts may proceed from unpopular decisions by institutions such as the European Economic Community and the World Trade Organization. How will these conflicts be resolved? The devolution of ethnic (nationalist) universitas functions historically has been very bloody. We know that the making of the modern nation-state involved a great deal of force in the repression of ethnicities and the assertion of one national ethnicity over all others. The reverse process could involve much more conflict.

At a glance, the world appears to be mimicking the paganistic days of Sodom and Gomorrah: void of order, hopelessly corrupt, and spinning its way into extinction. Unlike that time period, the prevailing hedonism will not be reborn by the birth of a savior, as in Yeats' poem "The Second Coming," but will plunge deeper into the pit of despair as the world is seized by a demon god who will reign with indifference and without mercy. Death, rather than birth, is civilization's destiny as the "[r]ough beast, its hour come round at last,/ Slouches towards Bethlehem to be born . . . ."[10] As our sophisticated world wavers on the edge of nuclear war, spearheaded by a nuclear bomb as the beast, one must ask whether Yeats' poem is a prophetic revelation. Does our present world mirror his vision of hopelessness?

Despite what appear to be insurmountable obstacles to peaceful stability, Stephen Crane feels that humans will prevail in their strug-

---

[10] W. B. Yeats, 'The Second Coming," in Richard J. Finneran ed., *The Collected Works of W. B. Yeats* vol. 1 (New York: Macmillan Publishing Company, 1989) 187.

gle to survive by forfeiting selfish demands for those that will benefit the whole of humanity. He acknowledges society's need for a harmonious community. In his work, "The Open Boat," the cook, oiler, captain and correspondent each grow to recognize the absurdity of their selfish regard for issues and things they previously considered priceless. Although temporary meanings failed the dinghy passengers, the one significant experience that seemed to give meaning to their present circumstances was their dependence on and support for each other. "They sat together in the same seat, and each rowed an oar. Then the oiler took both oars; then the correspondent took both oars . . . . It was all done with the most extraordinary care."[11]

Following the philosophy of community seen in Crane's story, the United Nations and many similar agencies have tried to artificially unite countries and people. However, until individuals of all different groups, such as the oiler, captain, cook and correspondent, realize the need to work together and appreciate one another, life will continue to be merely survival in an absurd world. Over the course of history, humankind has consistently reached the verge of annihilation and turned the tides to rescue the existence of humanity. Regardless of the face the new world order will don, people will celebrate cultural differences rather than making them a bone of contention. Rallying together for preservation as our forefathers did in days of old, humankind will pacify the swells of contention. Anticipating "the sea rippling with waves," we should join George Seferes to transcend "a little higher" in our celebration of humanity.

---

[11] Stephen Crane, 'The Open Boat," *The United States in Literature* (Glenview: Scott, Foresman and Company, 1976) 266–67.

BIBLIOGRAPHY

Allison, Graham T. *Essence of Decision: Explaining the Cuban Missile Crisis*. New York: Harper Collins Publishers, 1971.

Almond, Gabriel A. "Comparative Political Systems." *Journal of Politics* vol. 18, no. 3 (August 1956): 391–409.

Almond, Gabriel A. and Powell, Bingham Jr. *Comparative Politics: A Development Approach*. Boston: Little Brown, 1966.

Arnakis, George G. "The Role of Religion in the Development of Balkan Nationalism." Jelavich, Charles and Barbara eds. *The Balkans in Transition: Essays on the Development of the Balkan Life and Politics Since the Eighteenth Century*. Berkeley: University of California Press, 1963: 115–44.

Attalides, Michael A. "The Turkish Cypriots: Their Relations to the Greek Cypriots in Perspective." Attalides, Michael A. ed. *Cyprus Reviewed*. Nicosia: The Jus Cypri Association, 1977: 71–97.

Attila 1974: A Testimony on Film. Videocassette. Sept, and dir. Michael Cacoyannis. 1975. 98 min.

Averoff-Tossizza, Evangelos. *Lost Opportunities: The Cyprus Question*. 1950–1963. New York: Aristide D. Caratzas, 1986.

Baerentzen, Lars and Close, David H. "The British Defeat of EAM, 1944–45." Close, David H. ed. *The Greek Civil War. 1943–1950: Studies of Polarization*. London: Routledge, 1993: 32–55.

Barry, Brian. "Political Accommodation and Consociational Democracy." *British Journal of Political Science* vol. 5, no. 4 (October 1975): 477–505.

Black, Cyril E. "Russia and the Modernization of the Balkans." Jelavich, Charles and Barbara eds. *The Balkans in Transition: Essays on the Development of the Balkan Life and Politics Since the Eighteenth Century*. Berkeley: University of California Press, 1963: 145–72.

Brademas, John, *Amerikaniki Paideia Kai O Evriteros Cosmos (A World no Longer Narrow: International Education at American Universities)*. Athens: Athens Academy, 1985.

Brinkley, Douglas. *Dean Acheson: The Cold War Years 1953–71*. New Haven: Yale University Press, 1992.

Brubaker, Rogers. *Citizenship and Nationhood in France and Germany*. Cambridge: Harvard University Press, 1992.

Bureau of Intelligence and Research. "Intelligence Report No. 8047: Analysis of the Cyprus Agreements, July 14, 1959." *Journal of the Hellenic Diaspora: A Quarterly Review* vol. XI, no. 4 (Winter 1994): 10–31.

Campbell, John C. "The United States and the Cyprus Question, 1974–75." Coufoudakis, Van ed. *Essays on the Cyprus Conflict: In Memory of Stephen G. Xydis*. New York: Pella Publishing Company, 1976: 13–25.

Clerides, Glafkos. *Cyprus: My Deposition*. Vol. 1, 2, 3, and 4. Nicosia: "Alithia" Publishing, 1990.

Cleveland, William L. *A History of the Modern Middle East*. Boulder: Westview Press, 1994.

Clogg, Richard. *A Short History of Modern Greece*. Cambridge: Cambridge University Press, 1979.

Close, David H. "The Legacy." Close, David H. ed. *The Greek Civil War. 1943–1950: Studies of Polarization*. London: Routledge, 1993: 214–31.

Coufoudakis, Van. "American Foreign Policy and the Cyprus Problem, 1974–1978: The Theory of Continuity' Revisited." Couloumbis, Theodore A. and Iatrides, John O. eds. *Greek American Relations: A Critical Review*. New York: Pella Publishing Company, 1980: 107–29.

Coufoudakis, Van. "The Dynamics of Political Partition and Division in Multiethnic and Multireligious Societies—The Cyprus Case." Coufoudakis, Van ed. *Essays on the Cyprus Conflict: In Memory of Stephen G. Xydis*. New York: Pella Publishing Company, 1976.

Coufoudakis, Van. "United States Foreign Policy and the Cyprus Question: A Case Study in Cold War Diplomacy." Attalides,

Michael A. ed. *Cyprus Reviewed*. Nicosia: The Jus Cypri Association, 1977: 101–44.

Couloumbis, Theodore A. *Greek Political Reaction To American and NATO Influences*. New Haven: Yale University Press, 1966.

Couloumbis, Theodore A. *The United States, Greece, and Turkey: The Troubled Triangle*. New York: Praeger Publishers, 1983.

Craig, Gordon A. and George, Alexander L. *Force and Statecraft: Diplomatic Problems of Our Time*. New York: Oxford University Press, 1983.

Crane, Stephen. "The Open Boat." *The United States in Literature*. Glenview: Scott, Foresman and Company, 1976.

Cyprus: Republic of Cyprus 30 Years 1960–1990. Nicosia: Press and Information Office, 1990.

Cyprus, Annual Report of Cyprus Tourism Organization 1974–1975: Printing Office of the Republic of Cyprus, 1975.

Denitch, Bogdan. *Ethnic Nationalism: The Tragic Death of Yugoslavia*. Minneapolis: University of Minnesota Press, 1994.

Denktash, Rauf R. *The Cyprus Triangle*. London: Allen & Unwin, 1982.

Demographic Yearbook 1965. New York: United Nations, 1966.

Demographic Yearbook 1975. New York: United Nations, 1976.

Deutsch, Karl W., Burrell, Sydney A., et al. *Political Community and the North Atlantic Area: International Organization in the Light of Historical Experience*. New York: Greenwood Press, 1957.

Dillon, E. J. "The Fate of Greece." *Contemporary Review*. LXXII (July–December 1897): 1–34.

Di Palma, Giuseppe. *Surviving Without Governing: The Italian Parties in Parliament*. Berkeley: The Regents of the University of California, 1977.

Ehrlich, Thomas. *Cyprus 1958–1967: International Crisis and the Role of Law*. New York and London: Oxford University Press, 1974.

Ertekun, Necati M. *The Cyprus Dispute and the Birth of the Turkish Republic of Northern Cyprus*. Nicosia: K. Rustem & Brother, 1981.

Evans, Peter. *Dependent Development: The Alliance of Multinational. State, and Local Capital in Brazil*. Princeton: Princeton University Press, 1978.

Evriviades, Marios. "The Problem of Cyprus." *Current History (USA)*, vol. 70, no. 412 (Jan. 1976): 18–21, 38–42.

Featherstone, Kevin. "PASOK and the Left." Featherstone, Kevin and Katsoulas, Dimitrios K. eds. *Political Change in Greece: Before and After the Colonels*. London: Croom Helm, 1987: 112–33.

Galtung, Johan. "A Structural Theory of Imperialism." *Journal of Peace Research*. vol. 8 (1971): 81–117.

Geertz, Clifford. *Local Knowledge: Further Essays in Interpretive Anthropology*. New York: Basic Books, 1983.

Haas, Ernst B. "Turbulent Fields and the Theory of Regional Integration." *International Organization* vol. 30, no. 2 (Spring 1976): 173–212.

Hart, Parker T. *Two Nato Allies at the Threshold of War*. Durham and London: Duke University Press, 1990.

Hayden, Robert M. "Conflict in the Former Yugoslavia: The Partition of Bosnia and Herzegovina, 1990–1993." *Radio Free Euro/Radio Liberty Research Report* vol. 2, no. 22 (28 May 1993): 1–14.

Hill, George. *A History of Cyprus*. Vol. IV. Cambridge: At the University Press, 1952.

History of Modern Greece. Videocassette. Writ., dir., and prod. George P. Kontakos. Greek Video Records and Tapes Inc., 1988. 100 min.

Hitchens, Christopher. *Hostage to History: Cyprus from the Ottomans to Kissinger*. New York: The Noonday Press, 1989.

Horowitz, Donald. *Ethnic Groups in Conflict*. Berkeley: University of California Press, 1985.

Ioannides, Christos P. *In Turkey's Image: The Transformation of Occupied Cyprus into a Turkish Province*. New York: Aristide D. Caratzas, 1991.

Jelavich, Barbara. *History of the Balkans: Eighteenth and Nineteenth Centuries*. Vol. 1. Cambridge: Cambridge University Press, 1993.

Jelavich, Barbara. *History of the Balkans: Twentieth Century*. Vol. 2. Cambridge: Cambridge University Press, 1993.

Jervis, Robert. "Hypotheses on Misperception." Halperin, Morton H. and Kanter, Arnold eds. *Readings in American Foreign Policy: A Bureaucratic Perspective*. Boston: Little, Brown and Company, 1973: 113–37.

Jervis, Robert. "Offense, Defense, and the Security Dilemma." Art, Robert and Jervis Robert eds. *International Politics: Enduring Concepts and Contemporary Issues*. 3rd ed. New York: Harper Collins Publishers, 1992: 146–69.

Joseph, Joseph S. *Cyprus: Ethnic Conflict and International Concern*. New York: Peter Lang, 1985.

Karpat, Kemal. "Millets and Nationality: The Roots of the Incongruity of Nation and State in the Post-Ottoman Era." Braude, Benjamin and Lewis, Bernard eds. *Christians and Jews in the Ottoman Empire*. New York: Holmes & Meier Publishers, Inc., 1982: 141–69.

Khalaf, Samir. Lebanon's Predicament. New York: Columbia University Press, 1987.

Kirkpatrick, Jean J. *Dictatorships and Double Standards: Rationalism and Reason in Politics*. New York: An American Enterprise Institute Simon and Schuster Publication.

Kissinger, Henry A. *A World Restored: Metternich, Gastlereaah, and the Problems of Peace 1812–1822*. Boston: Houghton Mifflin, 1979.

Kissinger, Henry A. "Domestic Structure and Foreign Policy." Resenau, James N. Ed., *International Politics and Foreign Policy: A Reader in Research and Theory*. New York: Free Press of Glencoe, 1961.

Kitromilides, Paschalis M. "From Coexistence to Confrontation: The Dynamics of Ethnic Conflict in Cyprus." Attalides, Michael A. ed. *Cyprus Reviewed*. Nicosia: The Jus Cypri Association, 1977: 35–70.

Kostanick, Huey Louis. "The Geopolitics of the Balkans." Jelavich, Charles and Barbara eds. *The Balkans in Transition: Essays on the Development of the Balkan Life and Politics Since the Eighteenth Century*. Berkeley: University of California Press, 1963: 1–10.

Koumoulides, John. *Cyprus and the War of Greek Independence 1821–1829*. London: Zeno Booksellers & Publishers, 1974.

Kyriakides, Stanley. *Cyprus: Constitutionalism and Crisis Government*. Philadelphia: University of Pennsylvania Press, 1968.

Laitin, David D. *Hegemony and Culture: Politics and Religious Change Among the Yoruba*. Chicago: The University of Chicago Press, 1986.

Laitin, David D. "The Tower of Babel as a Coordination Game: Political Linguistics in Ghana." *American Political Science Review*. vol. 88, no. 3 (September 1994): 622–34.

Lijphart, Arend. "Consociational Democracy." *World Politics*. vol. XXI, no. 2 (January 1969): 207–25.

Lijphart, Arend. "The Comparable-Cases Strategy in Comparative Research." *Comparative Political Studies*. vol. 8, no. 2 (1975): 158–77.

Lijphart, Arend. *Democracy in Plural Societies: A Comparative Exploration*. New Haven: Yale University Press, 1977.

Loizos, Peter. "An Alternative Analysis: Part Two." *Cyprus. Minority Rights Group*. Rept. no. 30. London: Benjamin Franklin House, 1976.

Lustick, Ian. "Stability in Deeply Divided Societies: Consociationalism Versus Control." *World Politics* vol. 31, no. 3 (April 1979): 327–44.

Lustick, Ian. *State-Building Failure in British Ireland & French Algeria*. Berkeley: The Regents of the University of California, 1985.

MacDonagh, Oliver. *Ireland: The Union and Its Aftermath*. London: George Allen & Unwin Ltd., 1977.

Malcolm, Noel. *Bosnia: A Short History*. New York: New York University Press, 1994.

Markides, Kyriakos C. *The Rise and Fall of the Cyprus Republic*. New Haven: Yale University Press, 1977.

Migdal, Joel. *Strong Societies and Weak States: State-Society Relations and State Capabilities in the Third World*. Princeton: Princeton University Press, 1988.

The Military Balance 1974–1975. London: The International Institute for Strategic Studies, 1974.

Millar, T. B. "Conflict and Intervention." Ayoob, Mohammed ed. *Conflict and Intervention in the Third World*. London: Croom Helm, 1980: 1–11.

Moore, Patrick. "Conflict in Former Yugoslavia: Endgame in Bosnia and Herzegovina?" *Radio Free Europe/ Radio Liberty Research Report* vol. 2, no. 13 (August 1993): 17–23.

The North Atlantic Treaty Organization: Facts and Figures. Brussels: Nato Information Service, 1984.

Oakeshott, Michael. *On Human Conduct*. Oxford: Clarendon Press, 1991.

Odeh, B. J. *Lebanon: Dynamics of Conflict*. London: Zed Books Ltd., 1985.

Organski, A. F. K. *World Politics*. 2nd edition. New York: Random House, Inc., 1968.

Orr, C. W. *Cyprus Under British Rule*. London: Zeno Publishers, 1972.

Panteli, Stavros. *A New History of Cyprus: From the Earliest Times to the Present Day*. London: East-West Publications, 1984.

Perez-Dias, Victor. *The Return of Civil Society: The Emergence of Democratic Spain*. Cambridge: Harvard University Press, 1993.

Polyviou, Polyvios G. *Cyprus: Conflict and Negotiation* 1960–1980. New York: Holmes and Meier Publishers, 1980.

Polyviou, Polyvios. "The Problem of Cyprus and Constitutional Solution." Attalides, Michael ed. *Cyprus Reviewed*. Nicosia: The Jus Cypri Association, 1977: 212–54.

Press and Information Officers. *Cyprus: Republic of Cyprus 30 Years 1960–1990*. Nicosia: Press and Information Office, 1990.

Press and Information Officers. *The Cyprus Problem: Historical Review and Analysis of Latest Developments*. Nicosia: Press and Information Office, 1991.

Press and Information Officers. *Turkish Policy on Cyprus and Efforts to Solve the Cypriot Problem*. Nicosia: Press and Information Office, 1991.

Prison, Mark ed. *The Muslims of Bosnia-Herzegovina: Their Historic Development from the Middle Ages to the Dissolution of Yugoslavia*. Cambridge: Harvard University Press, 1994.

Psomiades, Harry J. "The United States and the Mediterranean Triangle. Greece, Turkey, and Cyprus." Attalides, Michael A. ed. *Cyprus Reviewed*. Nicosia: The Jus Cypri Association, 1977: 199–211.

Reich, Simon. *The Fruits of Fascism: Postwar Prosperity in Historical Perspective*. Ithaca: Cornell University Press, 1990.

Rumpf, E. And Hepburn, A. C. *Nationalism and Socialism in Twentieth-Century Ireland.* New York: Barnes & Noble Books, 1977.

Said, Edward W., Abu-Lughod, Ibrahim, et al. "A Profile of the Palestinian People." Said, Edward W. and Hitchens, Christopher eds. *Blaming the Victims: Spurious Scholarship and the Palestinian Question.* London: Verso, 1989: 235–96.

Shaw, Stanford. "The Ottoman View of the Balkans." Jelavich, Charles and Barbara eds. *The Balkans in Transition: Essays on the Development of the Balkan Life and Politics Since the Eighteenth Century.* Berkeley: University of California Press, 1963: 56–75.

Shlaim, Avi. "The Oslo Accord." *Journal of Palestinian Studies.* vol. XXIII, no. 3 (Spring 1994): 24–39.

Stavrianos, L. S. *The Balkans Since 1453.* New York: Rinehart & Company, Inc., 1959.

Stavrianos, L. S. *The Balkans 1815–1914.* New York: Holt, Rinehart and Winston, 1966.

Stavrianos, L. S. "The First Balkan Alliance System, 1860–1876." *Journal of Central European Affairs.* II (October 1942): 267–89.

Stavrianos, L. S. "The Greek National Liberation Front (EAM): A Study in Resistance Organization and Administration." *Journal of Modern History.* XXIV (March 1952).

Stavrianos, L. S. "The Influence of the West on the Balkans." Jelavich, Charles and Barbara eds. *The Balkans in Transition: Essays on the Development of the Balkan Life and Politics Since the Eighteenth Century.* Berkeley: University of California Press, 1963: 184–221.

Smith, Charles D. *Palestine and the Arab-lsraeli Conflict.* 2nd edition. New York: St. Martin's Press, 1992.

Smith, Ole L. "The Greek Communist Party, 1945–49." Close, David H. ed. *The Greek Civil War. 1943–1950: Studies of Polarization.* London: Routledge, 1993: 129–50.

Snyder, Jack. *The Ideology of the Offensive: Military Decision Making and the Disasters of 1914.* Ithaca: Cornell University Press, 1984.

Stephens Robert. *Cyprus: A Place of Arms: Power Politics and Ethnic Conflict in the Eastern Mediterranean.* New York: Frederick A. Praeger, 1966.

Stern, Laurence. "Bitter Lessons: How We Failed in Cyprus." *Foreign Policy*. (Summer 1975): 125–142.

Schumpeter, Joseph. *Capitalism. Socialism, and Democracy*. New York: Harper Torchbooks, 1950.

Stoianovich, Traian. "The Social Foundations of Balkan Politics, 1750–1941." Jelavich, Charles and Barbara eds. *The Balkans in Transition: Essays on the Development of the Balkan Life and Politics Since the Eighteenth Century*. Berkeley: University of California Press, 1963: 297–345.

Tatsios, George. *The Megali Idea and the Greek-Turkish War of 1897: The Impact of the Cretan Problem on Greek Irredentism. 1866–1897*. New York: East European Monographs, 1984.

Temperley, Harold. "The Situation in Crete." *Contemporary Review*. (September 1896): 317.

Theodoracopulos, Taki. *The Greek Upheaval: Kings. Demagogues and Bayonets*. London: Stacey International, 1976.

Thucydides, trans. *History of the Peloponnesian War*, by Rex Warner. London: Penguine Books, 1972.

Tsebelis, George. *Nested Games: Rational Choice in Comparative Politics*. Berkeley: University of California Press, 1990.

United Nations. *Yearbook of International Trade Statistics 1972–1973*. New York: United Nations, 1974.

Vanezis, P. N. *Makarios: Faith and Power*. London: Abelard-Schuman, 1974.

Vucinich, Wayne S. "Some Aspects of the Ottoman Legacy." Jelavich, Charles and Barbara eds. *The Balkans in Transition: Essays on the Development of the Balkan Life and Politics Since the Eighteenth Century*. Berkeley: University of California Press, 1963: 81–114.

Wallerstein, Immanuel. "The Rise and Future Demise of the World Capitalist System: Concepts for Comparative Analysis," *Comparative Studies in Society and History* vol. 16, no. 4 (September 1974): 387–415.

Waltz, Kenneth N. "Anarchic Orders and Balances of Power." Keohane, Robert O. ed. *Neorealism and Its Critics*. New York: Columbia University Press, 1986: 98–130.

Waltz, Kenneth N. *Man, the State and War: A Theoretical Analysis*. New York: Columbia University Press, 1959.

Waltz, Kenneth N. "Politcal Structure." Keohane, Robert O. ed. *Neorealism and Its Critics*. New York: Columbia University Press, 1986: 70–97.

Waltz, Kenneth N. "Reductionist and Systemic Theories." Keohane, Robert O. ed. *Neorealism and Its Critics*. New York: Columbia University Press, 1986: 47–69.

Woodhouse, C. M. *A Short History of Modern Greece*. New York: Frederick A. Praeger, 1968.

Woodhouse, C. M. *The Rise and Fall of the Greek Colonels*. London: Granada, 1985.

Xydis, Alexander G. "Cyprus: What kind of Problem?" Michael A. Attalides ed., *Cyprus Reviewed*. Nicosia: The Jus Cypri Association, 1977: 21–31.

Yearbook of International Trade Statistics 1972–1973. New York: United Nations, 1974.

Yeats, W. B. "The Second Coming." Richard J. Finneran ed., *The Collected Works of W. B. Yeats*. Vol. 1. New York: Macmillan Publishing Company, 1989.

Zarocostas, John. "Cyprus." Ayoob, Mohammed ed. *Conflict and Intervention in the Third World*. London: Croom Helm, 1980: 107–35.

PERSONAL INTERVIEWS

Christodoulou, Andreas. Press and Information Officer, Nicosia, June 26, 1992.

Clerides, Glafkos. Party Leader, Nicosia, June 27, 1992.

Evriviades, Marios. Press and Information Officer, Nicosia, June 23, 1992.

Kolotas, Frixos. Ambassador to Greece from Cyprus, Athens, December 22, 1992.

Lagakos, Efstathios. Member of the European Parliament, Athens, December 24, 1992.

Lyssarides, Vassos. President of the EDEK Socialist Party, Nicosia, June 26, 1992.
Polyviou, Polyvios. Lawyer, Nicosia, June 27, 1992.
Sarris, Michael. Division Chief at World Bank in Washington D.C., February 11, 1993.
Theodoropoulos, Theodoros. Ambassador retiree, Athens, December 23, 1992.
Triantafyllides, Michalakis. Attorney General, Nicosia, June 24, 1992.

NEWSPAPERS

The New York Times. February 12, 1973.
The New York Times. February 17, 1973.
The New York Times. March 10, 1973.
The New York Times. April 9, 1973.
The New York Times. April 16, 1973.
The New York Times. May 19, 1973.
The New York Times. July 6, 1973.
The New York Times. July 8, 1973.
The New York Times. July 30, 1973.
The New York Times. August 15, 1973.
The New York Times. July 16, 1974.
The New York Times. July 20, 1974.
The New York Times. January 3, 1995.
The New York Times. January 4, 1995.
The New York Times. January 21, 1995.
The New York Times. February 23, 1995.
The New York Times. February 27, 1995.
The New York Times. March 13, 1995.
The New York Times. March 21, 1995.
The New York Times. April 3, 1995.
The New York Times. April 4, 1995.
The New York Times. May 29, 1995.

MAPS

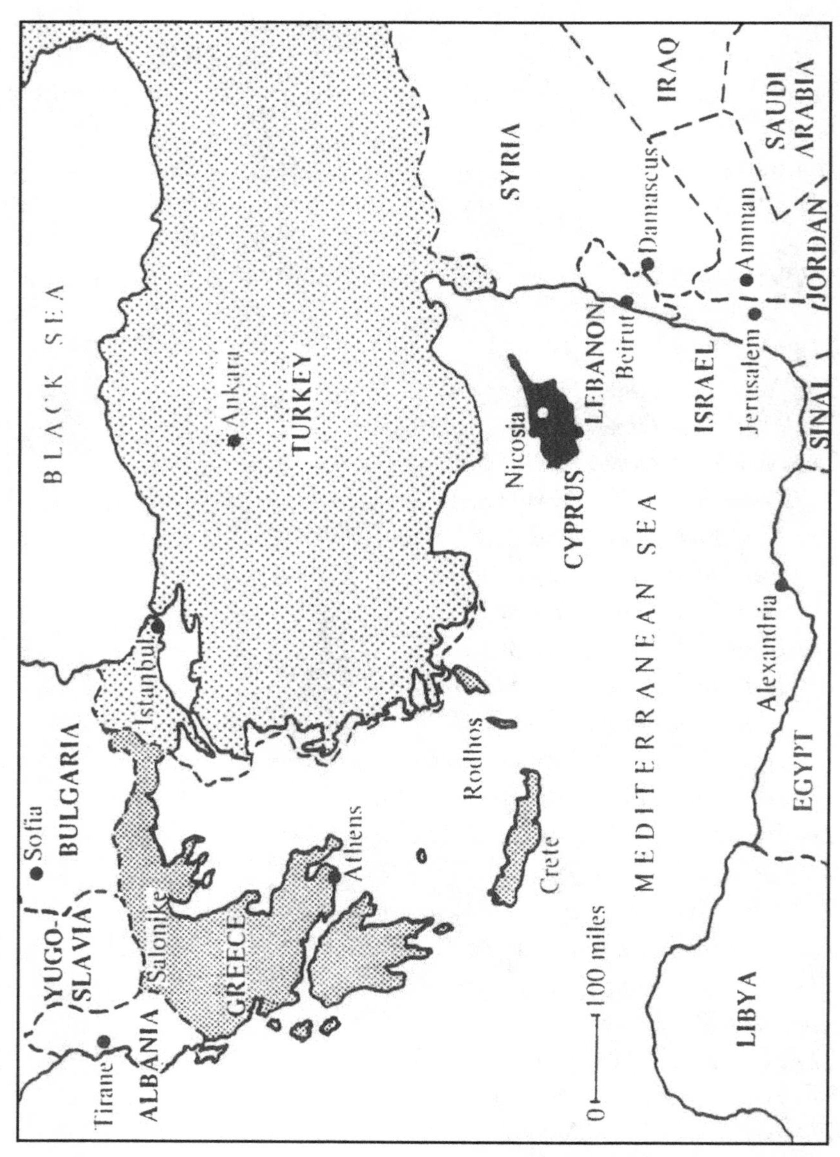

Coming from Markides, Kyriacos C. *The Rise and Fall of the Cyprus Republic*. New Haven: Yale University Press, 1977.

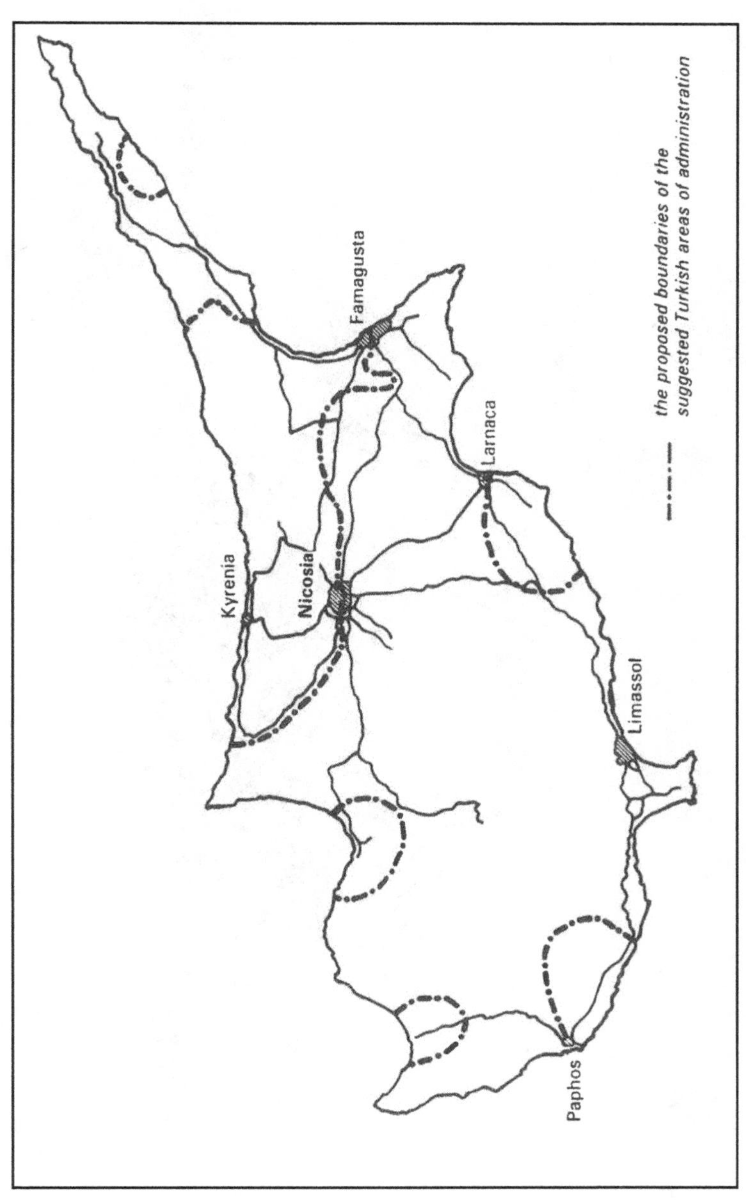

Coming from Polyviou, Polyvios G. *Cyprus: Conflict and Negotiation* 1960–1980. New York: Holmes and Meier Publishers, 1980: 240

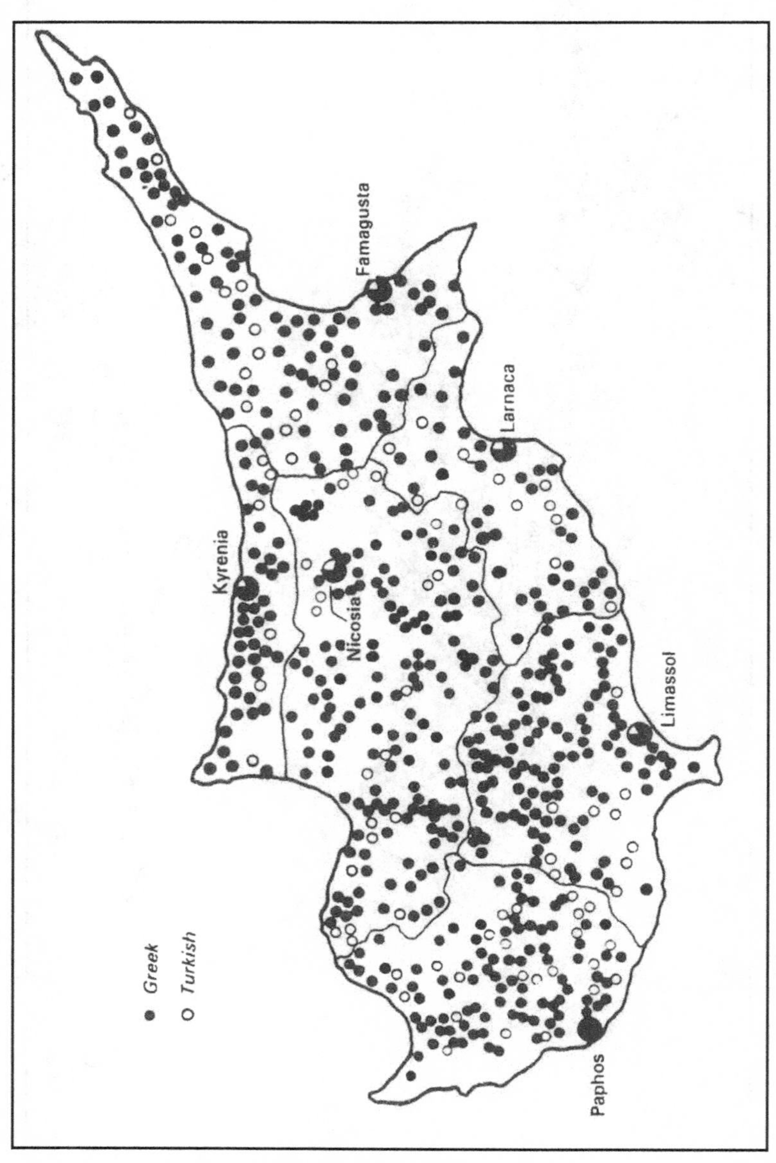

Coming from Polyviou, Polyvios G. *Cyprus: Conflict and Negotiation* 1960–1980. New York: Holmes and Meier Publishers, 1980: 238

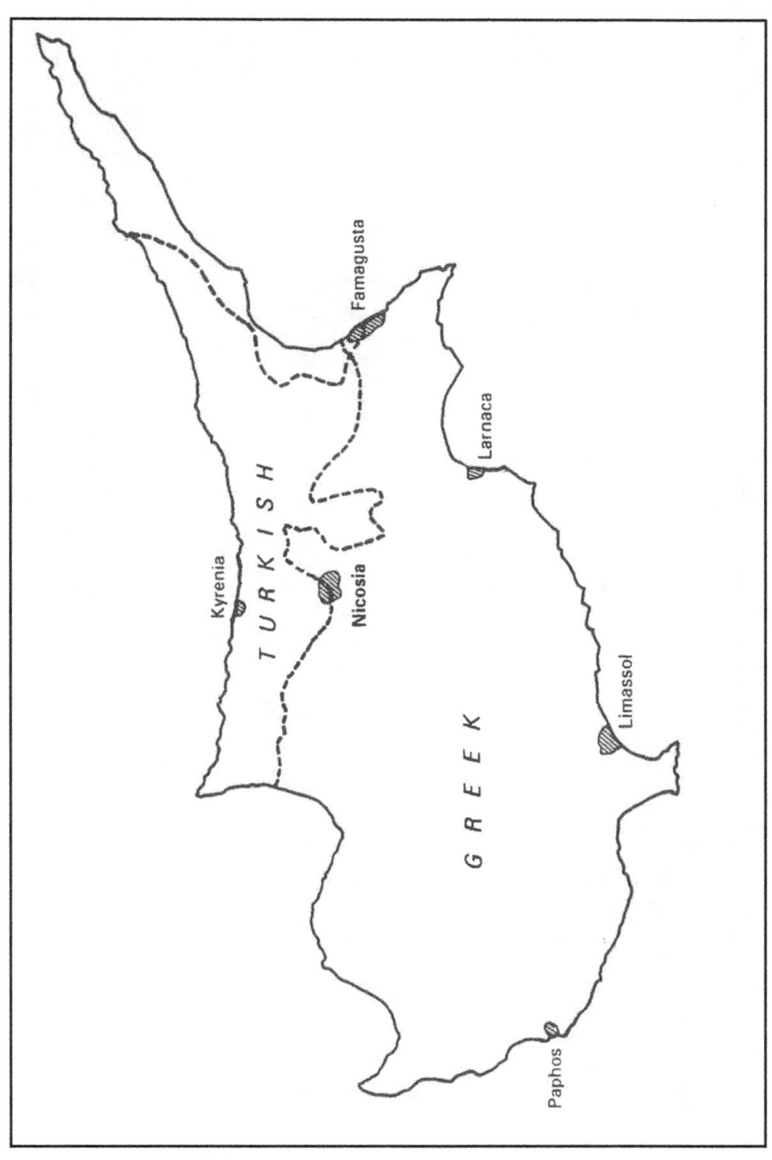

Coming from Polyviou, Polyvios G. *Cyprus: Conflict and Negotiation* 1960–1980. New York: Holmes and Meier Publishers, 1980: 241

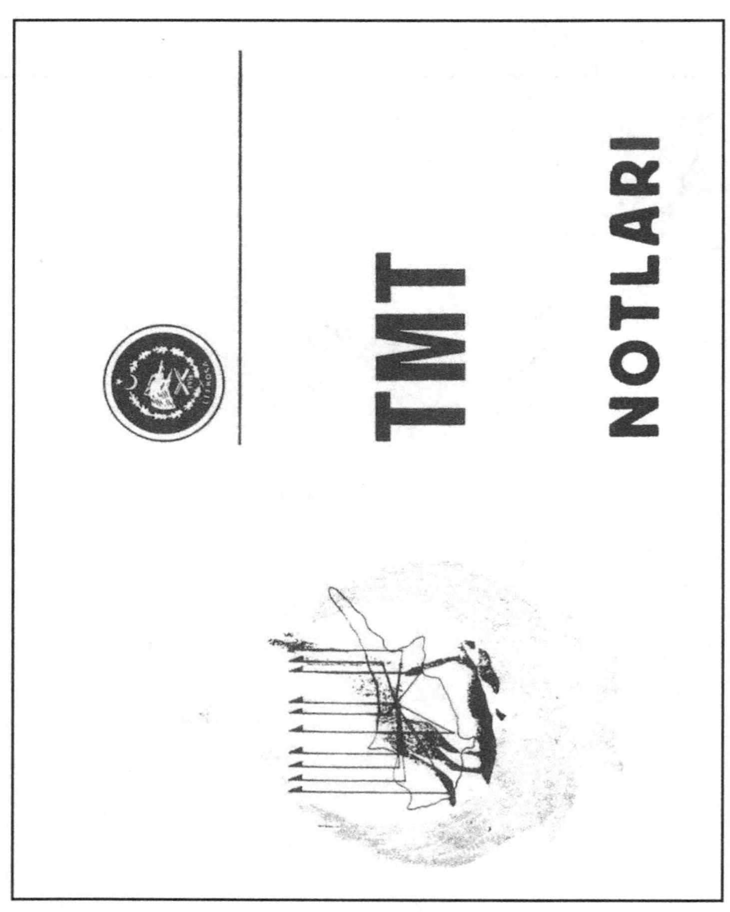

Coming from Ioannides, Christos P. *In Turkey's Image: The Transformation of Occupied Cyprus into a Turkish Province*. New York: Aristide D. Caratzas, 1991: 127

Figure 4: The two images of the *bozkurt* (gray wolf) represent TMT emblems as they appeared in the official publication of the organization entitled TMT Nollari (TMT Notes) (Lcfcoja [Nicosia]: Halkin Sesi, 1972). On the left, the *bozkurt* image is superim-posed on a map of Cyprus. The ten arrows arc rising from the points on the map where the ten command posts of the Miicahit force (military force) of TMT were located. All the arrows are linked to the central command post in Nicosia.

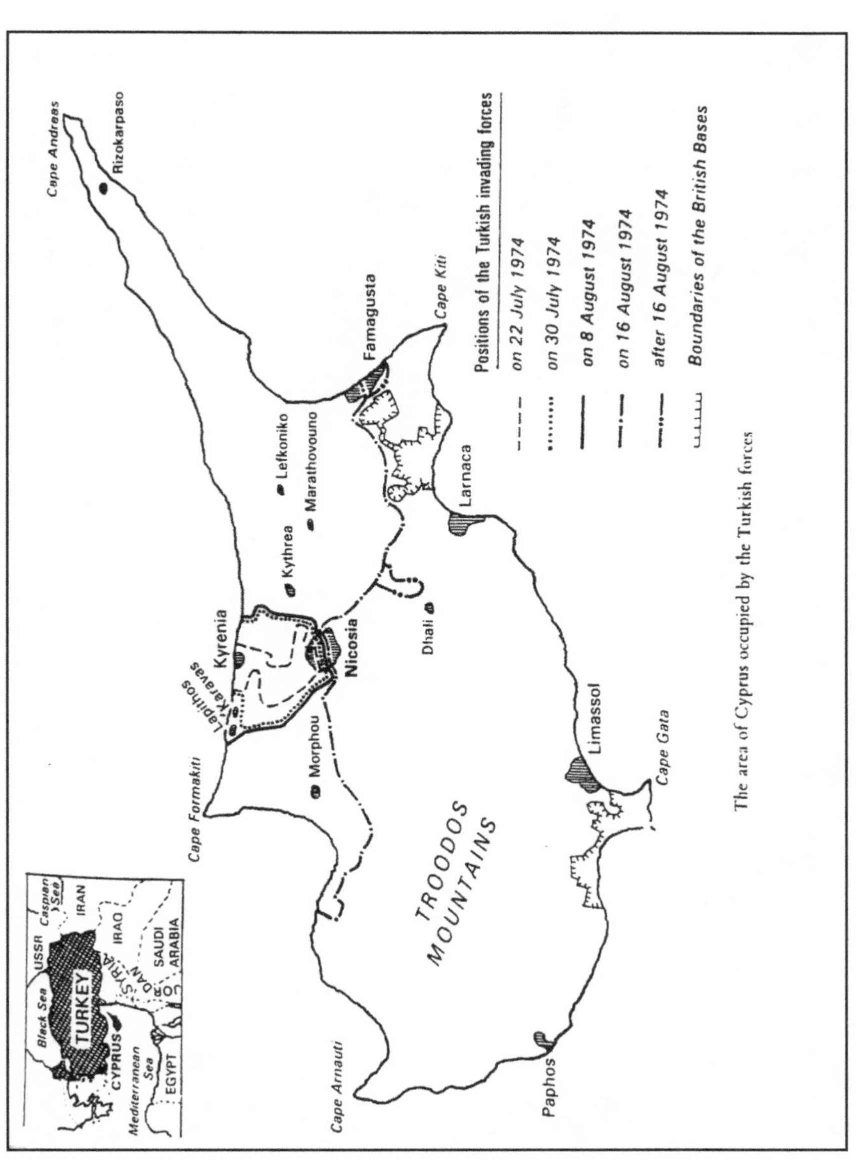

The area of Cyprus occupied by the Turkish forces

Coming from Polyviou, Polyvios G. *Cyprus: Conflict and Negotiation 1960-1980*. New York: Holmes and Meier Publishers, 1980: 239